hr mit **GO AHEAD 7!**

The McCarthy family from Dublin

The 'Gaeltacht' - areas in the west of Ireland where Irish is still spoken

A Celtic cross

Glendalough in the Wicklow Mountains

The Republic of Ireland

Luisa Strebel 7c

GO AHEAD

7

Cornelsen

Luisa Strebel 7c

Go Ahead 7

für die Jahrgangsstufe 7 an sechsstufigen bayerischen Realschulen

erarbeitet von	John Eastwood, Street, Somerset
	Klaus Berold, Kulmbach
	Elke Zahn, Bayreuth
unter beratender Mitarbeit von	Volker Anders, Mallersdorf-Pfaffenberg
	Gerlinde Eberhardt, Surberg
	Werner Epp, Kempten
	Gisela Fiedler, Nürnberg
	Günter Geiß, Weiden
	Renate Grieshaber, Kempten
	Renate Heidemeier, Eichstätt
	Konrad Huber, München
	Jürgen Kanhäuser, Rain
	Reinhold Schnell, Frickenhausen
Verlagsredaktion	Helga Holtkamp, Stefanie Gröne
redaktionelle Mitarbeit	Andrew Dowdall, Fritz Preuss, Barbara Swayne
Design und Layout	David Graham, London (*Units*) James Abram (*Anhänge*)
Bildredaktion	Béatrice Collette, Uta Hübner
zum Schülerbuch sind erhältlich	Workbook, CDs

Hinweise zu weiteren Bestandteilen im Lehrerhandbuch.
Bild-, Text- und Musikquellen auf Seite 152.

www.cornelsen.de

1. Auflage, 7. Druck 2008 / 06

Alle Drucke dieser Auflage sind inhaltlich unverändert und können im Unterricht nebeneinander verwendet werden.

Um die Wiederverwendbarkeit zu gewährleisten, darf in dieses Buch nicht hineingeschrieben werden.

© 2001 Cornelsen & Oxford University Press GmbH & Co., Berlin

Das Werk und seine Teile sind urheberrechtlich geschützt. Jede Nutzung in anderen als den gesetzlich zugelassenen Fällen bedarf der vorherigen schriftlichen Einwilligung des Verlages. Hinweis zu den §§ 46, 52 a UrhG: Weder das Werk noch seine Teile dürfen ohne eine solche Einwilligung eingescannt und in ein Netzwerk eingestellt oder sonst öffentlich zugänglich gemacht werden. Dies gilt auch für Intranets von Schulen und sonstigen Bildungseinrichtungen.

Druck: CS-Druck CornelsenStürtz, Berlin

ISBN 978-3-464-02621-2

 Inhalt gedruckt auf säurefreiem Papier aus nachhaltiger Forstwirtschaft.

CONTENTS / INHALT
Page Unit   What we learn in this unit

 1   IRELAND – OLD AND NEW

5	W & P	
6	Intro 1	Sit 1–3, Ex 1–3
8	Text 1	**Oliver can decide**, Ex 4–6
9	List	Ex 7
10	Act	
12	Intro 2	Sit 4–5, Ex 8–11
14	Text 2	**An urgent phone call**, Ex 12–14
15	Project	
16	Com	**Invitations**, Ex 16–17
16	TYE	1–5
18	Read	**Urban cowboys, urban cowgirls**

Revision
  Simple present – present progressive
  Simple past – present perfect
Simple past – past progressive
For/since
Phrasal verbs

2   KING ARTHUR

19	W & P	
20	Intro 1	Sit 1–3, Ex 1–3
22	Text 1	**The sword in the stone**, Ex 4–6
23	List	Ex 7
24	Act	
26	Intro 2	Sit 4–5, Ex 8–11
28	Text 2	**A new king**, Ex 12–14
29	Com	**Showing interest**, Ex 15
30	Project	
30	TYE	1–6
32	Read	**The three witches**

Question tags: *be, have, can* and *will*
Simple present and simple past
Have to

Had to
Prop word: *one, ones*

 3   THE BIG TIME

33	W & P	
34	Intro 1	Sit 1–2, Ex 1–4
36	Text 1	**Nothing to lose**, Ex 5–7
37	List	Ex 8
38	Act	
40	Intro 2	Sit 3–4, Ex 9–11
42	Text 2	**Absolutely fantastic**, Ex 12–15
43	Project	
44	Com	**Opinions**, Ex 16
44	TYE	1–5
46	Read	**Young people in sport**

If … simple present: *will, can, should*
If … simple present / simple present

Verbs with two objects

three 3

CONTENTS / INHALT

Page   Unit   What we learn in this unit

MOMENTS IN HISTORY

47	W & P		
48	Intro 1	Sit 1–3, Ex 1–4	Relative pronouns: *who, which, that*
50	Text 1	**On the battlefield**, Ex 5–6	
51	List	Ex 7	
51	Project		
52	Act		
54	Intro 2	Sit 4–5, Ex 8–11	Relative clauses without object
56	Text 2	**The monster king**, Ex 12–15	pronouns
58	Com	**Describing people and things**, Ex 16	Prepositions in relative clauses
58	TYE	1–5	
60	Read	**Haunted house**	

DOING THE D OF E

61	W & P		
63	Intro 1	Sit 1, Ex 1–2	Revision: Adverbs
65	Text 1	**Never again**, Ex 3–5	Adverbs with the same form as adjectives
65	List	Ex 6	Adjectives after *be, get, seem, look*
66	Act		
68	Intro 2	Sit 2–3, Ex 7–9	Present perfect progressive
70	Text 2	**You stole my purse**, Ex 10–12	*Must, mustn't, needn't*
71	Project		
72	Com	**Asking the way**, Ex 13	
72	TYE	1–5	
74	Read	**Poems**	

76	Sket 1	**The last question**
78	Sket 2	**Robin Hood the butcher**
80	Rev	**Revision exercises 1–15**
86	Rev	**Guided writing**
89		**Grammatical terms**	Grammatikalische Fachausdrücke
91		**Classroom phrases**	Redewendungen für den Unterricht
92		**Grammar**	Grammatikanhang
108		**English sounds**	Erklärung der Lautschriftzeichen
109		**Unit vocabulary list**	Wörterverzeichnis
128		**Tips**	Lerntipps
130		**Irregular verbs**	Unregelmäßige Verben
132		**List of names**	Liste der Namen
136		**Index**	Alphabetisches Wörterverzeichnis
150		**Activities vocabulary list**	Wörterverzeichnis **Activities**

Act = Activities   **Com** = Communication   **Ex** = Exercise   **Intro** = Introduction   **List** = Listening   **Read** = Reading
Rev = Revision   **Sit** = Situation   **Sket** = Sketch   **TYE** = Test your English   **W & P** = Words and pictures

4   four

UNIT 1
IRELAND – OLD AND NEW

WORDS AND PICTURES

This is the old Ireland. It's a country of green fields and farms. It's a place where you can travel along country roads and not see a car for miles.

Things happen slowly in the old Ireland. People haven't got much money, but they've got lots of time. They've got time to talk, to tell stories and to play their traditional music. The old Ireland is still there – but it's changing.

But there is also the new Ireland. You can see it in cities like Dublin, Galway, Limerick and Cork. It's a country of new office blocks, new companies and smart new shops and cafés. Ireland exports more computer software than any other country in the world except the US.

At one time people left Ireland in their millions and went to England, America and Australia where there was work for them. Now people are coming back to the new Ireland.

Ireland was once part of the United Kingdom of Britain and Ireland. Today the Republic of Ireland is a separate country. Northern Ireland is still part of the United Kingdom.

PROJECT

You can start looking for pictures of Irish people and places for your project work on Ireland. Maybe you can write to the Irish Tourist Board.

Unit 1 **INTRODUCTION 1**

  SITUATION 1

002

This is the McCarthy family. The children are Patrick (15), Fiona (13) and James (10). They're in the garden of their house in Dublin. Mum is holding the dog Nipper. Fiona is wearing a smart new top. They're all smiling except Pat. He doesn't like being in photos.

The McCarthys' home is a guest house. Mum runs the guest house. Dad is a computer technician. He works at Dublin Airport.

I'm playing tennis.
I play table tennis sometimes.

EXERCISE 1

Look at the pictures and put in the correct verb forms.

➤ Fiona *sees* her friends every day at school. In the picture she*'s talking* to Mary.
1 Mrs McCarthy has got a job. She (run) a guest house. It's ten o'clock now and she (make) the beds.
2 At the moment James and his friend (play) basketball in the garden. They (like) basketball.
3 Mr McCarthy (drive) to work every morning. In the picture he (sit) in a long queue of traffic.
4 Pat and his friend (go) to the swimming-pool now. They (go) there most weekends. They usually (walk) because it isn't far.

  SITUATION 2

003

I've just bought the new Raven CD.
I bought it last week.

Mum When are you going to do your homework, Fiona?
Fiona I've done it. I did it before tea.
Mum OK, and have you tidied your room?
Fiona Yes, I have. I did that yesterday.
Mum Well, I looked in there this morning, and it wasn't very tidy.

6 six

INTRODUCTION 1

EXERCISE 2

Complete the conversation. Put the verbs in the correct form.

James Have you finished with this video, Fiona?
Fiona 'Neighbours'? Oh, yes, I watched that yesterday. I (finish) with it now.
James I'll record 'Eastenders' on it then.
Fiona Yes, but don't use the other tape. It's got 'Home and away' on it. I (not watch) that yet.
James Oh, I (see) that on Tuesday. It (be) good. Sam arrives home at last.
Fiona Oh, now you (tell) me what happens. You are awful, James. I (not want) to know.
James But you (see) it before. They (show) the series last year.
Fiona Well, that (be) a long time ago. I (forget) most of it now.

SITUATION 3

Mum You've spilt something on your shirt, Pat.
Pat Oh, it's strawberry ice-cream. My friend Kevin did that on the bus. It happened when we were talking about a football game. He was holding an ice-cream, and suddenly it fell on my shirt. Sorry, but it wasn't my fault.
Mum Well, put it in the basket and I'll wash it.
Pat OK, thanks, mum.

EXERCISE 3

Make sentences from the table.

I was skiing in the Alps when ...

Kevin was holding his ice-cream	when we arrived at the station.
We were driving along the road	I was buying some food for the party.
When Ben came into the room,	when it fell on Patrick's shirt.
I was walking by the lake	the girl was lying on her back in the road.
When you saw me in the shop,	when the car started making a funny noise.
We were eating our burgers	Mrs Jenkins was explaining the project.
When the ambulance arrived,	when Leo DiCaprio walked into the café.
The train was already waiting	they were playing a Boyzone song.
When I switched on the radio,	when I suddenly saw someone in the water.

▶▶ Kevin was holding his ice-cream when it fell on Patrick's shirt.

Can you write a story? Work in groups of three or four pupils. The first pupil writes a sentence, the second pupil adds another sentence, and so on. Each sentence must take the story forward. If you can't think of a good sentence, maybe the others will help you. After about ten or twelve sentences you can try to end the story. Then decide on a title.

Use these notes to start your story.

- It was – o'clock
- I was – when suddenly
- I watched as • Then • It was
- I quickly ran – and • soon

seven 7

Unit 1 **TEXT 1**

  Oliver can decide

005   Mrs Cassidy lives in Wimbledon, but her sister Mrs McCarthy lives in Dublin. Mrs Cassidy and Oliver are visiting the McCarthys. Oliver is talking to Fiona and Patrick.

Oliver Are you glad your school holiday has started, Fiona?
5 *Fiona* Yes, I am. Last term I was really busy because I was in the school musical. Now I want to relax.
Pat Oliver doesn't want to relax. He wants to see the country. Maybe you two can go for a long walk in the Wicklow Mountains.
10 *Fiona* Oh, shut up, Pat. Oliver can decide what he wants to do.
Oliver What's that poster up there? Is that somewhere nice to go?
Fiona Oh, that's County Kerry. It's a long way away, in the south-west. I went there last month on a trip to the Gaeltacht.
Oliver The what?
15 *Fiona* The Gaeltacht, where people still speak Irish. Our class went to an Irish college for a week. We had Irish conversation classes, and in the evening there was a céilí.
Pat That means traditional Irish dancing.
Oliver So can you speak Irish?
20 *Pat* Conas a tá tú?
Oliver Er, …
Fiona That means 'How are you?'.
Oliver Oh, I see. I'm fine, thanks.

Fiona Well, that's enough Irish. What
25   about a computer game, Oliver?
Oliver Yes. I like computer games.
Fiona Pat's got some.
Pat I've got two new games, but they don't work on the old computer.
30 *Fiona* Oh, I forgot. You still haven't got the new computer.
Pat Mum took me to Computer World last week, Oliver, but they didn't have any computers.
35   The night before we went there, someone broke in and stole them all. When we arrived, they were putting a new window in.

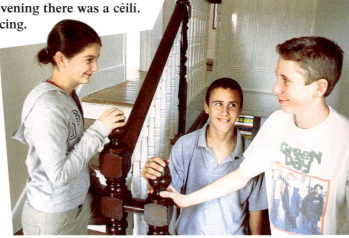

Oliver Oh, that's terrible. You can't play your new games.
Fiona I expect we can buy a computer somewhere else. 40
Pat On the internet, maybe.
Fiona Oliver, there's a disco at the community centre on Friday. Would you like to come?
Oliver Yes, great. Thanks.
Pat Fiona will be with her boyfriend. Who is it this 45
       week?
Fiona OK, I'll be with Connor. What's wrong with that?
Pat Nothing, nothing.
Fiona I can dance with Oliver too. If he wants to, of course. But my friend Emma hasn't got a 50
       boyfriend. And I think maybe you're her type, Oliver.
Pat Oh, shut up, Fiona. You're talking rubbish. Oliver can decide who he wants to dance with.

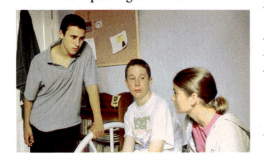

8 eight

TEXT 1

EXERCISE 4

Are the sentences right or wrong? Look at the text and find the information.

▶▶ Mrs Cassidy knows Mrs McCarthy well.
That's right. It says that Mrs McCarthy is 'her sister'.
1 Fiona's school holiday will start soon.
2 Fiona worked hard last term.
3 She has been to County Kerry in the south-west of Ireland.
4 There aren't any Irish speakers in Ireland now.
5 Patrick has played his two new computer games.
6 When Patrick went to Computer World, all the computers were missing.
7 Oliver wants to go to the disco on Friday.
8 Fiona thinks Emma will fancy Oliver.

EXERCISE 6

Rewrite the phrases in italics. Use *else* and these words: *everyone, everything, everywhere, someone, something, somewhere, nothing*.

▶▶ I want to keep these CDs and magazines.
I'm going to throw *all the other things* away.
I'm going to throw everything else away.
1 I don't want to go to the skate park. We always go there. I want to go *to another place*.
2 Why can't I stay out late? *All the other kids* can.
3 I can't buy Fiona a football for her birthday because she doesn't like football. I'm going to buy her *a different present*.
4 We've just got maths homework today, mum. There's *no other homework*, really.
5 Emily didn't go to the disco with Simon. She went with *another person*.
6 I found the letter in my pocket. But that was after I looked *in all the other places* first.
7 That's my desk. You can go and sit *in a different place*.
8 I don't like basketball. Let's play *another game*.

EXERCISE 5

Find the right words for these explanations. The words are all in the text.

▶▶ After the holidays you start a new school term.
1 If you have to do lots of things in a short time, you will be very … .
2 A drama with songs is called a … .
3 When people talk together, that's a … .
4 The last part of the day before you go to bed is the … .
5 An old song that people have sung for many years is a … song.
6 If someone took your money when you weren't looking, that means they … it.
7 A building where people can come together and do activities is a … centre.
8 Things that you don't want and can throw away are … .

EXERCISE 7

Listening

Listen to the conversation between Fiona, Emma and Oliver. Which picture shows the conversation?

Then complete the sentences. Put one word in each sentence.

A   B   C

1 Emma's brother works in a … .
2 He lives in a … in London.
3 Last year Emma visited the … of London.
4 Oliver hasn't visited Dublin … yet.
5 Fiona thinks Oliver should go there with … .

nine 9

Unit 1 — ACTIVITIES — **CEAD MILE FAILTE – A HUNDRED THOUSAND WELCOMES**

1 Saint Patrick of Ireland

Saint Patrick is the patron saint of Ireland. There are many legends about his life, but not all of them are true. He lived in the fifth century. People say that he was born in Wales. At the age of fourteen some pirates caught him and took him to Ireland. For six hard years he worked on farms. Then he ran away and went to France. One night, in his dreams, he heard a voice. It told him to go back to Ireland. He went and became one of the first Christian priests there. People loved to hear his message and started to build churches everywhere. He used something green to explain the Christian religion to them. Today, green is the national colour of Ireland. In many countries people wear green clothes on Saint Patrick's Day, March 17th.

Ask your teacher for internet addresses and try to answer these questions:

1 Patrick used 'something green' to explain the Christian religion. What is it?
Today, it has even become a symbol for Ireland.
2 There's a legend about Saint Patrick and the snakes. Find out what happened.

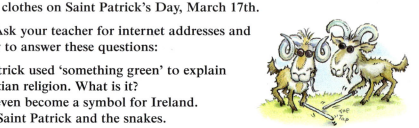

'It's difficult to choose between two blind goats.'

2 The Giant's Causeway

Many years ago, an Irish guy called Finn loved a lady from Scotland. But at that time there were no planes, trains or cars. And no ship could take him across the sea. You see, Finn was a giant and this makes life much more difficult … . Finn tried to find a different way to meet his darling and decided to build a stone path across the Irish sea. And today, these stepping stones still lead from the cliff into the dark green water, but nobody knows if Finn really met his lady for a giant's kiss.

Well, other people say that the Giant's Causeway was the work of a volcano 55 million years ago and that cold lava made these strange stones. Most of the 40,000 stones have six sides and the highest of them are 40 feet tall.

Try to find out Finn's full name from the internet.

10 ten

ACTIVITIES

3 The magic world of Ireland – Leprechauns

Leprechauns are a special kind of fairy in Ireland. They are little men about as high as your knee, and they usually wear a green hat and green trousers. Leprechauns are fairy shoemakers, and they can do all sorts of magic. Some are friendly, some are horrible, but all of them have a secret pot of gold which is hidden at the end of every rainbow. Leprechauns are very hard to find, and they can run very fast, but if you catch one, he will take you to the end of the rainbow and give you his pot of gold. If you like, you can have three wishes, too. But be careful! They are very clever little men and will try to trick you! On the internet you can see more pictures of Leprechauns. On some websites you can also hear some Irish music and see how Leprechauns dance.

4 The Irish language

A long, long time ago people called 'the Celts' came to Britain and Ireland. They spoke a Celtic language: 'Gaelic'. Today there are still many people in Ireland who speak Irish Gaelic (or 'Irish') because pupils learn it at school. Irish is also one of the country's two official languages.

Answer the following questions:

1 What's the other official language? Have a guess!
2 What does 'beag' mean in English? Check it in a Gaelic dictionary on the internet. Does it mean: ● big? ● small? ● bag? ● boy?

5 Irish potato cakes

Irish potato cakes are also called 'fadge'. For eight small potato cakes you need:

➤ 750g warm cooked potatoes
➤ ½ teaspoon of salt
➤ 25g melted butter
➤ 50g flour
➤ one egg

This is how you make them:
➤ Mash the potatoes.
➤ Mix the potatoes, salt, butter, egg and flour well.
➤ Roll out two circles, each about 22 cm in diameter and 1/2 cm thick.
➤ Cut each circle into quarters and fry them in a little butter for about five minutes.
➤ Eat them hot – if you like with a little sugar or melted butter on top.

eleven **11**

Unit 1   **INTRODUCTION 2**

010

SITUATION 4

It's Wednesday today. Oliver has been in Ireland for three days now. He's been at the McCarthys' house since Sunday evening.

Fiona Pat, can Oliver borrow your bike, please?
Pat Yes, sure. But it isn't very new, Oliver. I've had it for about four years – since my eleventh birthday, I think.
Oliver Oh, that's OK. Thanks, Pat.
Fiona I think it'll be the right size for you, Oliver.

We use 'for' and 'since' with the present perfect.

	Wie lange schon?		Ab wann?
	hours		three o'clock
	three days		Tuesday
for	a year	since	1995
	six months		June
	a long time		my birthday

→ page 94-95

EXERCISE 8

Put in *for* or *since*.

➡ The Cassidys have been in Dublin **since** the weekend.
1 The McCarthys have had the guest house … five years now.
2 Fiona hasn't had school … last Friday.
3 Oliver has known Fiona … a long time.
4 She hasn't been to Ireland … 1997.
5 Oliver has been at Brookfield School … two years.
6 Patrick has had the new computer games … a week now.
7 The Republic of Ireland has been separate from the United Kingdom … 1922.
8 Ireland has been a mainly Catholic country … about fifteen hundred years.

EXERCISE 9

Look at the pictures. Use phrases with *for* or *since* and say how long the people have been *in bed, in school, in the water, on holiday, on the train* or *with Emily*.

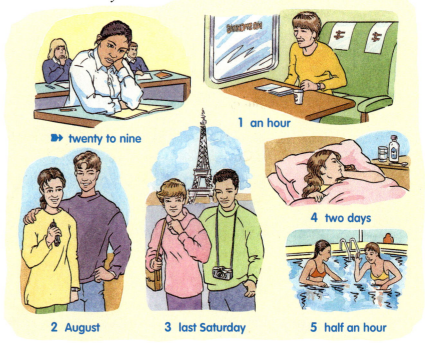

➡ twenty to nine
1 an hour
2 August
3 last Saturday
4 two days
5 half an hour

➡ Lehka wants to go home. She's been in school **since** twenty to nine.
1 Mrs Hurst is going to Manchester. She's been … .
2 Emily's new boyfriend is called Andy. …
3 Mr and Mrs Williams are in France. …
4 Kirsty is ill. …
5 The girls are swimming. …

12   twelve

INTRODUCTION 2

EXERCISE 10

Answer these questions.

▶ How long have you been in Class 7?
  For three weeks. / **Since** September.
1 How long have you been at your school?
2 How long have you lived in your house or flat?
3 How long have you known your best friend?
4 Think of something at home like your bike or your camera. How long have you had it?

Ask more questions. You can work with a partner.

▶ How long have you had that sweater?
▶ How long has Herr/Frau ... been your English teacher?

SITUATION 5

011

Fiona   Do you like Westlife, Oliver?
Oliver Yes, they're good.
Fiona   I think they're great. They're Irish, did you know? Two of them come from Dublin, and the other three come from Sligo in the north-west. They've just brought out this new CD.
Oliver Oh, can we hear it?
Fiona   You're sitting right by the CD player.
Oliver Give me the CD and I'll put it on then. ... Er, how do you switch this thing on?
Fiona   Oh, sorry. Someone's taken the plug out. I'll put it back in.
Oliver OK, here we go.
🎵 *I have a dream, a song to sing ...*

These are called phrasal verbs.

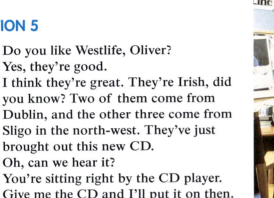

They've just brought out a new CD. **I'll put it on**.

→ page 111

EXERCISE 11

Put in these phrasal verbs: *fall off, find out, get in, hurry up, sit down, wash up.*

1 I'm going your way. Please ... .
2 ... or we'll be late.
3 I'm going to ... what happened.
4 Be careful that you don't ... .
5 Please ... .
6 Who's going to ... ?

Unit 1 TEXT 2

An urgent phone call

About a mile from Fiona's house, there's an old factory at the end of a lane. The factory has been empty for years now, and no one uses it. One of Fiona's friends got into the building through a window and opened a door from inside. There was a big room and a small office at one end. A group of friends started going there on their bikes. Emma brought a CD player, and Sean brought a football. They kicked it around and broke a window. They sat on the floor and talked. It was nice to have a secret place.

One day in the school holiday, some of the friends went to the old factory. There was Emma, Fiona, Connor, Claire, Michael, Sean, Helen, Sinéad and Fiona's cousin Oliver from England. When they arrived, they found about thirty large boxes. 'They're computers,' said Emma. 'What are they doing here? And how long have they been here?' 'I know,' said Sean. 'They're from Computer World. Yes, the address is on the boxes, look. There was a break-in last week, remember? These are the stolen computers. I expect they've been here since the break-in.'

'I think we should call the guards,' said Connor. 'Wait a minute,' said Michael. 'We shouldn't be in too much of a hurry. Let's all take home a new computer first.' 'Don't be silly,' said Emma.

Only Helen's mobile phone was working and she didn't want to call the police. 'Maybe we should tell our parents first,' she said. Meanwhile some of the kids started playing football. Someone put a CD on. Then something happened. The door opened and two men walked in. They stopped and looked at the young people. 'Get over there by the wall,' shouted one of them angrily. He was tall with fair hair and wearing jeans. 'Stand there. Shut up!' The other man took Helen's phone and threw it against the wall. The friends were afraid.

Fiona was sitting in the office with a book when she heard the crash. She knew who the men were. She opened the window and jumped out. She saw a white van with its doors open, but the men were inside the building. She got on her bike and rode away very fast. At the end of the lane she came to the main road. There was no phone box, so she went to the first house and rang the bell. A woman opened the door. 'Can I come in and phone the guards?' said Fiona. 'It's very urgent. Please!' The woman waited while Fiona phoned. She gave her name and the address of the house. It wasn't easy to explain everything, but she did her best. At last the guard said, 'All right, we're on our way. Stay where you are and wait for us.'

Five minutes later some guards arrived in two cars. 'Are you Fiona McCarthy? Get in the car, please. Leave your bike.' The cars drove along the lane. And yes, the van was still there. The two men were loading the last of the boxes. Both cars stopped and everyone jumped out. 'Stay there,' someone said to Fiona.

It was all over in a moment. One of the guards came back to the car and spoke to Fiona. 'OK, you can get out now,' he said. 'We've arrested them. And your friends are all OK. Here they are now.'

EXERCISE 12

Complete this report about the stolen computers. Put in the missing words.

> **Stolen computers in old factory**
> Thirty stolen computers are now back at Computer ... . After the ...-in last week, someone left the computers, still in their ... , in an old ... . Yesterday a ... of children ... the computers there. While the children were in the factory, ... men arrived in a ... . They ... the ... into the van, but one of the children, a 13-year-old ... called ... McCarthy, got away on her ... , rode along the ... and ... the guards from a house on the ... road. The guards arrived just at the right moment. They ... the men and took them away.

EXERCISE 13

What do you think Fiona said to the guard on the phone? Complete the conversation and then practise it in pairs.

Guard ... your name, please?
Fiona ...
Guard ... phoning from?
Fiona ... is 96 Dunbridge Road, and ... 436-5528.
Guard OK, ... problem?
Fiona We've ... computers. I was ... with my friends, and ... there. Then ... in a van. They've ... my friends. Please ... .
Guard Just a minute. ... ?
Fiona ... half a mile ... , near the canal. ... of a lane.
Guard And how ... that the ... stolen?
Fiona They're from ... . The address ... . There was ... weekend. Look, please ... . Those ... dangerous.
Guard All right. We're on ... . Stay ... and ... us. ... in five minutes.

EXERCISE 14

What *should* or *shouldn't* you do in these situations?

▶ You have found some stolen computers.
  You **should** tell the police.
  You **shouldn't** take a computer home with you.
1 Your mum is very busy because you've invited some friends to tea, and she is getting the meal ready.
2 You have found your friend's diary in your school bag.
3 It's a school day. You've just got up, but you're ill. You can't eat and you've got a terrible headache.
4 You borrowed your friend's watch yesterday, and now you've lost it.
5 A friend is giving you a CD for your birthday, but you've already got it.

PROJECT

Find some pictures of Irish people and places. Maybe you can find some in newspapers or magazines, or maybe someone in your family has photos of Ireland. You can also write to the Irish Tourist Board. (Ask your teacher for the address.) And maybe you can find something on the internet.

Make a class display about Ireland. Write one or two sentences about each photo. If you can, play some Irish music – traditional or pop. Do you know any Irish singers or bands?

The Corrs are a family band from Ireland – Jim Corr and his younger sisters Sharon, Caroline and Andrea. They've got fans in many countries. Their music is a mixture of pop and traditional Irish music.

This is the Blarney Stone. It's in a wall of Blarney Castle near Cork. If you kiss the Blarney Stone, you can 'sweet-talk' people and always get what you want.

Unit 1

COMMUNICATION

013

Invitations Einladungen

Fiona's mum	Would you two like to stay and have tea with us?
Emma	Oh, yes, I'd like to. Thank you.
Connor	That's very nice of you, Mrs McCarthy, but I can't stay. It's my guitar lesson at four.

So lädt man jemand ein	• Would you like to go to the concert with me?
	• Why don't you come with us?
So nimmt man die Einladung an	• Yes, OK. Thanks.
	• Yes, I'd like to / I'd love to. Thank you.
So lehnt man höflich ab	• I'd like to, but I'm afraid I can't. I've got a basketball game at four.
	• That's very nice of you, but I won't have time. I really need to finish my project.

EXERCISE 15

Kirsty is inviting Adam and Oliver to her party. Put the sentences in the right order and then act out the dialogue in groups of three.

6 *Oliver* I'd like to, but I can't. We're going to visit some relatives.
2 *Adam* A party? When is it?
4 *Adam* Yes, Saturday evening is OK. I'd love to. Thanks, Kirsty.
3 *Kirsty* Next Saturday evening.
5 *Kirsty* What about you, Oliver?
1 *Kirsty* Would you like to come to my party, you two?

EXERCISE 16

Work with a partner. Invite him/her to do these things.

1 come to our barbecue
2 go to the disco with me
3 play my new computer game

Then practise it the other way round. You can say *yes* or *no* to the invitations, but you must be polite. Think of two more invitations and ask your partner.

TEST YOUR ENGLISH

Dublin's playground

'Dublin's playground' is the Phoenix Park, two miles west along the River Liffey from the city centre. The main entrance
5 is in Parkgate Street. The Phoenix Park is one of the largest city parks in the world – more than twice as big as New York's Central Park. The wall
10 round the park is seven miles long.

The Phoenix Park is a lovely place. There are gardens and lakes and lots of trees. Three
15 hundred years ago it was a

royal deer park, and today there are still wild deer in the park. There are football, cricket and polo grounds. You
20 can hear concerts in the park. There are buildings in the park, too. One is the house where the Irish President lives and another is the residence of
25 the American ambassador to Ireland. There's also a castle with a visitor centre inside. At one end of the park is Dublin Zoo, open every day. Buses will
30 take you there from the city centre. There has been a zoo here since 1830. There are over 700 different animals and birds.

If you're tired, you can always
35 take a train ride around the zoo. But don't miss the lions because the zoo is famous for them. Do you know the lion at the start of an MGM film?
40 Well, that lion was born in Dublin Zoo.

16 sixteen

TEST YOUR ENGLISH

1 Answer these questions on the text.

1 How far is it from the centre of Dublin to the Phoenix Park?
2 Which is bigger, Central Park or the Phoenix Park?
3 Why are there deer in the park?
4 People can do sport in the park. Name three of the sports.
5 Who lives in the park?
6 Is Dublin Zoo open on Sundays?
7 How old is the zoo?
8 What has the MGM film company to do with Dublin Zoo?

2 A tourist guide in Dublin is answering questions. Look at the answers and complete the questions.

1 *Tourist* What … ?
  Guide The museum opens at ten o'clock.
2 *Tourist* … Dublin … any … ?
  Guide Yes, of course it has. It's got lots of night clubs.
3 *Tourist* How … Irish people … ?
  Guide Oh, we've always driven on the left.
4 *Tourist* … cost?
  Guide Tickets for the concert, did you say? They're £10.
5 *Tourist* Can you … ?
  Guide The castle? Yes, go along here and you'll see it on your left.
6 *Tourist* … ?
  Guide From the centre to the airport – oh, it's about ten kilometres.

3 Which word from the text is it?

1 There are some swings in the children's … .
2 I'll meet you at the … to the cinema.
3 You can see some interesting … animals at the zoo.
4 We've got a … at our house, my dad's old school friend.
5 It's cold outside. Let's go … where it's warmer.
6 We've been in the park … ten o'clock this morning.
7 Everyone has heard of U2. They're from … .

4 Oliver and Fiona are in a village on the coast near Dublin. Put in the missing words or the correct form of the words in brackets.

Oliver It's nice here. There's a great view. Look … all those boats.
Fiona Yes, I … (like) it here. We often … (come) here at weekends.
Claire Hi, you two.
Fiona Oh, hi, Claire. Hi, Helen.
Helen Hi. What … (you/do) here?
Fiona I … (show) Oliver around. … (he/never/be) to Ireland before.
Claire … (you/ride) your bikes here?
Oliver No, we … (come) on the train.
Helen We did, too. We … (arrive) a few minutes … . How long … (you/be) here?
Fiona About an hour. We're … to take the five o'clock train back.
Claire Where's your brother, Fiona?
Fiona Oh, Pat … (not/want) to come with us.
Helen I … (see) him when I went past your house. He … (wash) the car.
Claire What … a drink? … a café over there.
Fiona Oh, … (we/just/have) a cola. But you can have something, and … (we/come) and sit with you.

5 Mr McCarthy is asking Oliver and Fiona about their visit to the National Wax Museum in Dublin. Listen to the conversation and answer the questions.

014

1 Which of these names can you hear in the conversation?
  a) Madonna   d) Mary Robinson
  b) Julia Roberts e) the Simpsons
  c) the Spice Girls f) Marilyn Monroe

2 Answer *yes* or *no*.
  a) Did Fiona like the waxworks of Irish Presidents?
  b) Did she like the waxworks of rock stars?
  c) Did she like the Chamber of Horrors?
  d) Did Oliver like the Chamber of Horrors?

READING   Urban cowboys, urban cowgirls

'Just look at Gypsy, my new pony. Isn't he great? I bought him two weeks ago. I was lucky to get an extra £10 from my grandad and so I could pay the £90 for him at the Smithfield horse market. I'm Canice, Canice O'Byrne. I'm one of Dublin's
5 cowgirls and cowboys. We ride our ponies bareback through Ballymun. That's the place where we live. It's a part of Dublin, a very poor part with high tower blocks. We've got many problems with drugs and criminals here. But we're proud that we'll get out of all that. School? What for? Two out of three people are
10 without a job. School is boring, I don't go there every day. And looking after Gypsy is better than hanging around with nothing to do. They're trying to forbid ponies in Ballymun. I'm 13 now but they say I have to be 16 to keep a horse. Now I have to hide him every night. They are crazy, they can't take Gypsy away from me. Who says that horses are only for rich people? We'll be rich one day, too. We'll be famous jockeys
15 in America, not poor and without a job like our parents. Riding Gypsy through the streets of Ballymun is great, I like him very much. We'll get out of here, I can tell you. Here we go ... '

Why don't you help me? It's an awful place for ponies here, I'm hungry every day, I never find enough food and fresh water. My left foreleg has
20 been hurting for many cold nights because we always have to step over broken bottles, empty beer cans and heroin needles. Canice is a nice girl, but she doesn't know anything about horses. She has never learned to look after me properly. Why do these boys and girls play Wild West with us? I'm not a pet, you see. My life is torture. They keep us in the ghetto, in backyards and
25 public parks. One of my best friends, Billy-the-Kid, a wonderful black pony, broke his leg in a car crash a few weeks ago. Last night the DSPCA shot him. Why did they do that? Why can't I go back to the farm in the country where I lived before?

30 'We're trying to catch and save the Ballymun ponies, of course, but I'm afraid we had to shoot 160 of them in the last three years. Most of the Ballymun ponies are ill: broken legs, lots of diseases and not enough food. We can't save all the ponies. Our vets look after them in the middle of the night, when the cowboys and cowgirls are in their beds. The teenagers hide their ponies in the slums with old cars and lots of rubbish everywhere. There's a new law and you have to be 16 years
35 old to keep a pony. They want to get the ponies out of the city and back to the farms. The city is not the right place to keep some 1200 horses. It's torture for them. But just look at these kids: They want to fight for their ponies, their best
40 friends. These ten or thirteen year-olds probably dream of being cowboys in America one day. The real problem isn't the horses but how we can make sure that these kids will have a better future. In Ballymun drugs are a major problem, but pony
45 kids don't take drugs. The ponies also keep them from stealing cars. I can understand the kids – but please don't forget these poor animals.

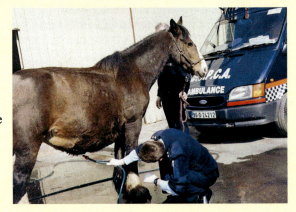

18 eighteen

UNIT 2
KING ARTHUR

WORDS AND PICTURES

015 Two thousand years ago, Britain was the home of people called Celts or Britons. The Celts were farmers, and they lived in villages. Today you can still see the work of Celts – a white horse 114 metres long on a chalk hill at Uffington.

The White Horse at Uffington

Then the Romans came across the sea and conquered most of Britain. They built roads and towns. The towns had stone buildings – flats, shops and public baths. But the Romans didn't conquer Scotland or Ireland. The emperor Hadrian decided to build a wall across Britain. Hadrian's Wall kept out the people to the north. Some of it is still standing.

Hadrian's Wall

The Romans left Britain in about the year 410. But soon other people arrived. They were the Angles and the Saxons (the Anglo-Saxons) from Denmark and north Germany. They conquered the country. The Britons tried to fight back, but the Anglo-Saxons pushed them west into Wales and Cornwall and north into Scotland. The Anglo-Saxon country was called England.

A king of the Britons called Arthur fought against the Anglo-Saxons. There are many stories about Arthur and his knights.

The Roman baths at Bath

A Saxon church in England

 You can start looking for stories and information about King Arthur and his knights for your project work. Find some pictures and see what clothes people wore in those days.

nineteen **19**

Unit 2   **INTRODUCTION 1**

 SITUATION 1

016

The McCarthy family are on holiday in Cornwall. Mum and dad, Patrick, Fiona and James are going out for the day.

Dad   So, what are we going to do?
Fiona   We can go to Tintagel, can't we?
Mum   Yes. It's on the coast, isn't it? There's a castle there. Or the ruins of a castle.
Patrick I don't want to see any old ruins. That won't be very interesting, will it?
James   King Arthur lived at Tintagel, didn't he?
Dad   That's right. You've read a book about him, haven't you?
Fiona   Those stories aren't true, are they?

Question tags: be, have, can and will → page 95-96

Positive ~ Negative
We're winning, **aren't we**?
You've got a pound, **haven't you**?

Jade can swim, **can't she**?
The test will be easy, **won't it**?

Negative ~ Positive
We aren't losing, **are we**?
You haven't got a ticket, **have you**?

Tessa can't swim, **can she**?
It won't be difficult, **will it**?

It's cold today, isn't it?

It isn't very warm, is it?

EXERCISE 1

Some pupils are doing a quiz in their English lesson. Complete the second part of each conversation.

▸ *Silke*   Is Tintagel in Wales or in Cornwall?
  Ingo   Tintagel? It's in Cornwall, **isn't it**?
1 *Gabi*   What can you hear in Edinburgh at one o'clock? A gun or a bell?
  Tanja   You can hear a gun, … ?
2 *Thorsten* What was the date when they arrested Guy Fawkes? Nov 5th or 10th?
  Susi   That's easy. It wasn't 10th, … ?
3 *Christian* What should you ring if you need an ambulance urgently, 333 or 999?
  Andrea I think I know. You … ring 999, … ?
4 *Frank*   How many legs has a spider got?
  Ute   It's got eight legs, … ?

5 *Andreas* Where is San Francisco? In California or Texas?
  Holger Oh, it's in California, … ? It isn't in Texas, … ?
6 *Markus* What will you see if you go to Madame Tussaud's, waxworks or fireworks?
  Heiko   You won't see fireworks, … ? I think … waxworks, … ?
7 *Tobias* What are the New York Yankees? A band or a baseball team?
  Maria   They're a baseball team, … ? Yes, I'm almost sure. … a band, … ?

 SITUATION 2

017

The McCarthy family are at Tintagel.

Fiona   King Arthur didn't really live here, did he?
James   Yes, he did.
Fiona   You don't believe those stories, do you?
James   Of course I do. You heard what dad said, didn't you?
Mum   You two always get into an argument, don't you? No one really knows. Perhaps Arthur lived here and perhaps he didn't.

INTRODUCTION 1

Question tags: simple present and simple past

Positive ~ Negative
You watch 'Neighbours', **don't you?**
Ben lives in London, **doesn't he?**
My cousins came last year, **didn't they?**

Negative ~ Positive
You don't watch football, **do you?**
He doesn't live here, **does he?**
They didn't stay long, **did they?**

→ page 96

EXERCISE 2

Complete the sentences. Put in the question tags.

▶ You like Cornwall, **don't you?** – Yes, it's great.
1 You don't want to go home, … ? – No, I'm enjoying the holiday.
2 Lots of people visit Tintagel, … ? – Yes, most of them in summer.
3 This path goes around the coast of Cornwall, … ? – That's right.
4 King Arthur lived there, … ? – Well, that's what they say.
5 You didn't bring a camera, … ? – No, I left it in the caravan.
6 We walked a long way yesterday, … ? – Yes, we walked miles.

SITUATION 3

018

Lehka I've got my ticket for the musical. There was a huge queue. I had to wait twenty minutes.
Oliver What musical is that?
Lehka 'Arthur'. The drama club's musical about King Arthur and his knights.
Oliver Oh, yes, of course.
Lehka If you want a ticket, you'll have to hurry.
Oliver I have to go and see Mrs Jenkins first. I'll get my ticket afterwards.

EXERCISE 3

Complete the sentences. Use a pronoun and *have to / has to / had to / I'll have to* and one of these verbs: *borrow, buy, feed, get, think, tidy, wait, wash*.

▶ There are clothes and CDs on Amy's bed and on the floor. She **has to tidy** her room.
▶ We had a very nice meal, but afterwards we **had to wash up**.
1 Our bus was late yesterday. … a long time for it. And it was raining.
2 It's my mum's birthday next week. … a present for her soon.
3 The kids are in bed, but it's half past seven, time to get ready for school. … up now.
4 Adam had some maths homework yesterday. The questions were difficult. … carefully about them.
5 Mrs Foster is looking after Rusty the dog. It's his tea time now, so … him.
6 Sophie wanted to buy a magazine, but she didn't have enough money. … some from Jessica.

You can play this game. Imagine you are very late for school because you stayed in bed too long, ate your breakfast very slowly and missed the bus. What can you tell the teacher? Think of a good excuse.

▶ Sorry I'm late. I hurt my leg, and I had to go to the doctor.
▶ Sorry I'm late. A spaceship landed in our garden, and I had to show it to some reporters.

Who can find the best excuse?

twenty-one **21**

Unit 2 TEXT 1

The sword in the stone

019

There was once a British king called Uther Pendragon. He was a good king. He had a lot of help from a magician called Merlin. Merlin was very clever, and he also knew about the future.

The Duke of Tintagel fought a battle against Uther. Uther killed the duke and won the battle. The duke had a beautiful young wife called Igraine. Merlin used his magic on Igraine, and she fell in love with Uther. Uther loved Igraine, too. They married and lived in the castle at Tintagel. (Well, that's the story. No one knows if it's really true, or if Arthur was a real person.)

One day Merlin said to Uther, 'You're going to have a son. You must give the child to me, and I can find a safe home for him.' Merlin was looking into the future. He saw the death of Uther and his queen. He wanted to keep the child safe until he was old enough to be King of Britain.

A son was born to Uther and Igraine, and they called him Arthur. They didn't want to lose him. But Merlin said to Uther, 'I've always helped you, haven't I? You know that, don't you? Now you have to do what I say.' Merlin took the baby away from Uther's castle and gave him to a knight called Hector. Merlin didn't tell Hector who the baby was. Hector and his wife had to look after little Arthur, but they were glad to have him. They already had an older son called Kay, and now Kay had a younger brother.

Uther and Igraine didn't have any more children, and two years later they both died. No one knew that they had a son.

When Uther died, all the most important knights wanted to be king. 'We haven't got a king now, have we?' they said. 'So I'm going to be king.' They fought a number of battles. At the same time, the Saxons came across the sea and conquered a large part of the country. It was a bad time for Britain.

Merlin often visited Kay and Arthur. Arthur was a very happy child. Of course he didn't know that Hector wasn't his real father. And Arthur was a clever boy. He was good at riding and archery. Kay was clever, too. He was older than Arthur, and he wanted to be better than him at everything. But the boys had a lot of fun together.

When Arthur was fourteen, Merlin knew that he was ready to be king. Merlin put a large stone outside a church in London. He put a sword in the stone, and on the stone were the words 'Only the true King of Britain can pull out this sword.'

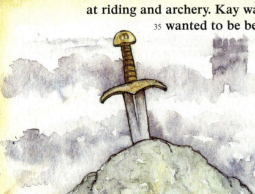

Lots of people came and looked at the sword in the stone. A lot of knights tried to pull it out, but no one was strong enough.

TEXT 1

EXERCISE 4

Put in the simple past forms of the verbs and put the sentences in the right order.

1. But Merlin (take) Arthur away from them and (give) him to Hector.
2. He (put) a sword in a stone and (write) some words on the stone.
3. He (win) a battle against a duke and (marry) the duke's wife Igraine.
4. But the sword (stay) in the stone and (not move).
5. Once there (be) a king called Uther.
6. When Arthur (be) fourteen, Merlin (use) his magic.
7. Then Igraine (have) a son.
8. Two years later Uther and Igraine (die).
9. A lot of knights (see) the sword and (try) to pull it out.
10. His parents (give) him the name Arthur.

EXERCISE 5

Write two sentences about people in Text 1.

➡ Uther Pendragon
➡ Uther was a British king and Arthur's father. He killed the Duke of Tintagel and married Igraine.

1 Merlin 3 Arthur
2 Igraine 4 Hector
          5 Kay

EXERCISE 6

Put in these prepositions: *about, across, after, against, for, from, in, of, outside, to*.

➡ We remember Arthur long after his death.
1. There are lots of stories … him and his knights.
2. Uther Pendragon was King … Britain.
3. Uther had some help … Merlin the magician.
4. Uther fought … the Duke of Tintagel.
5. Tintagel is … Cornwall.
6. Uther and Igraine gave their baby … Merlin.
7. Merlin found a safe home … Arthur.
8. Merlin put a stone … a church in London.
9. The Saxons came … the North Sea.

EXERCISE 7

020 Listening

Listen to the conversation. Fiona is telling Connor about her family's holiday in Cornwall. Then answer the questions.

1. How did the McCarthys travel to Cornwall?
   a) in the car b) on a plane c) on the train
2. Where did they stay?
   a) in a caravan b) in a cottage c) in a hotel
3. What did they do when they had to stay in all day?
   a) They played games. b) They read books.
   c) They watched television.
4. What did they do at Newquay?
   a) They did some surfing. b) They went to an arcade.
   c) They played football on the beach.
5. How many times did they go to Newquay?
   a) once b) twice c) three times

twenty-three 23

Unit 2 ACTIVITIES

KING ARTHUR AND HIS KNIGHTS OF THE ROUND TABLE

1 Why a Round Table? Here's the Legend.

021

A few days before Arthur and Guinevere's wedding, Arthur got a present from a friend: a big round table for him and his knights. 'When you meet your knights,' his friend explained, 'they can't have an argument or secrets because you're all sitting face to face. Nobody can say that he is more important than somebody else.'

'But a king sits at the head of a table,' Arthur remembered, 'this table hasn't got a seat for me, the king.' Guinevere took his hand as she told him, 'My lord, all your men have the same rights as you when they sit at this table. The same right to speak and the same right to decide on a serious matter.'

'Well, all right. That's fair enough. But they will still fight about who sits where, won't they?' Arthur asked.

At this moment Merlin said, 'Never mind. There's an easy answer to your question.' He put his hands on the table – and suddenly they could read the names of 140 knights in the fine dark wood of the table. 'There's Sir Kay's name, Sir Bedivere, … aha, and Sir Lancelot, but I have never heard of Gareth, Tristan and, … .' 'Wait and see,' Merlin smiled, 'some of them are already here and some haven't arrived yet.'

2 Make your own legend about Arthur and his knights

There are so many legends about King Arthur and his knights. No one knows which one is true. People have added more moments of magic to the life of this famous king. You can do that too! Go ahead and write a new legend. Each pupil makes five magic cards with Arthur symbols (a letter, a boat, a stone, …). Get in groups of four people: Shuffle the cards and take five. Use the cards and write a new legend about King Arthur. You can use some of the following sentences if you want to:

- On a cold Sunday morning, Arthur and … were riding through a dark forest when suddenly they met a man called …
- He asked them: 'Who … ? And what … ?' Arthur answered …
- Arthur asked: 'Would you like to come with us? I think we need somebody like you at Tintagel.'
- Then he told him: 'But we've got a task for you. I'm fighting against … . / I'm looking for … because … Can you help me?'
- After some time they told him to … because they wanted to …
- The man answered: 'Why not? I know a lot about … I'm sure I can … for you.'
- Before they could … , the man told them, ' … '
- Their new friend's suggestion that they should … was a great idea.
- In the end they found a … which helped them to …
- And so the man became a Knight of the Round Table.
- … (Find your own sentence.)

24 twenty-four

CHRISTMAS

ACTIVITIES

1 Under the Mistletoe

Why don't you hang up some mistletoe in your classroom? If you meet someone under it, you may kiss him or her – even your teacher – if you like … !

2 Frosty, the Snowman

SONG 022

Frosty, the snowman, was a
    jolly happy soul
With a corncob pipe and a button nose
And two eyes made out of coal

Frosty, the snowman, is a fairy-tale they say
He was made of snow, but the children know
How he came to life one day

There must have been some magic
In that old silk hat they found
For when they placed it on his head
He began to dance around

Frosty, the snowman, was alive as he could be
And the children say he could laugh and play
Just the same as you and me

(…)

For Frosty, the snowman, had
    to hurry on his way
But he waved good-bye
Saying 'Please don't cry
I'll be back again some day'

Look at Frosty go – over the
    hills of snow!

3 Poem: The Chimney (Anon.)

023

When Santa Claus got
    stuck up the chimney,
He began to shout,
'You girls and boys
    won't get any toys
if you don't pull me out!
My beard is black,
I've got soot on my sack
And my nose is
    tickling too!'
When Santa Claus got
    stuck up the chimney,
Atishoo, atishoo,
    attisssshhhooooooo!!

twenty-five 25

Unit 2   **INTRODUCTION 2**

024
🎵 **SITUATION 4**

Amy	I really enjoyed 'Arthur'. It was a great musical. And you were good, Royston.
Royston	Oh, thanks. Well, I only had a small part. I didn't have to say very much.
Amy	How many times did you have to practise those songs?
Royston	Lots of times. In the last week it was every day.
Amy	Maybe I should join the drama club. Do you have to learn all your words?
Royston	Yes, of course you do. But if that's a problem, you can do something else. You can make costumes. You don't have to act.

Have to	*Present*	*Past*
Positive	We have to go now. My mum has to work today.	I had to go to the doctor yesterday.
Negative	We don't have to go yet. My dad doesn't have to work today.	I didn't have to go to school.
Question	Do you have to learn these words? Why does Adam have to wait?	Did you have to stay in bed? → page 97-98

EXERCISE 8

Complete the conversation. Use a form of *have to*.

➡ *Mum* You're late, aren't you, Ben? … (you/have/stay) Did you have to stay after school?
Ben Well, no, … (I/not/have to/stay), but I wanted to wait for Adam. He … (have to/see) one of the teachers about something.
Mum Ben, you really must do something about your room. It isn't very tidy, is it?
Ben Oh, … (I/have/tidy) it now? I … (have to/do) my homework. I … (have to/work) on my project.
Mum I told you yesterday, didn't I?
Ben Well, I … (have to/do) homework yesterday, too.
Mum You … (not/have to/work) the whole evening. You still had time to tidy your room.
Ben Why … (it/have to/be) so tidy?
Mum Don't be silly, Ben. Look, … (you/have to/leave) your clothes on the floor all the time?
Ben It's my room. You … (not/have to/look) in it.

INTRODUCTION 2

SITUATION 5

025

Arthur These shields are good.
Kay Yes, they are, aren't they? I tried one the other day, the red one over there.
Arthur Yes, that's a nice one. I like the green ones, too. But I think this one is my favourite.
Kay I like the one with the horse.

one = a shield
this one = this shield
the green ones = the green shields
the one with the horse = the shield with the horse

→ page 98

EXERCISE 9

You are buying things in England. Say what you need.

➡ I'd like a tennis racket, **a cheap one**. (cheap)
➡ I need two shirts, **white ones**. (white)
1 I want a sweater, … (blue).
2 I'm looking for a radio, … (small).
3 I need some socks, … (green).
4 I'd like some pens, … (black).
5 I'm looking for a coat, … (long).
6 I need some shoes, … (brown).
7 I want to buy a mobile, … (cheap).
8 I need a diary, … (big).

EXERCISE 10

Find the word pairs.

1	arms	A	daughters
2	hills	B	death
3	horses	C	flats
4	houses	D	future
5	life	E	legs
6	north	F	months
7	present	G	mountains
8	sons	H	phrases
9	sword	I	ponies
10	weeks	J	shield
11	words	K	south

➡ 1E arms and legs

EXERCISE 11

Complete the conversations. Put in *one, ones* or *it*.

➡ Emily Are these the photos of the school trip?
  Anita No, they're old **ones**. I took this **one** in Edinburgh.
  Emily Oh, it's good, isn't it?
1 Sophie What about this colour? Do you like … ?
  Jessica Yes, it's a nice green. They're lovely sweaters. But the blue … are the nicest.
  Sophie Yes, they are. I think I'll buy … .
2 Adam These sweets are nice. Would you like … ?
  Ravi Oh, thanks. I like these red … .
  Adam The yellow … are my favourites.
3 Royston Let's go to a café.
  Oliver There's … over there, but I think …'s expensive.
  Royston Well, let's go to the … by the post office.
4 Kirsty Have you got a pen? I had … , but I've lost … .
  Amy Is a blue … OK?
  Kirsty That's fine, thanks. I'll give … back at the end of the lesson.
5 Fiona Let's look at these computer games. I want to buy … for James. It's his birthday at the weekend.
  Emma This … is good. I played … last week at Claire's house.
  Fiona OK, I'll get that … .

Unit 2   TEXT 2

🔴 A new king

026

Every year there were games in London for all the knights. Kay was now a young knight, so Hector took him to London to the games. Arthur went with them. He had to carry Kay's weapons and look after his horse. They stayed at an inn. Kay knew about the sword in the stone, and he wanted to pull it out.

5 On the first morning, Hector, Kay and Arthur left the inn and rode to the games. Kay was wearing his new armour, and he had a nice new shield. He was very excited. But then
10 Arthur noticed that he was suddenly quiet. Kay said to Arthur, 'Don't tell our father, but something terrible has happened. I've forgotten my sword. I've left it at the inn. Please go and
15 get it.' 'All right,' said Arthur.

Arthur rode back to the inn. When he got there, he found the door locked. 'I can't get in,' he thought. 'What should I do now? Kay must have a sword, so I'll have to find one.' He rode through the streets. Suddenly, outside a church, he saw a large sword in a stone.
20 'I can take that one, can't I?' he thought. 'No one is using it.' He jumped down from his horse, pulled out the sword and rode away to the games.

Kay was waiting for Arthur. 'Sorry I was
25 so long,' said Arthur. 'There was no one at the inn. I had to find another sword. I found this one outside a church.' 'It's all right,' said Kay. 'The games haven't started yet.' When Kay saw the sword,
30 he knew it was the one from the stone.

Kay held the sword in his hands. It was a wonderful feeling. He took the sword to Hector. 'Look, father,' he said. 'I've got the sword. Am I the new king now?'
35 Hector said nothing. He looked at Kay. 'Where did you get that sword?' he asked. Kay looked down at the ground for a moment. 'Well, I have to admit it,' he said. 'Arthur gave it to me.'

Hector, Kay and Arthur went back to the church. A crowd of people followed them. Hector put the sword back in the stone. He tried to pull it out again, but it didn't move. Kay tried too, but he wasn't strong enough. Then Arthur put his hands around the sword. He didn't have to pull very
40 hard because out it came like a knife from butter. And so Arthur became the King of Britain.

When Arthur learned that Hector and Kay were not his father and brother, he was very sad. 'You have been a good father to me,' he said to Hector. 'But now you are our king,' said Hector. Arthur was a great king, and he won battles against the Saxons. He lived in a castle with his knights. They were called the Knights of the Round Table because they sat at a large round table
45 with one hundred and forty chairs. They had lots of exciting adventures. Kay had a marvellous time there. He enjoyed living in Arthur's castle and being one of his famous knights.

28 twenty-eight

EXERCISE 12

Answer the questions on Text 2.

1. Why did Hector take Kay to London?
2. What was Arthur's job at the games?
3. Where did Hector, Kay and Arthur stay?
4. What did Kay forget on the first morning?
5. Why didn't Arthur get Kay's sword from the inn?
6. Where did he find a sword for Kay?
7. Why did Arthur become King of Britain?
8. Did Kay have a good time when Arthur was king? Explain why or why not.

EXERCISE 14

Explain what *one* or *ones* means.

➤ Those are the two brothers. *The younger one* is Arthur. • *The younger one* = the younger brother
1. There are holes in Merlin's shoes. He should get *some new ones*. • *some new ones* = …
2. Are there many inns in the town? We'll need to find *one* soon • *one* = …
3. Kay has got a new sword. It's a *really good one*. • *really good one* = …
4. There are lots of knights at the games. *Which ones* are Knights of the Round Table? • *Which ones* = …
5. There are some men outside the inn. Hector is *the one* on the white horse. • *the one* = …

TEXT 2

EXERCISE 13

Imagine you are Kay. Write your diary of the day when you first went to the games. Say what happened when Arthur pulled out the sword. Write six sentences or more. You can start like this:

In the morning we rode to the games. On the way I suddenly noticed that I didn't have …

Showing interest

Sein Interesse ausdrücken

Emma My aunt is a detective.
James A detective? Is she really? That's interesting. Has she got a gun?
Emma No, she hasn't. But she sometimes watches people and follows them.
James That must be exciting.

COMMUNICATION

 027

I've got my own website.	● Oh, really? What have you put on it?
We live in a caravan.	● Oh, do you? / Do you really? How big is it?
I'm going to be in a play.	● Really? That's interesting. What play is it?

EXERCISE 15

Show interest in what these people are telling you. Use *Has she? Did you?* etc and then ask a question.

➤ *Richard* Have you heard? Laura has won £500.
   You *Has she* really? How *did she* do that?
1. *Tony* I played a game of American football yesterday.
   You Oh, … you? And … win?
2. *Michael* Do you know what my brother is doing? He's travelling round the world.
   You …
3. *Rebecca* When I was at the airport, I saw one of the Spice Girls.
4. *James* You must meet my grandma. She loves computer games.
5. *Tom* Did you know I've got seven sisters?
6. *Kathy* Have I ever told you I once saw a ghost?

twenty-nine **29**

Unit 2

PROJECT

King Arthur and his knights had lots of exciting adventures. There are lots of stories where they fight against their enemies. There are also stories about Arthur's wife, Queen Guinevere, and how a knight called Lancelot fell in love with her. Choose a story and write it as a play in English. Work in groups. When you've finished, you can practise the play and then act it in front of the class.

TEST YOUR ENGLISH

Stonehenge

It all started one evening years ago. Mum and dad were out, and my 16-year-old sister Tracy was looking after me. I wanted to watch the football game on television, but Tracy was
5 watching a programme about an old stone circle called Stonehenge. It was boring and I wasn't really watching, but suddenly I noticed a long line of people. They were walking slowly into the circle. They were all wearing long
10 white gowns. The sun was going down behind the stones, and it was getting dark, but the people had torches in their hands. A voice said that 2,000 years ago they were the priests of the Britons and that they were called Druids.
15 What were they doing? My eyes didn't move from the screen. I was almost afraid.

Then we heard the car outside. 'Oh God,' said Tracy. 'Look at the time. Hurry up, Kevin, you should be in bed.' So I didn't see the end of
20 the programme. Afterwards I lay in bed and thought about Stonehenge. Who built it? The Druids? Why? And how did they move those heavy stones?

Since that evening I've always been interested
25 in Stonehenge. I've visited it more than once,
I've read books about it, and I've got information about it from the internet. I soon found out that the Druids didn't build Stonehenge. People started building it about 5,000 years ago. No one knows why. Perhaps 30 it was a temple, and perhaps it was an observatory, something to do with the sun. But the stones are the really interesting thing. The big ones are over five metres tall. The people had to build ramps and pull the stones 35 up them with ropes. Some of the other stones came from south-west Wales, about 200 miles away, and each of them weighed four tons. How did they bring the heavy stones all that way? These questions are all part of the 40 wonderful puzzle and magic of Stonehenge.

1 Look again at the text and complete these sentences.

1 Stonehenge is a famous … .
2 At first Kevin thought the TV programme was … .
3 Suddenly he saw the Druids in their … .
4 They were carrying torches because it … .
5 Kevin's eyes never left the television … .
6 Kevin didn't see the whole programme because he … .
7 Since then Kevin has always found Stonehenge … .
8 It isn't true that the Druids … .
9 People needed ramps and ropes because the stones … .

2 Put in the question tags.

1 Tracy is older than Kevin, … ?
2 You've been to Stonehenge, … ?
3 Lots of people visit Stonehenge, … ?
4 Kevin doesn't want to go there again, … ?
5 The journey won't take long, … ?
6 The Druids didn't bring the stones here, … ?
7 Kevin can find more information on the internet, … ?

TEST YOUR ENGLISH

3 Put the words in the right group.

rumora • stecal • hucrhc • toca • keud • reporem • gnu • nin • inefk • neueq • ritsk • dwors

things to wear	buildings	weapons	important people
armour	…	…	…
…	…	…	…

4 Look at the pictures and complete the story of Amy and Kirsty's visit to Stonehenge.

One day Amy and Kirsty … . Amy's mum … .
The journey … . At last they … . Amy's mum … .
They walked … and … . A man … old.

1
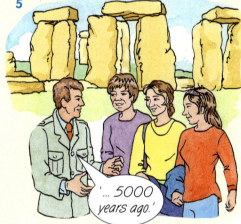

2 '90 minutes later'

'… 5000 years ago.'

5 Kevin is talking to his friend Steve. Use the words in brackets in their correct form and put in the right words.

028

Kevin What did you do … the weekend?
Steve Not much. I … (play) football in the park … Mike and Carl.
Kevin We … (go) to Stonehenge.
Steve Oh, … (I/never/be) there. Is it good?
Kevin Well, Saturday was 21st June, the … (long) day. Lots … people go there … about five o'clock in the morning, when the sun comes … .
Steve … (you/do) that on Saturday?
Kevin No, we got … later. But we … (see) the Druids. They … wearing their white gowns. Did I … you there was a TV programme … them? I think it was … year. It was … (real) interesting.
Steve Those Druids are just … (person) in costumes. And Stonehenge is just … few old stones.

6 Listen to the interview between a reporter and a woman called Sarah. Sarah and her team are trying to move a big stone from Wales to Stonehenge. Answer the questions.

1 How far will the whole journey be?
2 How far have they come after one day?
3 How many people were there on the first day?
4 How far did Sarah want to move the stone on the first day?
5 How many people did she hope to have in her team?
6 Will most of the journey be on land or on water?
7 Why have some people already left the team?

thirty-one 31

READING The three witches

They were always together those three – Claire, Vicky and Rebecca. The other kids called them the three witches. They didn't look like witches or carry broomsticks, but
5 they were interested in magic and ghosts and things like that. They were talking outside Mr Megson's room before the maths lesson. Today it was a test, and nobody was looking forward to that because Mr Megson's tests were always difficult. He was a sadist, everyone knew that.
10 'I heard the owl last night,' said Claire. 'It was in the tree outside my window. It hooted three times. When I heard it, I walked round in a circle and I said: *Oh, clever owl, you know best. From Mr Megson there'll be no test.*' 'That's great,' said Vicky.

Now it was Vicky's turn to tell the other two about
15 her spell. 'I found Mr Megson's photo in the school magazine,' she said. 'I gave it to Finn, my pet snake. I put it in the box with him.' 'Did he eat it?' asked Rebecca. 'Yes. Well, most of it.' 'Good. That should do it.'

20 'I sent a text message,' said Rebecca. 'I used a magic code. Nobody knows the code because it's locked in a box. I opened the box with this key.' She showed them the special key with the two wings. 'Then I sent the message to his mobile. It said: *That test will go out of your head, or you'll never get out of bed.*'
25 'Good,' said Vicky. 'What do you mean, never get out of bed?' asked Claire. 'We don't want to kill him, do we? Just make him ill.'

Just then another maths teacher, Mr Thorpe, arrived. He said to everyone, 'Mr Megson had to go to the hospital, so I'm going to give you a test today. And it won't be an easy one, like Mr Megson gives you. It's going to be a difficult one.'
30 Mr Thorpe was right. It was a difficult test. He was a bigger sadist than Mr Megson. The three witches were glad that their spells were working, but they weren't glad about Mr Thorpe's test. Claire was doing very badly because she was worrying about the spells. 'How ill is Mr Megson?' she thought. She wanted to cry. 'Will he ever get out of bed again? Did we go too far with our spells?'

35 At the end of the lesson Claire and her two friends hurried after Mr Thorpe as he left the room. 'Sir,' she said. 'What's the matter with Mr Megson? Is he ill?' 'No, he isn't ill,' said Mr Thorpe. 'His wife has just had twins. I expect he'll be back next week. You'll be glad to see him, won't you?' 'Oh yes,' said Claire. And the funny thing is that she was telling the truth.

UNIT 3
THE BIG TIME

WORDS AND PICTURES

029 You've heard of the Spice Girls – Geri, Victoria, Mel B, Mel C and Emma.
5 The girl band hit the big time a few years ago when 'Wannabe' went to number one in
10 Britain. Suddenly they were popular all over the world. Geri left the group in 1998, but the
15 other four stayed together.

Victoria, 'Posh Spice', married David Beckham, the Manchester United and England footballer. 'Posh' and 'Becks' were big time. They became
20 rich and famous – not like ordinary people. All the time their faces were in newspapers and magazines and on television.

Film stars are big time, too. Leonardo DiCaprio and Kate Winslet starred in 'Titanic'. He was
25 the poor boy, and she was the rich girl. They fell in love on the journey across the Atlantic to New York. But then oops! The ship hit an iceberg and started to sink slowly into the sea …

Who else is in the big time? Think of at least
30 five other people and say why they are famous.

PROJECT For your project work you will need to choose someone famous and speak or write about them. You can start thinking about this now and looking for pictures.

thirty-three 33

Unit 3   **INTRODUCTION 1**

SITUATION 1

Starting a band?

You're starting a band? And you want to succeed? You're going to make the big time? Let's admit it – your chances aren't good. But if you read these hot tips first, your chances will be much better.

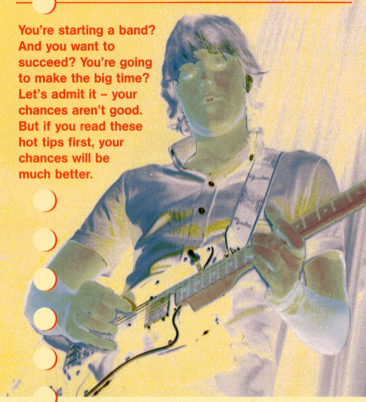

- Work hard. If you aren't ready for some hard work, you can forget it. You won't get far if you don't practise.
- Take your time. It won't happen overnight. If at first you don't succeed, you must try again.
- Get some help. You'll need a manager. If you try to organize everything, you'll have no time left for your music.
- Do lots of gigs. And just hope that somebody from a record company is in the audience. If they notice you, maybe you'll get a contract.
- Enjoy it. Pop music is fun. Yes, you must work hard if you want to succeed. But if you don't enjoy making music, you shouldn't do it.
- Remember the other things in life. If you don't do your homework, you'll soon be in trouble. And you'll be a very boring person if you talk about pop music all the time.

Sentences with 'if'

If ... simple present ... , ... will/can/should etc ...

If **you** **ring** the bell, someone **will open** the door.
If **I** **bring** my camera, we **can take** some photos.

... will/can/should etc ... if ... simple present ...

Those flowers **will die** soon if no one **gives** them any water.
You **should put up** your hand if you **don't understand**.

→ page 99

If you leave me, I'll be sorry.   *If you leave me, I'll be sad.*

EXERCISE 1

Look again at the tips in the magazine. Find the sentences with *if*. Then answer these questions.

1   Does the word *if* come at the beginning of a sentence, in the middle or at the end?

2   Write down the subject and verb after *if*.

   ▶ *if you aren't ready, if you don't practise, ...*

   What can you say about these forms? Are they present or past?

3   What about the other part of the sentence without *if*? Write down the subject and verb.

   ▶ *you can forget, you won't get, ...*

   Look at the first word after the subject, e.g. *can*, *won't*. One of these words occurs more often than the others. Which word is it?

34   thirty-four

INTRODUCTION 1

EXERCISE 2

Complete the conversation. Use the simple present or *will*.

Mum When are you going to do your homework, Ben?
Ben After the football game. If I do (do) it now, I won't see (not see) the end of the game.
Mum You've been in front of that television most of the evening. If you … (not do) your homework soon, it … (be) too late.
Ben I've only got three or four maths questions. If I … (do) them right after the game, there … (not be) any problem.
Mum Why do you always leave things to the last minute? You … (be) tired tomorrow if you … (stay) up late. And if you … (leave) it until tomorrow morning, there … (not be) time. You can't do it while you're eating your breakfast.
Ben Oh, please can I watch this game now? It's really exciting.
Mum You … (not learn) much if you … (watch) television all the time, you know.

EXERCISE 3

Complete the sentences in your own words.

1. If it rains tomorrow morning, …
2. I'll be tired if …
3. If I get everything right in the next test, …
4. If our teacher doesn't give us too much homework tonight, …
5. If the weather is nice at the weekend, …
6. It'll be great if …

031

SITUATION 2

Luke There's something wrong with this video recorder. If you record something, it doesn't play back. There's no picture.
Oliver Well, we haven't had the recorder long. Maybe it's the tape.
Luke It can't be the tape. If you use another one the same thing happens. It doesn't work.
Oliver Well, that's a nuisance. I want to record a film tonight.

EXERCISE 4

Look at the table and make sentences.

If	it's hot,	you go to the website.
	you take six from fifteen,	it sinks.
	you click on the picture,	it burns.
	you throw paper on a fire,	people drink more.
	you drop a stone into water,	it hurts.
	you drop a brick on your foot,	you get nine.

More sentences with if
If … simple present … ,
 … simple present …
If you play the tape, it doesn't work.
If you're ill, you need a doctor.
→ page 100

▶ If it's hot, people drink more.

thirty-five 35

Unit 3 **TEXT 1**

  Nothing to lose

032 The scene is a bedroom in Finchley, North London. It's Nathan Freeman's room. Nathan (16) is there with his friends Crystal (16), Jodie (17) and her stepbrother Philip (15). They're a pop band, and they're called Spider. Nathan's house is where they meet and practise their songs. Luckily, Nathan's parents don't mind. They think the band is great.

5 **Jodie** OK, how does this sound? 'Oh, I feel really excited.' What rhymes with 'excited'?
Nathan Oh, I don't know. 'Invited'?
Philip 'Manchester United'?
Jodie Oh, very funny. Why are brothers so annoying? How can we write a song when nobody here takes it seriously? We need new songs.
10 **Crystal** Oh, I don't agree. We don't need new songs. We've written lots of good ones already. Well, you've written them.
Nathan Yeah. People like our songs. Especially 'Baby, you're mine'. They always cheer when we do that one.
Crystal Our gig at the fashion show last week was
15 great. They all loved it. We were a big hit.
Nathan Do you know what we need? A record contract.
Jodie Well, we know that.
Philip What about our demo tape? You sent it to those record companies, didn't you, Jodie?
20 If they like it, we'll get a contract.
Jodie They don't listen to demos. They get hundreds of them every week. Everybody knows that.
Crystal If we do something really special, someone might notice us.
Nathan That reminds me. I read in the paper that it's Prince Harry's
25 birthday in September, and he's going to have a disco at Buckingham Palace for a few hundred of his friends.
Jodie Well, so what?
Nathan There's going to be live music. They're going to need a band.
Philip What? You mean we can play for them? They might invite us?
30 **Jodie** Don't be silly, Phil.
Nathan Well, don't laugh, but maybe we should write a letter and say why don't we come and play for you?
Jodie That won't do any good.
Crystal Well, I think it's a good idea, actually.
Philip Just think – playing my drums at Buckingham Palace. 35
Jodie In your dreams.
Crystal It might work. I mean, we've got nothing to lose, have we? If they throw the letter in the bin, so what? But if they say yes, well, that'll be our big break. 40
Philip Great! Come on, let's do it then.
Jodie Give me a piece of paper, Nathan. Thanks. OK, 'Dear Prince Harry … '
Nathan We should write to the Queen. It's her place, isn't it? 45
Jodie I'll start again, OK, 'Dear Queen … '
Crystal 'Dear Queen Elizabeth … '
Jodie OK. 'Dear Queen Elizabeth, …'

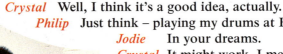

36 thirty-six

EXERCISE 5

Here are the answers to some questions about Text 1. Can you ask the questions?

➡ At Nathan's house.
   Where do the band practise their songs?
1 They both think the band is great.
2 She's trying to write a song.
3 'Baby, you're mine' is the most popular.
4 At a fashion show.
5 She sent it to some record companies.
6 In the newspaper.
7 At Buckingham Palace.
8 Yes, she thinks it's a good idea.
9 If they do, it'll be a big break for the band.
10 Jodie is writing it.

EXERCISE 7

Rewrite the sentences. Use *might*.

➡ Maybe the band are at Crystal's house.
   The band *might* be at Crystal's house.
➡ Perhaps the Queen will invite us to the Palace.
   The Queen *might* invite us to the Palace.
➡ Maybe they won't listen to the tape.
   They *might not* listen to the tape.

EXERCISE 8

033

Listening

Sally is a radio reporter. She is interviewing a boy called Richard. He wants a ticket to a Britney Spears concert in London. Listen to the conversation and then answer the questions.

1 How long has Richard been in the queue?
2 Does Richard like Britney Spears as a person or as a singer?
3 How many times has he met her?
4 Does Richard agree that Britney Spears is going to marry Prince William?
5 Does Britney Spears come from a big city or a small town?
6 What does Britney Spears like to do in her free time?
7 What is Richard's favourite Britney Spears song?

EXERCISE 6

Can you say it in English? These sentences are all in the text.

➡ Ich weiß es nicht.
   I don't know.
1 Sehr komisch.
2 Der Meinung bin ich nicht.
3 Das stimmt.
4 Weißt du, was wir brauchen?
5 Das wissen wir.
6 Da fällt mir was ein.
7 Ja, und?
8 Sei nicht blöd.
9 Lach nicht.
10 Das wird nichts nützen.
11 Es könnte gehen.
12 Wir haben nichts zu verlieren, oder?
13 Also, machen wir's.
14 Ich fange noch mal an.

1 Perhaps my parents will drive us to the gig.
2 Maybe your friends are in the music room.
3 Perhaps this song isn't any good.
4 Maybe we'll go to the concert on Saturday.
5 Perhaps the band has a website.
6 Maybe Beckham won't play today.
7 Perhaps I'll watch this film about the Spice Girls.
8 Maybe there's a piano at school.

TEXT 1

Unit 3 ACTIVITIES — BEING BIG TIME

034

1 'At Your Side' by The Corrs — a big-time Irish band

When the daylight's gone,
   and you're on your own
And you need a friend,
   just to be around
I will comfort you, I will
   take your hand
And I'll pull you through,
   I will understand
And you know that …

I'll be at your side
There's no need to worry
Together, we'll survive
Through the haste and hurry
I'll be at your side, when you
   feel like you're alone
And you've nowhere to turn,
   I'll be at your side

If life's standing still, and
   your soul's confused
And you cannot find what
   road to choose
If you make mistakes, you
   won't let me down
I will still believe, I won't
   turn around
And you know that …

I'll be at your side
There's no need to worry
Together we'll survive
Through the haste and hurry
I'll be at your side
If you feel like you're alone
And you've nowhere to turn
I'll be at your side
I'll be at your side

I'll be at your side
There's no need to worry
Together we'll survive
Through the haste and hurry
I'll be at your side, if you
   feel like you're alone
You've got somewhere to go
'Coz I'm at your side
I'll be at your side
I'll be right there for you
I'll be at your side

2 The Corrs — FAQs

These are FAQs – frequently asked questions. Fans ask these questions about The Corrs very often.

- Where are they from?
- What are their names?
- Why do the girls all look the same?
- How old are they?
- When did they first start playing together?
- Who plays which instrument in the band?
- Are any of them married?

You are running a The Corrs fanclub and have got the chance to interview the band. Write down the interview. The questions and photos and the information on page 15 might help you, but you can also make up your own questions and answers.

ACTIVITIES

3 Test yourself: Are you going to be big time one day? Answer the following questions and write down how many As, Bs, … you've got. Count your points.

1 You want Madonna as lead singer in your band but she hasn't answered your letter. So …
- you forget about the idea of a band and decide to become a maths teacher. **B**
- you write another letter to Britney Spears. **C**
- you ask your music teacher for the names of girls who would make a good pop singer. **E**

2 Your band is doing the first gig at a club, but only three people have come: your mum, the guitar player's little sister and a strange man in a black coat. What will you do?
- You cry in your mother's arms. **B**
- You love playing, so you go ahead and perform as well as you can. **F**
- You start playing and watch the strange man. Maybe he will give you a record contract. **D**

3 You're giving a radio interview but no one calls in to ask you about your music and your band. What are you going to do?
- You stay cool because you've told all your friends to phone after a few minutes. **E**
- You go home and take your tapes with you. **B**
- You complain to the manager of the radio station and everyone at home can hear you. **A**

4 You earn 20,000 ” on your first tour of South Germany. What are you going to do with the money?
- You spend all the money playing arcade games and buy expensive clothes. **B**
- The band buys new instruments and some extra equipment for the next CD. **E**
- You give exciting parties for lots of famous people so that you'll be in the magazines every week and everybody will know about your band. **D**

5 After a concert a crowd of cheering fans are waiting for you outside. What are you going to do?
- You push them away and get into your car – it shows them that you're really cool! **B**
- You write your name on people's bodies or on their tickets and you kiss all the girls – or, if you are a girl, you kiss all the boys. **F**
- You throw some CDs into the audience and hide until morning. **C**

Results: A = – 5, B = 0, C = 1, D = 2, E = 5, F = 10

Less than 8 points:
Forget it, you don't really like doing gigs with a band. You think fans are awful and you're looking for an easy job where you can earn a lot of money. I'm afraid you have to look for something else! Maybe the manager of a big company? Be sure you do some extra school work.

8 to 15 points:
You know that it's a hard job to become a pop star. You must practise for hours and hours every week. Think it over again: Do you really love music or do you just want to be famous? Have you ever thought about being a film star? Join the drama club at your school. Start wearing cool sunglasses when you meet your friends.

More than 15 points:
Great! You'll make it! You really love music, your band and your fans! You're good-looking and you get along with people very well. You will be big time if you try hard.

thirty-nine **39**

Unit 3 **INTRODUCTION 2**

  SITUATION 3

035

The next day the band sent this letter to the Queen. Nathan posted it on his way to school.

These are indirect objects.

They sent **the Queen** a letter.
They sent a letter to **the Queen**.
→ page 100

12 Finchley Road
15 July 20—

Dear Queen Elizabeth,

We hope you don't mind that we're writing this letter to you. We are two girls and two boys, and we're a pop band called Spider. We're also sending you a tape with some of our songs. We'd like to perform at Prince Harry's birthday party in September. We think he'll like our music. What do you think?

If you invite us to the party, we'll be good. We don't use bad language, and we don't do drugs. You can safely invite us to the Palace, and we'll be no problem. Please give us a chance. If we get a break, we might just have a great future. We're looking forward to your answer.

Love and xxxx,
Nathan, Crystal, Jodie and Phil

It's your lucky day. Somebody's sent you a present.

EXERCISE 9

Who gave who a present at Christmas? Use these words: *a boat, a book, a candle, some chocolates, some drums, a mobile phone, a poster, some socks.*

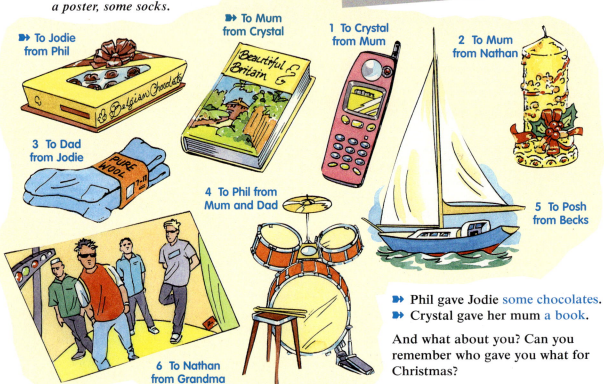

➡ Phil gave Jodie some chocolates.
➡ Crystal gave her mum a book.

And what about you? Can you remember who gave you what for Christmas?

40 forty

INTRODUCTION 2

EXERCISE 10

Look again at the pictures in exercise 9 and write a sentence about each present.

- What about the candle? Crystal gave it to her mum.
- What about the socks? Jodie gave them to her dad.

1. What about the drums?
2. And the poster?
3. And tell me about the mobile phone.
4. And the boat?
5. What about the chocolates?
6. What about the book?

SITUATION 4

036

Mum	I'm surprised you've got an answer. And I'm amazed they've actually said yes.
Nathan	I can't believe it.
Dad	We can buy you a new guitar.
Mum	We'll buy some new equipment for all of you. We'll talk to the others about it. And we'll have to get you something new to wear.
Nathan	It's OK, mum. You bought me a guitar last year. And you got all those clothes for us, remember?

Can I get you a drink?

Thanks, but someone is already getting one for me.

EXERCISE 11

Fiona is doing a course in music at an activity centre. She's talking to Claire and Helen. They're learning to play musical instruments. Choose the right answer from the words in brackets.

Claire	Can you lend me (me / to me) your flute, please, Fiona? I've got my first lesson after lunch.
Fiona	OK, but can you give it back … (me / to me / for me) at four o'clock?
Claire	Oh, it's a nice flute. Is it new?
Fiona	Yes, my parents bought it … (to me / for me) last year.
Helen	They've got some flutes here. The teacher was giving them … (the older pupils / to the older pupils) yesterday. I expect they had to give … (them / to them / for them) back to him afterwards.
Claire	Oh, well maybe I won't need yours then, Fiona.
Fiona	OK, well it's lunch time now. I'll have to go and get my purse.
Claire	I've got some money. I can buy … (you / to you / for you) a sandwich if you like.
Fiona	Oh, thanks. Well, can you lend … (me / to me) some money, please? I'll pay it back … (you / to you) later.

→ page 100

forty-one 41

Unit 3   TEXT 2

Absolutely fantastic

037

After Spider played at Prince Harry's party, this report appeared in a popular magazine.

Four young people aged between 15 and 17 years old played pop music in front of 750 guests at Prince Harry's birthday party in Buckingham Palace on Friday. Nathan Freeman, Crystal King, Jodie Hobbs and her stepbrother Philip Minako are the four members of the band Spider.

They were a big hit with Harry and his guests. The prince thought they were 'absolutely fantastic', and he said it was 'a wonderful evening'.

'We practised every day in the weeks before the show,' said Jodie. 'We worked very hard. And we were really nervous on the day. We knew it was our big chance, and we didn't want to make a mess of it. We just started to play, and it went OK. They seemed to like the music. They all cheered and stamped their feet when we played 'Baby, you're mine'.

We had to do it twice. And the Prince clearly had a good time because he danced with three or four different girls.'

Two months ago, Spider decided to write a letter to the Queen. They told her they would like to play for her grandson on his birthday. They also sent her a tape of their music. 'We weren't very hopeful actually,' said Nathan, 'and maybe the letter was a bit cheeky, but three weeks later we got an answer. And the answer was yes. We still can't believe it. I still think I'm going to wake up in a minute and it'll all be a dream.'

The band get a lot of help from their parents. 'My mum prints posters for us,' said Nathan. 'And my parents have bought us some new equipment. They don't mind if we practise at our house. We're really lucky.

Other parents might complain about the noise. I know people in another band, and they've got nowhere to practise.'

They started the band after Nathan sang at his bar mitzvah. 'He sang beautifully, in my opinion,' said his dad. 'After that he knew what he wanted to do. He got together with Crystal, (on keyboard) and her best friend Jodie (on guitar).' 'And Philip played the drums for them,' added Philip's mum, Mrs Hobbs. 'They all seem to get on very well together.'

Until now Spider have performed only in schools. But things will be different in future. 'This is our big break,' said Crystal. 'A top record company has offered us a contract. And we're going to be on 'Top of the Pops' in two weeks. I think we're on our way to the big time.'

42 forty-two

EXERCISE 12

A reporter wrote this story about Spider at Buckingham Palace. But he made lots of mistakes. Can you write his report correctly?

On Tuesday afternoon, five boys played church music in front of Prince William and his guests. William thought the team were 'not bad'.

'Before the show we didn't do much work on our music,' said one member of the club. 'And when we played 'Baby, it's time', they all laughed and jumped up and down.'

The five sent a polite e-mail to William's father three weeks ago and sent him a poster. He invited them to the Tower. And their friends bought them a new car. They still think it's all a mistake.

Now a top fashion company has offered them a tour. And in four weeks they're going to be on 'Neighbours'.

EXERCISE 13

Put in the missing word and complete the sentences. Each missing word is in the text.

1 I'm sure this is just a dream. I'm going to w… up soon.
2 The computer has p… out the e-mail from Prince Harry.
3 If there's something wrong with your new guitar, you should take it back to the shop and c… .
4 The band has already a… on two TV shows.
5 Mr and Mrs Freeman have bought some new e… for the band.
6 I'm very h… that we're going to get a break at last.
7 I think the gig was OK. Everything s… to go all right.
8 The company has o… us a chance to make a record.

EXERCISE 14

Imagine that you are a member of Spider. After the party, you are writing a report about it for the school newspaper. Use these notes.

- last Friday – band – 750 people – Harry – Palace
- yes – true – not a joke
- all start – July – decide – letter – Queen
- say – would like – play – party
- amazed – say – yes
- before – work hard – nervous
- but – OK – like – music
- play 'Baby …' – twice
- now – company – contract
- soon – TV
- we – way – big time
- dream – not believe

You can start like this:

Last Friday our band Spider played in front of 750 people …

EXERCISE 15

Mum worries a lot. She always thinks something bad is going to happen. Complete what she is saying to her children. Use *will* or *might* and choose one of the words in brackets.

➡ If you don't wear a coat, you**'ll be cold**. (hot/cold)
➡ If you don't hold the swing with both hands, you **might fall off**. (fall/jump)
1 If the neighbours hear your music at night, they … . (explain/complain)
2 If you don't go to the bus-stop now, … . (miss/lose)
3 If you try to do your homework too quickly, … . (mistakes/opinions)
4 If your rabbits don't get enough to eat, … . (die/hurt)
5 If you don't keep the money safe in your pocket, … . (hold/steal)
6 If you aren't more careful on your bike, … . (adventure/accident)

Choose a favourite film star, pop singer or sporting hero. You can work on the same person in pairs or groups. Find a picture of the person and put it on the classroom wall together with a few sentences of information. One of you can give a short talk to the class about your favourite star. Your teacher will give you more information about what you can do.

Unit 3 **COMMUNICATION**

Opinions Meinungen

So fragt man nach einer Meinung	• What do you think of /about the problem?
Seine Meinung äußert man mit	• I think it's a good idea. In my opinion, everybody should have a mobile phone.
So stimmt man einer Meinung zu	• Yes, I agree with you. Yes, that's right.
Man widerspricht einer Meinung	• *direkt* Well, I think it's a terrible idea. But it'll be expensive, won't it?
	• *höflich* I'm afraid I don't agree.

Reporter What do you think of the new 'Star Wars'?
Girl Not much. Actually, I think it's boring.
Boy Well, I think it's great. It's a fantastic film in my opinion.

EXERCISE 16

Du führst mit deinem Partner/deiner Partnerin ein kurzes Gespräch. Folgende Punkte sollen darin vorkommen.

- *Du fragst ihn/sie nach seiner/ihrer Meinung über das neue Computerspiel 'Alphastar'.*
- *Er/Sie meint, dass es ein sehr langweiliges Spiel sei.*
- *Du widersprichst und behauptest, dass es ein interessantes Spiel sei.*
- *Er/Sie sagt, es sei langweilig. 'Superworld' sei viel besser.*
- *Du antwortest, dass du davon gehört hast, es aber nicht kennst.*
- *Er/Sie fragt, ob du es bei ihm/ihr spielen möchtest.*
- *Du reagierst darauf.*

TEST YOUR ENGLISH

Prince William

In thirty or more years from now, if the British haven't burned down Buckingham Palace, Prince William will probably become King William V. But that's a long way in the future.

5 William, 'Wills', was born in June 1982. His father is Prince Charles, the Queen's son. His mother was Princess Diana. She showed Wills that life for the royal family can be fun. When she learned that he liked Cindy Crawford, Diana invited the supermodel to tea with her and Wills. You can imagine how Wills felt when his mum died in a car accident in Paris in September 1997.

Wills is 1 metre 82 tall, and he has fair hair and blue eyes. Lots of girls think he's lovely.

10 Wills went to Eton, a very expensive school, where he met the sons and daughters of other very rich people. His best subjects were French and art. He likes sport and fast cars. Two of his favourite bands are Pulp and the Spice Girls, and his favourite Spice Girl is Emma, Baby Spice. He's also a big Britney Spears fan. At school he had a poster of Pamela Anderson, one of the stars of Baywatch, a popular TV show.

15 Wills doesn't like the media – newspaper and TV reporters. His younger brother Harry likes all the attention, but Wills is shy. He tries to keep away from crowds and reporters. Of course it isn't easy for a future king to be alone – there are two detectives by his side everywhere he goes.

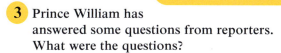

TEST YOUR ENGLISH

1 Answer these questions on the text.

1 What will probably happen to Prince William one day?
2 How did he meet Cindy Crawford?
3 How old was William when his mother died?
4 What colour are William's eyes?
5 What language did he learn at school?
6 What does he think about the Spice Girls?
7 How did Pamela Anderson become famous?
8 Are William and Harry both shy?

2 Complete this information about Princess Diana. Put in the missing words or the correct form of the words in brackets.

Princess Diana ... born into a very rich family. Once, ... she was a little girl, she ... (meet) Prince Charles, ... future husband. At the ... of 19, she was ... (work) as a teacher of young ... (child) in London. Then in 1981 she ... (marry) Prince Charles, the ... (old) of the Queen's three sons. Almost overnight, a shy young woman ... (become) a beautiful princess. Her photo was everywhere. In a few years Charles and Diana ... (have) two sons, William and Harry.

But there ... (be) problems. Diana was more popular ... Charles, but she ... (not be) happy. Her husband loved another woman. In 1992 Charles and Diana decided ... (go) their separate ways. Diana stayed popular and famous. She ... (fall) in love again. The papers ... (be) full of stories ... her. Maybe she wanted ... (marry) again. But then the story suddenly ... (end) one night in Paris.

3 Prince William has answered some questions from reporters. What were the questions?

1 *Reporter* ... the Spice Girls?
  William Yes, but I like other bands, too.
2 *Reporter* ... of Pam Anderson in your room?
  William No, I haven't got that poster now.
3 *Reporter* ... ?
  William My favourite film star? I don't know.
4 *Reporter* ... a car?
  William Yes, I am. I'm going to buy a really fast one.
5 *Reporter* ... ?
  William Yes, I did. I enjoyed my trip to Canada very much.
6 *Reporter* ... very often?
  William Yes, of course. I often see my father. That's a strange question.
7 *Reporter* ... ?
  William No, I don't think it is true. I'm not a shy person.

4 Here is some information about Prince William for visitors to Madame Tussaud's in London. Can you translate the information for German visitors?

Prince William is tall, and he looks like his mother. He's very popular, and all the girls love him. William went to school at Eton, not far from London. He enjoyed school because there were no reporters there. Wills is a bit shy. But he's been lucky. He's met famous people. Once he and his brother Harry met the Spice Girls. (You can see them in the next room.) What does William think about his future? He'll have to wait a long time before he can be king.

039

5 Listen to the conversation between Paul and Kirsty. Which picture shows what happened?

READING   Young people in sport

Mia Hamm

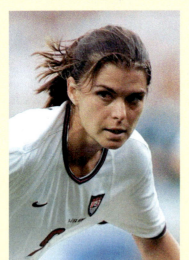

Mia Hamm plays football, what the Americans call 'soccer'. She plays for the US, and they're the World Champions. Mia is the best woman soccer player in the world and one of the most famous and most popular women in world sport. She was US soccer's Female Athlete of the Year five times in five years. Her face is in newspapers and magazines, on posters and in TV advertisements all over America.

Mia's father was in the Air Force, and his wife and six children had to move around with him. Mia was born in Alabama, but she also lived in California, Texas, Virginia and Italy. At 14 Mia was the star of girls' school soccer in Texas. At 15 she played for the US Women's National Team, their youngest player ever. That was back in 1987.

Mia is a quiet, almost shy person. But it's different when she's playing football. She's very quick, very strong and very dangerous. She scores lots of goals, more than any other player in the history of the game. But she's also a team player. She always talks about how the team performed and not just about Mia Hamm.

In 1999 Mia started a company called the Mia Hamm Foundation. An important part of its work is about females in sport. Mia wants to give other girls and women the chance to succeed in their sport.

Jenson Button

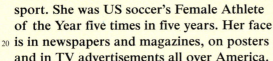

Jenson Button lives with his father John near Oxford. John loves motor-racing, and his company makes go-karts. Jenson was driving go-karts almost before he was walking. He won races against much older boys. Soon he was British champion in his age group. John knew he had a future Formula One driver on his hands.

John took Jenson to races all over Britain and in other countries. He missed a lot of school lessons. 'I didn't worry. He's clever enough,' says John. 'He didn't seem to fall behind the others.'

All these journeys to races were expensive, and John didn't have much money. Once, when they were driving home from a race in Scotland, they had to borrow money for petrol.

But Jenson won lots of races, and people started to notice him. Soon they wanted to sponsor him. He went into motor-racing, and he did well in Formula Ford. Then he got his big break. 20-year-old Jenson was talking to his friends in the pub when his mobile phone rang. It was Sir Frank Williams. He offered Jenson a Formula One contract. Jenson became a member of the Williams team. In the year 2000 he became the youngest ever British driver in a Formula One race.

On his way to the big time, Jenson lost a few races, and he had a few accidents (luckily no serious ones). Perhaps the worst moment was when he failed his first driving test at 17. The problem of course was that he drove too fast.

UNIT 4
MOMENTS IN HISTORY

WORDS AND PICTURES

 Early in the morning of 28th September 1066, Norman soldiers landed on the south coast of England. There were no English soldiers on the coast because King Harold of England and his army were in the north. They were fighting a battle against another enemy, invaders from Norway.

A couple of weeks later, Duke William of Normandy defeated Harold at the Battle of
5 Hastings and soon conquered the country. He gave the land to his Norman lords. William's knights made sure that the English did what the King wanted. Many English people now felt like strangers in their own country. The ordinary people spoke English, but the King and the lords and all the important people spoke French. It
10 took another 250 years before a King of England spoke English again. After all that time it was difficult to say who was Anglo-Saxon and who was Norman. The Normans
15 became part of the English mixture.

In the 16th century there was another important moment in English history. It was the time of Henry VIII, the one with six wives. Henry had an argument with the Pope and broke away from Rome. He became the head of a new Church of England.

Henry's daughter, Elizabeth I, was Queen for 45 years.
20 Her most dangerous moment came when King Philip of Spain tried to invade England in 1588. But the Spanish Armada did not defeat England. Many of their ships sank in a sea battle and in terrible storms.

At this time the theatre was very popular in
25 England, and William Shakespeare was beginning to write his plays.

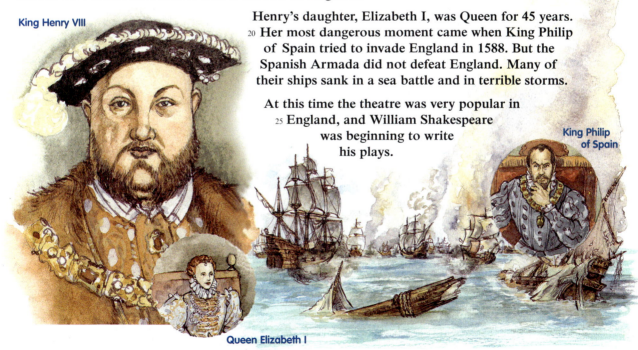

King Henry VIII

King Philip of Spain

Queen Elizabeth I

PROJECT Your project will be about the 'Bayeux tapestry'. Find out what it is and what story it tells.

forty-seven **47**

Unit 4   **INTRODUCTION 1**

 SITUATION 1

041

The McCarthys are visiting friends in York.

Mum   Let's go to the Viking museum.
James What's a Viking?
Mum   They were people who sailed here from Scandinavia. It was over a thousand years ago, even before the Normans. I'm sure the museum has got a poster which tells you all about them.
Pat   The Vikings were great. They killed everyone that got in their way.

Mum   What a stupid thing to say, Pat. Let's go to the museum. You can ride on a car that takes you back in time to when York was a Viking city.

the person who …
the thing which …

→ page 101

EXERCISE 1

Complete these sentences about people and things in history. Put in *who* or *which*.

 The people who built Stonehenge lived a long time before the Druids.
 The Roman emperor Hadrian built a wall which kept out the people to the north.
1 The person … pulled the sword out of the stone was Arthur.
2 The Anglo-Saxons were farmers … lived in villages.
3 The people from Scandinavia … invaded England were called Vikings.
4 The land … belonged to the Anglo-Saxons fell into the hands of the Normans.
5 The tapestry … tells the story is at Bayeux in Normandy.
6 Many of the Spanish ships … sailed to England did not get home again.
7 Guy Fawkes was a Catholic … tried to blow up the Houses of Parliament.
8 Shakespeare wrote many plays … are still popular today.

EXERCISE 2

Complete the sentences. Use *who* or *which*.

 This is the bus which goes to the Tower.
1 William was the king … .
2 That's the museum … .
3 Mr Moss is the teacher … .
4 The Spanish were the first Europeans … .
5 No one can find the sword … .

This bus goes to the Tower.

William conquered England.

This museum opened last month.

Mr Moss took us to Hadrian's Wall.

The Spanish arrived in California.

This sword was in the stone.

48   forty-eight

INTRODUCTION 1

SITUATION 2

042

Tom Who are the people in this photo?
James They're waxworks of Vikings that we saw at a museum in York. We went there with some friends who we were visiting.
Tom Is that the Jorvik Museum?
James That's right. It's really good.

EXERCISE 3

Say it in one sentence. Use a relative clause with *who*, *which* or *that*.

➡ The Freemans bought some equipment. The band needed it.
  The Freemans bought some equipment that the band needed.
1 The McCarthy family visited some people. They met them on holiday.
  The McCarthy family … they met on … .
2 Crystal saw the poster. Jodie put it on her bedroom wall.
3 Everyone liked the songs. Spider sang them.
4 They played for all the guests. Harry invited the guests to his party.
5 Nathan is watching a music programme. He recorded it last night.
6 What's the name of that film star? Crystal fancies him.

Look at these relative clauses.

Subject pronoun	The woman **who / that** spoke to us is Philip's mum. (**She** spoke to us.)
	The letter **which / that** came today was for me. (**It** came today.)
Object pronoun	The woman **who / that** we saw earlier is Philip's mum. (We saw **her**.)
	The letter **which / that** I was reading came today. (I was reading **it**.)

➡ page 101-102

SITUATION 3

 043

James You see this Viking? Well, Pat has got a friend whose mum looks just like her.
Tom Oh, which friend is that?
James Vicky Megson. She's the girl whose dad once gave us a lift to the school disco. Remember?
Tom Oh, yes. Maybe her mum is a Viking then.

You're the girl whose mum works in a sports shop.

EXERCISE 4

Explain who these people are or were. Use *who* or *whose*.

➡ Fiona – she lives in Dublin
  Fiona is the girl who lives in Dublin.
➡ Kay – his father looked after Arthur
  Kay was the boy whose father looked after Arthur
1 Philip – he plays the drums
2 the Spice Girls – their song 'Wannabe' went to number one
3 Emma – her older brother works in London
4 the Normans – they conquered England in 1066
5 Nathan – his parents bought some new equipment for the band
6 Elizabeth I – her ships defeated the Spanish Armada
7 Spider – they played at Buckingham Palace

forty-nine **49**

Unit 4   TEXT 1

On the battlefield

044

It was a cool day in early autumn. Ethel (15) and her brother Wilfred (12) walked out of the village, across the big field and into the forest. Ethel had a basket for the berries that they wanted to pick that afternoon.

There were pigs in the forest, and once they saw some deer. About two miles into the forest they heard a noise in the distance, the kind of noise which you can hear when somebody is working with iron and making a knife or an axe. People were shouting, too.

After another mile they came out of the forest and then stopped suddenly. In front of them, in the distance, were two armies. There were thousands of men. On the left, at the top of a slope, was a long line of soldiers with shields. Down on the right of the battlefield was the other army.

'It's a battle,' said Ethel. 'Those down there are the Normans. Duke William's men. They're from over the water. Some of them fight on horses, look.'
'And the ones at the top are ours?'
'Yes, that's King Harold and his men.'

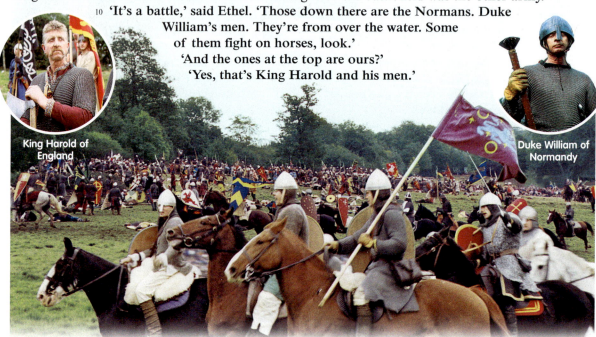

King Harold of England

Duke William of Normandy

The Normans were attacking the English. The English soldiers stood in a line with their shields in front of them. The Normans charged into the English line and swung their swords. The English swung their axes. Ethel and Wilfred watched in horror as some English soldiers attacked a Norman whose horse was on the ground.

After a while there were fewer English in the line. On the slope there were a lot of dead bodies – dead men and dead horses. The battle stopped while everyone had a rest.

'Why are the Normans here?' asked Wilfred.
'William wants to conquer us and be king,' said Ethel. 'His soldiers have burned the villages and farms along the coast. Mum and dad heard it from someone who was travelling through the village.'

'What will happen if Harold loses?'
'William will be king. Dad says the Normans will burn our village too and kill us and all our animals.'

'I'm scared,' said Wilfred. 'Me too. We ought to go home,' said Ethel. 'And it'll be dark soon.'

Then at last something happened. The Normans shot a lot of arrows in the air. They fell on the English soldiers. Then the Normans charged up the slope again and into the wall of shields. This time they broke through. The English fought hard, but they were tired, and the Normans were stronger. King Harold fell under the Norman swords.

Ethel and Wilfred left the basket behind them and ran back through the forest.

50   fifty

TEXT 1

EXERCISE 5

Match these sentences to the pictures below and write them in the correct order.

1. Some time later the Normans shot some arrows into the air.
2. This time they broke through the English line.
3. The English fought with their axes against the Normans on horses.
4. The Norman knights killed King Harold.
5. The Normans attacked the English line, but they didn't break through.

➡ A3 The English fought with their axes against the Normans on horses.

A

B

C

D

E

EXERCISE 6

When Ethel and Wilfred got back to their cottage, they told their mother about the battle. Write the conversation from the notes. You can practise it in groups of three.

Mum	late • where?
Ethel	see battle • other side – forest
Wilfred	Normans • thousands – men
Mum	battle – over? • happen?
Ethel	Normans – win • kill – Harold
Wilfred	happen – now? • Normans – kill?
Mum	leave – today • go – find – father • quick

EXERCISE 7

045

Listening

Oliver is telling Kate what his family did at the weekend. Listen to the conversation and then complete the sentences. Put one word in each space.

1. First Oliver's family went to … .
2. When the Normans arrived in England, they made a … for the army.
3. It's about … miles from Hastings to Battle.
4. Battle is a small … .
5. The Normans built a … at Battle.
6. At the place where Harold died, there's a … in the ground.

Battle Abbey

PROJECT

Find the scenes in the Bayeux tapestry which tell the story of 1066, how the Normans sailed to England and defeated Harold. Choose what you think are the most important pictures and then copy them. Then you can work in pairs. You should photocopy a picture or print it out from the internet. (Search for 'Bayeux tapestry'.) Write one or two sentences in English above the picture. Then put all the pictures together in the right order and make a display in the classroom.

Unit 4 ACTIVITIES — HOW ROBIN HOOD GOT THE SHERIFF'S HORSE

046 Welcome to the 12th century! In Sherwood Forest our friend Robin Hood, the famous outlaw, and his Merry Men were doing their job just like they did every day.

Usually things went right …

… but sometimes things went wrong.

One Friday morning, a potter was driving through the forest on his way to the market.

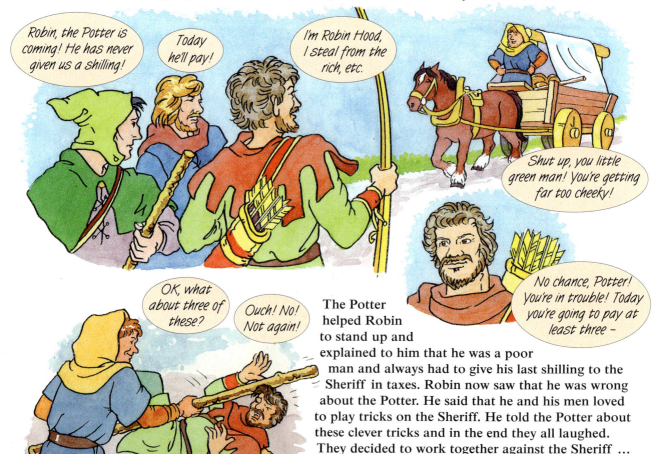

Look at the clever potter's answer!

The Potter helped Robin to stand up and explained to him that he was a poor man and always had to give his last shilling to the Sheriff in taxes. Robin now saw that he was wrong about the Potter. He said that he and his men loved to play tricks on the Sheriff. He told the Potter about these clever tricks and in the end they all laughed. They decided to work together against the Sheriff … The Potter lent Robin his clothes and a little later, Robin, 'the Potter' drove to Nottingham market to sell his new friend's goods.

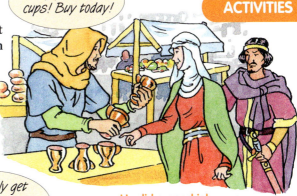

He sold so many that there were just five cups left when the Sheriff's wife came along. He gave them to her as a present. She was surprised and happy – but the Sheriff, her husband, was jealous. He invited Robin to an archery contest. The prize was a bag of gold. Of course the Sheriff never wanted to give away the money, he thought he could make a fool of the 'Potter'. But it turned out that the Potter was very good at archery, and this made the Sheriff very angry.

He did a good job.

Robin could even split the arrow in two.

So off they went and as they were riding through Sherwood Forest, the Sheriff had a wonderful dream: with the help of the Potter he was arresting Robin Hood, the famous outlaw. And of course he didn't really need to give the Potter his prize. What a great day this would be! But suddenly a crowd of Merry Men stood in their way.

Finally the Sheriff understood what was going on …

And so it happened that the Sheriff had to give Robin his horse, his sword, his money, his clothes, …

It was a long and hard journey home.

The free cups became very expensive for the Sheriff in the end. The Merry Men gave the Potter his share and gave the rest of the money to the poor just as usual …

… but sometimes Robin forgets that he died 800 years ago.

fifty-three **53**

Unit 4   **INTRODUCTION 2**

 SITUATION 4

047 Oliver, Ben and Mrs Preston are at the Tower of London.

Mum   That building there is the White Tower. It's the part William built. The other buildings came later.
Ben   Where are the weapons we saw last time? There were swords and guns.
Oliver   Yes and the heavy armour they wore. That was interesting.
Mum   I think it's all in the White Tower. Come on, let's go and see.

Relative clauses	
With object pronoun	We were visiting some people **who / that** we know.
	These are the photos **which / that** I took.
Without object pronoun	We were visiting some people we know.
	These are the photos I took. → page 103

You can use these object pronouns, but you don't need them.

EXERCISE 8

Write sentences from the table.

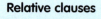

Baseball is the game	Ravi supports.
Smash Hits is the magazine	Jessica rode.
Maths is the subject	Sophie always watches.
East Enders is the soap opera	Ben likes playing.
Lollipop is the horse	the Jewells sometimes visit.
Arsenal is the team	Lehka reads.
Midway Farm is the place	Mr Williams teaches.

➡ Baseball is the game Ben likes playing.

EXERCISE 9

Explain what the words mean. Use a relative clause with these verbs: *carry, eat, not know, like, open and close, play, ride, speak, wear, win.*

➡ A bag is something you **carry**.
➡ A friend is somebody you **like**.
1 A game …   5 A uniform …
2 A meal …   6 A prize …
3 A door …   7 A stranger …
4 A bike …   8 A language …

 SITUATION 5

048
Mum   What next?
Ben   Where are the places they kept all those prisoners in?
Oliver   And I want to see the axe they cut off people's heads with. There was something about it in the guide that I was looking at.
Mum   Well, if you really must.

Prepositions in relative clauses   → page 103
That's the boy I was talking **about**. (I was talking **about** the boy.)
The hotel that we stayed **at** was nice. (We stayed **at** the hotel.)

54   fifty-four

INTRODUCTION 2

EXERCISE 10

'Shakespeare's London flat' is a new attraction for tourists. But some of the things in it might not be genuine. What is the guide saying as she shows a group of visitors around the flat?

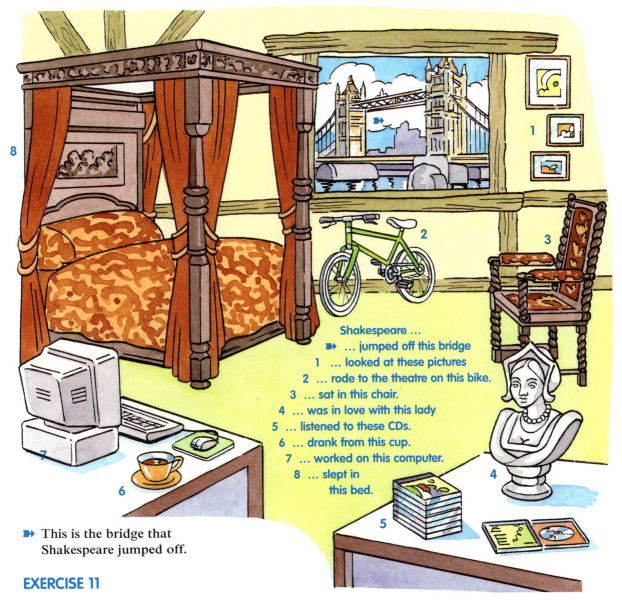

Shakespeare ...
➡ ... jumped off this bridge
1 ... looked at these pictures
2 ... rode to the theatre on this bike.
3 ... sat in this chair.
4 ... was in love with this lady
5 ... listened to these CDs.
6 ... drank from this cup.
7 ... worked on this computer.
8 ... slept in this bed.

➡ This is the bridge that Shakespeare jumped off.

EXERCISE 11

Complete the definitions. They all have relative clauses.

➡ A magician is someone who can do magic.
➡ Butter is something that you put on bread.
➡ A pen is something that you write with.
1 An activity is ... do.
2 An exercise book is a book you can ... .
3 A seat is something ... .
4 Shoes are things ... on your feet.
5 A caravan is a home ... with you on holiday.
6 A weapon ... that people ... .
7 A maze is something ... to find ... through.
8 A forecast is ... that ... you what ... happen.
9 An audience is a group of ... watching or listening.

Some of these sentences must have a relative pronoun, but some don't have to have one. Which are the sentences where you can leave out the relative pronoun?

fifty-five **55**

Unit 4 TEXT 2

The monster king

049

Henry VIII is one of the most famous people in English history. Everyone has heard of Henry and his six wives.

Henry Tudor became King of England in 1509. He was 17 years old and a very popular young man. Henry was good at dancing, riding and archery. He played several musical instruments, and he wrote songs.

He also liked spending money – on new clothes, for example. The one thing he didn't like was work, but there were ministers who did the boring things for him.

Henry married Catherine of Aragon, the daughter of the King and Queen of Spain. Henry wanted a son. He wanted more Tudor kings after him. Boys came first in those days, as they do in the royal family today.

Catherine had six children, but they all died except one – a girl, Mary. After 18 years of marriage, Henry was beginning to worry. And he wanted to marry Anne Boleyn, a young lady he was having an affair with. He decided to divorce Catherine, but he had to ask the Pope first. And that's where the problem started. The Pope said no, and Henry was furious. He decided to have his own church, and in 1534 he became head of the 'Church of England'. So now it wasn't the Pope who made the rules – it was Henry.

Henry divorced Catherine and married Anne. Seven and a half months later, a baby was born – another daughter, Elizabeth. Henry was furious (again). Soon he decided to execute Anne because of her affairs with other men. (Of course Henry was happily having affairs with other women.) A man with a sword cut off Anne's head in the Tower of London. Henry was playing tennis at the time.

Eleven days later Henry married Jane Seymour, and she did what Henry wanted – she gave him a son, Edward. But Jane died soon afterwards.

Henry's fourth marriage was to Anne of Cleves. When he saw her for the first time, he thought she looked more like a horse than a princess and not as beautiful as her picture. (Henry didn't worry about other people's feelings.) He quickly divorced Anne, and three weeks later he married somebody he really fancied. This was the 20-year-old Catherine Howard. Henry was happy. But when he found out about her love affairs, she went the same way as Anne Boleyn – to the Tower. (But for her it was an axe not a sword.) Finally Henry married a 31-year-old widow called Catherine Parr.

Henry was a monster. As he got older, he became very fat because of all the huge meals he ate, and he had a terrible temper. Catherine looked after him in his last few years, until he died in 1547.

Catherine of Aragon
Anne Boleyn
Jane Seymour
Anne of Cleves
Catherine Parr
Catherine Howard

56 fifty-six

TEXT 2

EXERCISE 12

Answer the questions on Text 2.

1. What did people think of young Henry?
2. What were Henry's favourite activities? Name four of them.
3. Who was Henry's first wife?
4. Why did he decide to divorce her?
5. Why did he want his own church?
6. Why did Henry send Anne Boleyn to the Tower?
7. What gave Henry the idea that Anne of Cleves was beautiful?
8. Who was Henry's sixth and last wife?

EXERCISE 13

Look at the table and choose three of Henry's wives. Write a paragraph about each of them.

	Name	Married	End of marriage	Children
1	Catherine of Aragon	1509	divorced 1533	Mary I
2	Anne Boleyn	1533	Tower 1536	Elizabeth I
3	Jane Seymour	1536	died 1537	Edward VI
4	Anne of Cleves	Jan 1540	divorced Jul 1540	no
5	Catherine Howard	Jul 1540	Tower 1542	no
6	Catherine Parr	1543	Henry died 1547	no

Right then, who's next?

➡ Henry's … wife was … . He married her in … and … in … . Henry and … had a son/daughter called … , later King/Queen … of England.

EXERCISE 14

Look at the explanations and give the word. All the words are in the text.

➡ the story of the past
   history
1. very angry
2. to give or pay money for something
3. to end a marriage
4. very big
5. a woman whose husband is dead
6. something you can play music on
7. you can cut down a tree with it
8. not interesting

EXERCISE 15

Find the sentence pairs and complete the second sentence.
You can use *ought to/oughtn't to* or *should/shouldn't*.

An axe can be dangerous.	We … pick some for mum.
You need to be more careful.	You … swing it around like that.
It's half past five in the morning.	We … switch the lights on.
There are lots of berries here.	You … put it in the bin over there.
It's getting dark.	We … find some level ground.
What's all this rubbish doing here?	You … wake me up so early.
We can't play football on this slope.	We … talk in the theatre. It's not polite.
The audience wants to listen to the play.	You … make so many mistakes.

➡ An axe can be dangerous. You shouldn't swing it around like that.

Unit 4 **COMMUNICATION**

050

Describing people and things
Leute und Dinge beschreiben

What does he look like?	How old / tall is she?	Can you describe her?
Alter	• He's about 15 / in his twenties / between 30 and 35 years old.	
Größe	• She's quite tall.	
Haare	• She's got short black / fair hair.	
Gesicht	• He's got blue / brown eyes.	
	• He's got a beard. / She has glasses on.	
Kleidung	• The boy was wearing a grey sweater and a baseball cap.	

What does it look like?	How big / What colour is it?	Can you describe it?
Form	• It's quite big / very small.	
	• It's long and thin. / It's round.	
Farbe	• It's green and yellow.	
Material	• It's made of plastic / wood / glass.	
Merkmale	• It's quite old.	
	• It's got my name / photo on it.	
	• There's a picture of a spaceship on it.	

Detective What did the man look like?
Sophie He was tall and thin and in his thirties. He was carrying a bag.
Detective What kind of bag?
Sophie A blue bag with the word 'Sport' on it in white letters.

EXERCISE 16

Can you describe these three people?

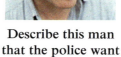

Describe this man that the police want to interview.

Describe this umbrella that you lost last week.

TEST YOUR ENGLISH

The Mary Rose

The Mary Rose was Henry VIII's favourite ship. When in 1545 the French tried to invade England, the Mary Rose was one of the ships that sailed against them. It was an old ship,
5 but it was fast and it had ninety new guns. Henry was there when it left Portsmouth with about 600 men. He was watching from a castle on the shore. The Mary Rose fired at the French fleet, but then as it was turning, it
10 began to take in water. This was probably because it was carrying too many men and too much equipment. Henry watched in horror as it sank into the sea a mile from the shore. Almost everyone on the ship lost their lives.
15 The Mary Rose stayed at the bottom of the sea for 437 years. In 1982 a big crane lifted it very slowly and carefully out of the water.

Today you can see part of the Mary Rose in a museum in Portsmouth. The wood needs to be wet, so they have to spray it with water the
20 whole time. In the museum you can see lots of other interesting things that were in the Mary Rose: weapons, clothes, shoes, plates, knives, bottles, candles and even musical instruments.

TEST YOUR ENGLISH

1 Choose the correct answers.

1 When the Mary Rose sank, it was …
  a) fighting a war against France. b) sailing around the world. c) taking some wood to Portsmouth.
2 When the ship sank, Henry was …
  a) looking out from a building on the coast.
  b) in his castle in London.
  c) on another ship about a mile away.
3 Most people on the Mary Rose …
  a) got onto another ship. b) died.
  c) swam to the shore.
4 Today the Mary Rose is
  a) at the bottom of the sea. b) in a museum. c) on the French coast.
5 Were there any musical instruments on the Mary Rose?
  a) Yes. b) No. c) No one knows.

2 Each of these sentences has two mistakes in it. Write the correct sentences.

1 When the English fleet sailed out, a lot people were watch from the shore.
2 The ship it sinked was the Mary Rose.
3 When he heard the new, the French king smiled happy.
4 We ought go to the Portsmouth and see the Mary Rose.
5 Those plates at that we was looking came from the ship.

3 Use the words in brackets in their correct form and put in the right words.

Henry VII – the father of the famous Henry VIII – … (become) king after a long war between different groups in England. Under Henry, England was … (quiet) than before, and people … (be) glad about that. But Henry … (have, be) careful because he had enemies … wanted … (get) him out and have a different king.

Henry was very mean with his money. He took lots … money from ordinary people, but he … (not like) spending it.

Henry VIII spent all the money … his father so … (careful) saved. He … (wear) expensive clothes and … (eat) expensive food. He also … (fight) some expensive wars against France, Scotland and Spain. He was trying … (be) a big star in Europe. When he died, there was almost … money left.

4 Look at the pictures and tell the story of Henry VIII and Anne of Cleves. You can start like this:

When Jane Seymour … , Henry was very … because … . But then …

5 The day after the Mary Rose sank, Henry was talking to his wife, Catherine Parr. Listen to their conversation. Answer the questions.

1 Does Henry think he will win the war against France?
2 Henry names two things that he can't do now. What are they?
3 Which wife did Henry love the best and why?
4 What does Henry say about his leg?
5 What is Henry going to have for tea? Name four things.

fifty-nine 59

READING   The haunted house

On a cold December morning, a young man called Christopher Gordon came to Gwynllan, a little village in North Wales.
5 He worked in a town not far away, and so he was looking for a small house in Gwynllan for his family.

When he got out of his car,
10 he saw some children and asked them: 'Excuse me, I want to buy a small house for me and my family. Do you know somewhere nice
15 with a big garden around it?' The children laughed. 'Oh yes,' one of the girls told him, 'there's a lovely old house with a nice garden on the
20 hill over there. No one has lived in it for ten years or so. It isn't very expensive, I'm sure, ... because ...'. Her friends pulled her away from
25 Christopher, and they ran down the street. Christopher thought: 'They're very strange children, aren't they? But that house sounds wonderful.'

30 He was very hungry, and so he went to the village pub for some sandwiches. 'Where are you from?' the friendly landlord asked him. 'I haven't seen you here
35 before.' 'Well, you're right. I'm not from Gwynllan,' said Christopher, 'but I'd like to live here. I've heard about that house on the hill. I need a big garden for my family, and
40 perhaps it's not too expensive.' The landlord shouted to all the farmers in the pub: 'Hey, here's someone who wants to buy the haunted house!'

45 'Haunted house?' Christopher asked. 'Well, I don't believe in ghosts. But why is this house haunted? Is there a story about it?' 'Not just a story. It's true,' said one of the farmers, 'there's a ghost in that house, you know.'

'Don't be silly,' Christopher 50 laughed, 'there aren't any ghosts in this world.'

'I'm not so sure about that,' said the landlord. 'Sometimes we can see a light in the house 55 on the hill, although no one has lived in it for years.' 'Yes, and sometimes you can hear a cat at night, although we've never seen one there, a woman added. 'Please keep 60 away from that dangerous place.'

'I can't believe this,' thought Christopher. He said goodbye to the people in the pub, went up the 65 hill and walked through the garden to the front door. He looked around. There were spiders everywhere. No one was around. Suddenly he heard a 'meeow'. He 70 looked around, but there was no cat. He felt a bit nervous. Perhaps it was better to leave this place and go home. Perhaps the stories were true. 'Don't be stupid,' he thought. 75 'No one lives here. There can't be any ghosts. I'll knock on the front door, but no one will answer.'

He knocked. Nothing happened. He knocked again, but again 80 nothing happened. He turned round and looked at the garden. Then the door behind him opened with a creaking sound. An old man with long white hair was standing 85 in the doorway. Behind his left foot Christopher saw – a black cat! 'Can I help you?' the old man asked politely. His voice was very quiet. 'Yes, errrm, sorry to disturb 90 you. I heard the house is for sale. I think I'd like to buy it, but the people in the pub told me there's a ghost here. Of course I don't believe these stories.'

The old man smiled. 'I've heard the story 95 too,' he said. 'It's very silly. It simply isn't true. You see, I've lived here for four hundred years, and I've never seen a ghost here.'

60 sixty

UNIT 5
DOING THE D OF E

🔘 052 In Britain about a hundred thousand young people do the Duke of Edinburgh's Award every year. Everybody calls it the 'D of E'.

WORDS AND PICTURES

You have to go on a camping expedition. Most people walk, but you can also cycle or even ride a horse.

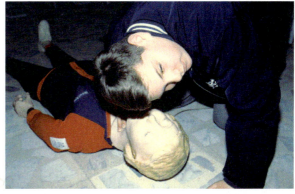

There are lots of other possible activities. You can learn useful things like first aid. You can learn to dance. You can do sport. You can do surfing or water skiing. Some people even do paragliding.

There are three Awards: Bronze, Silver and Gold. You have to be 14 before you can start on your Bronze Award. The rules are tougher as you go from Bronze to Gold. For the Bronze expedition you have to walk 15 miles in two days, but for Gold it's 50 miles in four days.

PROJECT On the next page you'll see someone who lives near Birmingham and is doing the D of E. Birmingham is a big city in the English Midlands. Your project is to find out about a British city such as Glasgow, Manchester or Cardiff.

sixty-one **61**

Unit 5 **INTRODUCTION 1**

  SITUATION 1

053

Scott Gardner lives in Dudley, a town near Birmingham in the Midlands. Scott and his friends are doing their D of E Bronze Award. They're really enjoying it.
5 Today they're with some disabled kids who are spending an afternoon at the Black Country Living Museum in Dudley. The Black Country got its name from the thick black smoke which once poured from the factory chimneys there.

10 At the museum you can see some factories, shops and houses as they were in the old days. There are old buses and trams, and there are boats on the canal. There's even a fairground. Scott is slowly pushing
15 Alex around in his wheelchair. They're just going past the fairground.

Scott That ride looks good, but it's a pity you can't take a wheelchair on it.
Alex Oh, it doesn't matter. These
20   sweets taste nice, don't they?
Scott Yes, they're OK. Oh, look. Here's the school. We can go in here because there's a ramp. I can get you up there if I push hard.
25 Alex School doesn't sound very exciting.
Scott We can go to a lesson. It'll be like it was a hundred years ago.
Alex So we'll have to sit there quietly and listen.
30 Scott It might be fun.
Alex OK, but if we get bored, we'll go, right?
Scott Oh, we're too early. It says the next lesson isn't until three o'clock.
Alex Well, let's take a trip along the canal first.

Adjectives	Adverbs
She had a **quiet** voice.	She spoke **quietly**.
You must be **careful**.	You must do it **carefully**.
	→ page 104

fast, hard, long, early

This is a fast car. I can go fast in it.

These words are adjectives AND adverbs.

62 sixty-two

INTRODUCTION 1

EXERCISE 1

Put in the missing adverbs. Form them from these adjectives: *angry, careful, early, excited, good, hard, long, quiet, slow*. But be careful: not all the adverbs end with *-ly*.

▶ 'Look, there's a fairground!' Alex said **excitedly**.
1. We'll have to sit … at our desks and not say a word.
2. Scott and Alex listened … as the teacher explained.
3. When someone in the class laughed, she shouted … .
4. We haven't got much time, so we won't stay … at the museum.
5. Let's go a bit faster, Scott. We're going too … .
6. Scott is good at first aid. He did very … in his test.
7. The D of E isn't easy. You have to work quite … .
8. Scott delivers newspapers at seven o'clock on Sunday morning, so he has to get up quite … .

EXERCISE 2

Make sentences from the list. Use an adjective (*bad, clear*) or an adverb (*badly, clearly*).

▶	The plane flew through a storm. But it landed	bad / **badly**
▶	I like your jacket. It looks very	clear / **clearly**
1	It wasn't very warm in the church. I felt quite	safe / **safely**
2	The little girl was really angry. She stamped her foot	shy / **shyly**
3	We ought to go home now. It's getting	cold / **coldly**
4	The team didn't play so well. Actually they played	urgent / **urgently**
5	I don't like this yoghurt. It tastes	**smart** / smartly
6	The new girl doesn't say much. She seems very	furious / **furiously**
7	I can't read what you've written. You don't write very	funny / **funnily**
8	Nobody knew about our date. We met	secret / **secretly**
9	Mr Williams wants to see you. Hurry up. It sounds	dark / **darkly**

be
get (werden)
become
stay
seem
look (aussehen)
sound
feel
smell
taste

▶ The plane flew through a storm. But it landed safely.
▶ I like your jacket. It looks very smart.

You can play this game. Think of sentences where most of the words start with the same letter.

▶ **A**fterwards **A**my **a**te **a**n **a**wful **a**pple **a**ngrily.
▶ In **B**righton **B**en **b**uilt a **b**ig **b**ridge **b**adly.

Choose four or five different letters and think of sentences with each letter. Try to use adjectives and adverbs. Who can make the longest sentence? And who can make the funniest?

Verb + adjective

We'll have to be **quiet**.
We might get **bored**.
That ride looks **good**.
This D of E thing sounds **interesting**.
These sweets taste **nice**.

→ page 105

sixty-three **63**

Unit 5   **TEXT 1**

  Never again

054

This is Scott's diary of his D of E expedition.

Tuesday lunch time

We're sitting on the top of a big hill we've just climbed. We're enjoying a rest as we listen to Sting on Nick's radio. It's cloudy but warm, and we're drinking lots of water. I've taken several photos of the marvellous views.

There are eight of us – four boys and four girls. The other boys are my friends Matthew, Jamie and Nick. Two of the girls, Alice and Natalie, are from our school, but there are two from another school who have joined our group for this trip. They're called Donna and Louise.

Our teacher Mr Hibbert drove us to the start this morning in the very old and very uncomfortable school minibus. The journey from Dudley took about an hour. Before he waved us goodbye until tomorrow, Mr Hibbert took a photo of us all with Matthew's camera.

Tuesday evening

We're camping in the forest. We've had our tea. I had ham rolls and a cup of tomato soup. The soup wasn't exactly hot, but it tasted quite nice. The girls cooked sausages. They smelled great.

We've also put our tents up, and it hardly took a minute. I'm really glad we practised this back home in the garden. Donna has lost her purse. (Why did she bring a purse? There aren't any shops here.) She and Alice have just had an argument about it. I expect it's at the bottom of her backpack.

We've come a long way today. I've got a blister on my left foot. We're all tired, so we'll probably sleep well.

Wednesday lunch time

We didn't sleep well. It was freezing. Even inside my sleeping bag and with two thick pairs of socks on, my feet felt cold. Now it's a sunny day, and we're hot and thirsty. And I've got more blisters. When I did the practice walk, I had hardly any problems with my feet, so why now? I was up at seven and felt terrible, like death. I ate two half-frozen jam rolls I brought with me yesterday. Why did I ever start this D of E thing? It's torture. Never again.

Wednesday afternoon

The last part of the walk was on level ground, so it was the easiest part. After lunch we had a problem with the map-reading and walked the wrong way for half a mile. Natalie said it was my fault, but actually it was hers. Then Jamie's knee started hurting, and we had to walk more slowly. My backpack was getting heavier all the time.

64 sixty-four

TEXT 1

Now it's over, and we're waiting for Mr Hibbert. Late as usual! If he takes another photo of us, it'll look different from the one he took at the start. Everyone looks filthy and exhausted. But soon we'll be back in the world of hot water, television and nice meals. Wonderful! The pain was worth it, of course. I'll have my Bronze Award soon, and I'm already looking forward to Silver and the three-day expedition.

EXERCISE 3

Look at the words and imagine which people in the story said them.

➡ I can't find my purse.
   It was Donna who said that. She lost her purse.
1 Can you take a photo of us with my camera, please?
2 Sorry, I can't walk very fast because of my knee.
3 I've brought a radio, so we can listen to music.
4 It was Scott's fault that we didn't take the right path.
5 I've got more blisters on this expedition than on the practice walk we did.
6 Donna and I both go to King Edward's School.
7 I'll see you all tomorrow afternoon.

EXERCISE 5

Put in *hard* or *hardly*.

➡ I hope you're working hard at your maths, Oliver.
➡ I'm thirsty. And there's hardly any water in this bottle.
1 I like a soft bed better than a … one.
2 Are you sure you've done all your homework? You've spent … any time on it.
3 No, Donna isn't my friend. Actually I … know her.
4 I'm sure you'll get your Bronze Award if you try … enough.
5 You can't be tired already. We've come … any distance.
6 I can't do this puzzle. It's quite … actually.

EXERCISE 6

Listening

You are ringing the Black Country Living Museum in Dudley. Listen carefully to the information and then answer the questions.

1 When is the museum open on Sundays?
2 What is the shortest time you should spend there?
3 How much does a 13-year-old visitor pay to go in the museum?
4 Are the fairground rides free, or do you have to pay for them?
5 What is the name of the old inn at the museum?
6 What is the address of the museum's website?

EXERCISE 4

Explain the meaning of the words in *italic*. Use *very* + adjective.

➡ Your shoes are *filthy*.
   (filthy = very dirty)
1 After the expedition we were *exhausted*.
2 The journey seemed *endless*.
3 The food was *terrible*.
4 I had a *huge* backpack.
5 In the night it was *freezing*.
6 We had a *marvellous* time.
7 I was *amazed* at the result.
8 My parents were *furious*.

hard = hart / schwer / schwierig
hardly = kaum
→ page 105

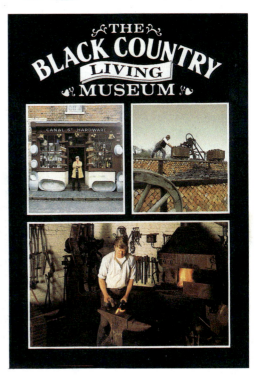

ACTIVITIES

A: *Forget about the band. I'm not going to London with her. Only because we don't have as much money as her. She thinks we can't afford mobile phones, so I've taken hers!*

B: *Never mind Crystal, we're all excited. Come on, I'm sure you've left it at home. Remember, this is an important day for our band!*

C: *Leave me alone, Crystal! You're so mean. Don't accuse me of something I haven't done. You can stay at home if you like, the band don't need you!*

What can Philip do now? What do you think is the best answer? Do you think he took the mobile? Why is Crystal so angry? Should Mr Freeman calm them down?

2 How can we get the new ELVIS jeans?

They cost £49, and that's expensive. You think they look great, but your parents say that jeans for £29 will do. What can you do to get the extra £20? Here are some suggestions from our friends. Which do you think is a good idea? In your opinion, who won't get a pair of ELVIS jeans from his or her parents? Why?

Emma — I've earned £10 at the supermarket. Will you give me another £10, please?

Patrick — I just don't want to be the only one in my class without them. Everyone wears ELVIS jeans! Ask Fiona!

Oliver — I'll pay £5 out of my pocket money. Can you give me the extra £15, please?

Crystal — All my jeans are over two years old. They're much too short anyway! I would rather get one pair of ELVIS jeans than three cheap ones!

Philip — I've been to so many shops. £49 is a special offer! Usually ELVIS jeans are £59 or more …

Fiona — I'm helping you in the garden every weekend. A gardener might be much more expensive than £20!!! Don't be so mean, mum!

Ravi — Grandma always gives me £20 on my birthday. I'll be 14 in April – so you can buy my ELVIS jeans now and take her money then, OK?

Sophie — So what, I need more pocket money anyway. £5 a week is not enough. All my friends get at least £10. Come on, hurry up, mum!

3 Holiday by Madonna

SONG 057

Listen to the song! With a partner decide where these verbs go in the song: *bring, come, find, forget, have, make, need, put, shine, turn.*

chorus   If we took a holiday
Took some time to celebrate
Just one day out of life
It would be, it would be so nice

Everybody spread the word
We're gonna ✶[1] a celebration
All across the world
In every nation
It's time for the good times
✶[2] about the bad times, oh yeah
One day to ✶[3] together
To release the pressure
We ✶[4] a holiday   *chorus*

You can ✶[5] this world around
And ✶[6] back all of those happy days
✶[7] your troubles down
It's time to celebrate
Let love ✶[8]
And we will ✶[9]
A way to come together
And ✶[10] things better
We need a holiday   *chorus*

Write the words in your exercise book. Find photos or draw a picture for the song.

sixty-seven **67**

Unit 5 **INTRODUCTION 2**

SITUATION 2

058

Matthew We've been walking for about two hours. I need a rest.
Natalie Oh, shut up, Matthew. You've been complaining the whole way.
Nick Anyway, we haven't been going two hours.
Matthew This backpack weighs a ton.
Natalie We're all carrying backpacks, aren't we?

Where's the bus? I've been waiting for ages.

The present perfect progressive

Positive	We've been doing this walk for two days.
have / has been doing	Your teacher has been waiting for you since two o'clock.
Negative	You haven't been looking at the map.
haven't / hasn't been doing	Emma hasn't been doing the Silver Award very long.
Question	How long have you been putting this tent up?
have / has ... been doing?	Has Alice been talking to those new girls?

→ page 106-107

EXERCISE 7

What have they been doing? Talk to a partner about the people in the pictures. Use these verbs: *cut down, pick, read, see, shoot, surf, watch.*

▶ Kim

1 Steve

3 Tara

2 your parents

4 Charlotte

5 Tom

6 your brothers

▶ What has Kim been doing?
She's been shooting arrows.
1 What ... ?
He's ... ghost stories.
2 What have your ... ?
They've been ... the sights.
3 ... 4 ... 5 ... 6 ...

68 sixty-eight

INTRODUCTION 2

EXERCISE 8

Put in the verb forms. Use the present perfect progressive.

Kathy Sorry I'm late.
Tom That's OK. I haven't been waiting (I/not wait) long. What … ? (you/do)
Kathy … (I/talk) to Mrs Jenkins about the D of E expedition.
Tom Oh, I haven't heard about that.
Kathy Well, everyone … (talk) about it.
Tom … (I/not spend) enough time on the D of E really. … (I/work) for my uncle in his shop for the last few weekends, so I haven't had much spare time outside school. And my friend Gary … (try) to start a band. I might play the guitar in it.
Kathy Really? How long … (you/play) the guitar?
Tom Well, not long. But … (I/practise).

SITUATION 3

059

Mr Hibbert is talking to a new group of pupils who want to do the Bronze Award.

'You have to do a two-day expedition. I expect you know that you must travel on foot, of course. You mustn't use buses or trains or have a lift in a car. And you must carry a backpack which weighs a quarter of your own body weight. But you needn't carry more than that. You can give me some of your equipment, and I'll take it to the camp site for you. You needn't carry all your food and equipment for the whole journey.'

you must = du musst
you needn't = du musst nicht
            du brauchst nicht
you mustn't = du darfst nicht

→ page 107

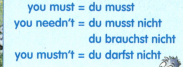

EXERCISE 9

Mr Hibbert is still talking. Rewrite each second sentence with *must*, *needn't* or *mustn't*.

▶ Your clothes are important. Please make sure you wear the right clothes.
   You must wear the right clothes.
1 The idea is that you walk. It's against the rules to travel in a car.
2 Stay in a group. It's important that the group stays together.
3 I'll take most of your equipment to the camp site. You don't have to carry all of it.
4 You know about the report, don't you? Everyone has to write one.
5 There won't be any shops on your route. You don't have to take a lot of money.
6 You've all done first aid. Please don't forget your first aid box.
7 You'll need to cook something. The rule is that you cook your own food.
8 You can start at nine o'clock if you like. There's no rule that says you start at six.
9 Try to get on with other people in the group. It isn't a good idea to have arguments about every little thing.

sixty-nine 69

Unit 5   TEXT 2

You stole my purse!

060

It was a pity, Natalie thought, that they weren't getting on very well with the two girls
5 from the other school. Louise seemed OK, and she talked to Natalie and Alice about the Backstreet
10 Boys concert in Birmingham the week before. But Donna wasn't so friendly and didn't seem interested in anything Natalie said to her. Now they were back in two pairs – Natalie and Alice in front, then Louise and Donna, with the boys behind them – as they walked down the hill.

15 At the camp site they all put up their tents and then had their tea. Natalie and Alice offered the other two girls some of their sausages, and so Louise shared some of her food with them. But Donna didn't want to. 'I don't like sausages,' she said. 'I'm going to have some soup.'

After tea Donna was tired. She didn't want to talk to anybody, so she lay down in the tent. Scott was writing his diary in the boys' tent. The others were sitting outside. Suddenly Donna came out of
20 the tent. She looked very upset. 'Donna, what's the matter?' asked Louise. 'Have you been crying?' 'It's my purse,' said Donna. 'I've been looking through my things, and I can't find it.' Then Alice spoke. 'Everything is in a mess in there,' she said. 'You needn't worry. It'll be in there somewhere.' Donna turned and shouted at Alice.
'Give it to me!'
25 'Pardon?'
'Give me back my purse. I know you've got it.'
'What do you mean? I haven't got your purse.'
'It was in my backpack, and now it isn't there. There's all my money in it.'
30 'Well, I didn't take it. Maybe you dropped it somewhere on the way.'
'You stole it!'
'Look, I'm telling you. I did not steal your purse.'
35 'I know you've got it, so give it to me.'
'You're saying that because I'm black, aren't you? You think a black person must be a thief. Well, you're just stupid, do you know that?'
'You were in the tent on your own earlier, when
40 you were fetching a spoon. It can't be anyone else.'
'You're crazy.'
'Come on,' said Natalie. 'You mustn't argue.'
But no one was listening to Natalie.

The girls didn't sleep very well that night. They
45 were upset after the argument. It was cold, and they were uncomfortable in their sleeping bags. Alice felt angry with Donna. Donna was worried about her purse, and there was a stone in the ground right under her sleeping bag. She was awake for ages.

70   seventy

TEXT 2

In the morning they had a quick breakfast. Alice didn't speak to Donna. When they were packing their things, Louise said to Donna, 'You ought to take everything out of your backpack and make sure the purse isn't in there.' 'I did that last night,' said Donna. 'There isn't anywhere else to look.' But she did it again. She took everything out – clothes, map, lunch box, chocolate, first aid box, and so on – and then slowly put it all back in again. Finally she rolled up her sleeping bag. And there, under the sleeping bag, there was something she felt in the middle of her back during the night. But it wasn't a stone in the ground. It was her purse.

EXERCISE 10

There is at least one thing wrong in each of these sentences. Can you say what really happened in the story?

➤ Donna talked to Natalie and Alice about a pop quiz.
Louise talked to Natalie and Alice about a pop concert.
1 They took down their tents before tea.
2 Donna had sausages because she said she didn't like tomato pizza.
3 When Donna was lying down, Scott was doing his homework.
4 Donna was upset because her camera wasn't in the shed.
5 Alice thought Donna was the thief.
6 Natalie fetched a knife from the cottage.
7 The girls slept well in their beds and didn't stay awake long.
8 Alice felt something hard under her head.
9 In the afternoon Donna found her stereo behind her backpack.

EXERCISE 11

Put in the missing letters and complete the words. Each missing word is in the text.

1 You mustn't get upset. Don't c... .
2 I usually eat my cornflakes with a s... .
3 That was a nice camp s... we stayed at yesterday.
4 I can't sleep. I've been a... for hours.
5 Nick didn't feel very well, so he l... down in the tent.
6 It's our holiday tomorrow. I'm just p... my case.
7 Please don't a... . Just do what I tell you.
8 Natalie didn't have any water, so Scott s... his with her.

EXERCISE 12

Put in these words:
something, anything, someone/somebody, anyone/anybody, somewhere, anywhere.

'Some' in positive sentences	'Any' in negative sentences
We've got **some** bread.	There isn't **any** butter.
We've got **something** to eat.	There isn't **anything** else.
	➔ page 125

Emma What are you doing?
Fiona It's my mobile. I can't find it ... .
Emma When did you last have it?
Fiona When we came in here. Oh, there's ... at the bottom of my bag. Oh no, it's my purse. No, I've lost my mobile.
Emma It must be ... , Fiona.
Fiona Maybe ... has stolen it.
Emma We're the only people in here. There isn't ... else. Have another look in your bag.
Fiona If it's stolen, I won't get it back. I can't do ... about it.
Emma Look, I'll ring your number. If the phone's in your bag, we'll hear it.

PROJECT

Choose a British city that you would like to know more about: Liverpool, Edinburgh, Bristol, Sheffield, ... Write a short report about it. Write one or two sentences about each of these:

- where it is
- industry/work
- population
- buildings
- history
- tourist attractions

You can add information about other things you are interested in, for example sport. If possible, include some photos in your report.

seventy-one 71

Unit 5 **COMMUNICATION**
061

Asking and telling the way

Wegbeschreibungen

So fragt man nach dem Weg	• Excuse me, can you tell me the way to Princes Street? • Do you know where the American Museum is?
So gibt man Auskunft	• Go straight on / straight ahead, past the cinema. • Turn right / left at the traffic lights. • Take the next / first / second turning on the right / left. • It's in front of you / on your right / on your left.

Tanja Excuse me, can you tell me how to get to New Street Station, please?

Officer Yes, go along Newhall Street here until you get to New Street. Turn left and then take the first street on your right. Go straight ahead and you will see the station right in front of you.

Tanja Thank you very much.

EXERCISE 13

You are in Corporation Street, Birmingham. Work with a partner. Ask the way to these places.

1 the Tourist Information Centre
2 the Town Hall
3 the Cathedral
4 the Post Office
5 Great Western Arcade

Your friend has just arrived at New Street Station. Send a short text message to his mobile and tell him the way to Bull Street.

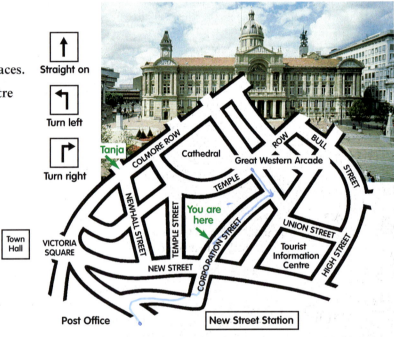

TEST YOUR ENGLISH

Birmingham

by Harriet Martin, aged 14

I like living in Birmingham. It's a big city, but it's also a very friendly place. The people are a real mixture – over one in five are non-white. There are lots of people of West Indian and Asian origin, and Birmingham has its China Town, too. It feels like an international city.

We live near the centre, and it's only a short bus ride to the shops. There's also lots to do. There
5 are theatres and cinemas and an ice-rink. And there are some nice buildings in the city centre, in Victoria Square, for example. The old central library was nice, but they pulled it down and put a huge piece of concrete in its place.

Of course there are some things about Birmingham which are not so good. There are some horrible parts. There are poor and homeless people. There's too much traffic and too much noise.
10 And too much crime. Sometimes you feel it isn't safe to walk around on your own when it's dark.

I was born in Birmingham and I've always lived here. Maybe one day I'll move somewhere else, but it'll be hard to leave all my friends behind. When I visit another town, everything feels strange. Birmingham feels like home.

72 seventy-two

TEST YOUR ENGLISH

1 Answer the questions.

1 Say which two of these words best describe Birmingham in Harriet's opinion.
 a) boring b) horrible c) large d) nice
2 Complete the sentence: Under four fifths of the people in Birmingham are ... .
3 How many different kinds of things are there to do in Birmingham?
 a) very few b) not many c) very many
4 Complete the sentence.
 The new library ... as the old one.
5 Which one of these does Harriet not say about Birmingham?
 a) It can be dangerous at night.
 b) Some places in the city aren't very nice.
 c) There aren't enough shops.
6 Which best describes her feelings about the city?
 a) At the moment it's where she belongs.
 b) She wants to leave as soon as possible.

2 Explain the meaning of these words and phrases.

1 people of Asian origin
2 an international city
3 an ice-rink
4 a library
5 horrible
6 homeless people
7 traffic
8 somewhere else

3 Harriet's class are talking with their teacher about their home town. Use the words in brackets in their correct form and put in the right words.

Teacher I enjoyed ... (read) what you've all ... (write) about Birmingham. It's a place ... you all seem ... (like).
Sarah But it's only the second city. It isn't ... big as London.
Richard Birmingham is ... (good) than London. I ... (not like) Londoners. I hate ... (they), actually.
Teacher You can't ... (real) mean that, Richard. You can't hate six million people.
Richard Well, OK, but I think people are ... (friend) here than in London.
Harriet There are some nice places in the city centre. Brindley Place, ... example.
Lauren But some parts look ... (awful).
Jack There's a ... of crime in Birmingham.
Richard Well, that's the same ... most other cities. It's ... (bad) in London than here, ... it?
Teacher What ... (you/think), Rebecca?
Rebecca Er, sorry?
Teacher You ... (look) out of the window for the last five minutes. And you ... (not do) your homework last night.
Rebecca Oh, sorry. There ... (not be) time. I ... (have/help) my dad.

4 Translate this information about Birmingham into German.

Birmingham in the English Midlands has a population of about one million and is the second largest city in England. It has a history as an important centre of heavy industry, but today it is a lively, modern city. Traditionally it has not been a place for tourists, but now there are many things that Birmingham can offer visitors. If you want to see a film or go to a show, you'll find what you're looking for. The city has some interesting museums and a good number of parks. Another attraction is the 32 miles of canals that tourists can enjoy. So why not take a trip on the canal the next time you're in Birmingham?

 062

5 13-year-old Stacey lives in a village near Oxford with her mum. She's been visiting her dad in Birmingham. Listen to the conversation and then complete the sentences.

1 At the weekend Stacey and her dad went to ... and ... .
2 In the future they might go to ... or to ... .
3 Stacey's train is at ... .
4 She'll travel to the station in ..., and she'll get home from Oxford Station in ... .
5 Stacey likes Birmingham better than the place where she lives because ... .

seventy-three **73**

POEMS

New Computer
063 by Kenn Nesbitt (adapted)

We have bought a new computer
that's the fastest ever seen.
It has terabytes of memory
and a forty-eight inch screen.

It has disk drives by the dozen
It has twenty-seven mice,
and it even has a microwave
included in the price.

It can teach you how to mambo.
It can play the violin.
It can calculate the distance
from Botswana to Berlin.

When we went and bought
 it yesterday
we thought it pretty neat,
but today our new computer
is already obsolete.

Merlo the Magnificent
064 by Kenn Nesbitt (adapted)

I am Merlo the Magnificent
I can do magic with my hand.
I'm a master prestidigitator;
 greatest in the land.

Yes, at making things invisible
I'm really the premier.
There is nothing that I cannot make
 completely disappear.

I'm undoubtedly the best
at getting things to disappear,
so the one thing that I can't explain is:
 why are you still here?

POEMS

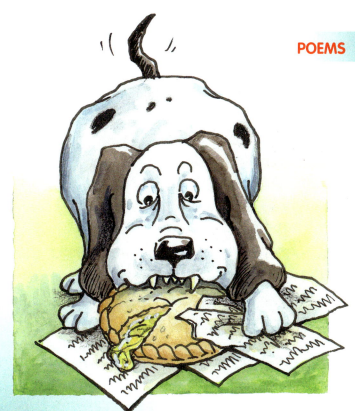

🟡 **My Homework**
065 by Lauren (adapted)

My dog ate my homework,
It's not a lie.
He ate it along with a whole apple pie.

My sister ate my homework,
It's not a lie.
She ate it real fast and started to cry.

My mom ate my homework,
It's not a lie.
She ate it and I thought she would die.

My dad ate my homework,
It's not a lie.
He ate it and kissed my mom goodbye.

I ate my homework,
It's not a lie.
I ate it, oh I don't know why.

🟡 **Words**
066 by Grandpa Bob Tucker (adapted)

There are some words so hard to read.
Some confuse like feet and feed.
Do you know of go and dough?
There's sew and sow, then there's so!

Sometimes a word is hard to spell.
But it's important for show and tell.
So work real hard to spell and read 'em.
'Cause all your life you'll really need 'em.

🟡 **Whether**
067 (Anon.)

Whether the weather be fine
Or whether the weather be not
Whether the weather be cold
Or whether the weather be hot –
We'll weather the weather
Whatever the weather
Whether we like it or not!

seventy-five 75

SKETCH 1   The last question

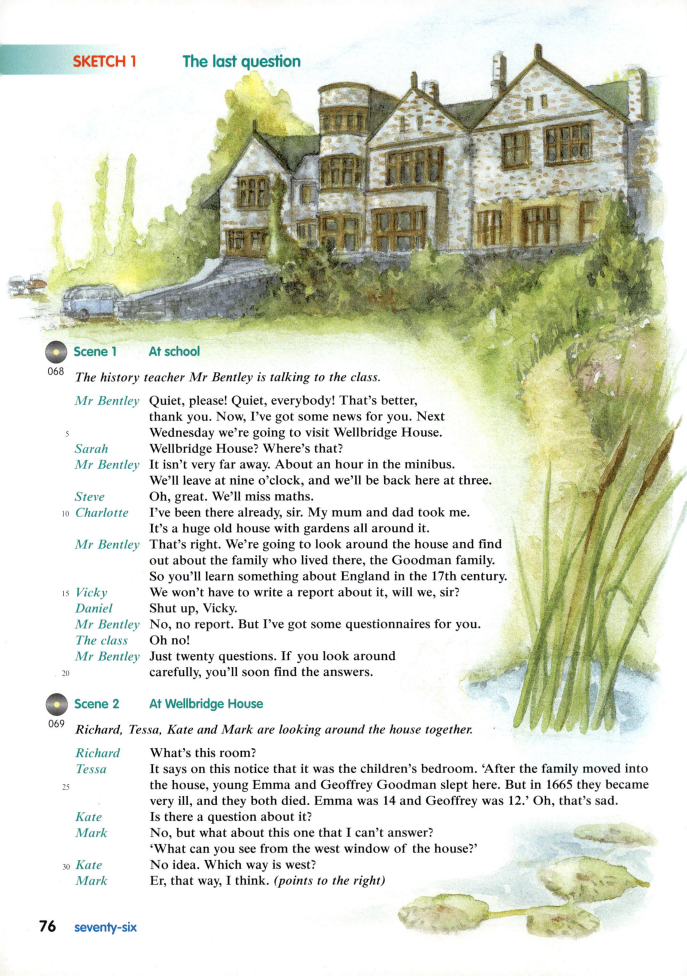

Scene 1   At school

068

The history teacher Mr Bentley is talking to the class.

Mr Bentley   Quiet, please! Quiet, everybody! That's better,
             thank you. Now, I've got some news for you. Next
             Wednesday we're going to visit Wellbridge House.
Sarah   Wellbridge House? Where's that?
Mr Bentley   It isn't very far away. About an hour in the minibus.
             We'll leave at nine o'clock, and we'll be back here at three.
Steve   Oh, great. We'll miss maths.
Charlotte   I've been there already, sir. My mum and dad took me.
             It's a huge old house with gardens all around it.
Mr Bentley   That's right. We're going to look around the house and find
             out about the family who lived there, the Goodman family.
             So you'll learn something about England in the 17th century.
Vicky   We won't have to write a report about it, will we, sir?
Daniel   Shut up, Vicky.
Mr Bentley   No, no report. But I've got some questionnaires for you.
The class   Oh no!
Mr Bentley   Just twenty questions. If you look around
             carefully, you'll soon find the answers.

Scene 2   At Wellbridge House

069

Richard, Tessa, Kate and Mark are looking around the house together.

Richard   What's this room?
Tessa   It says on this notice that it was the children's bedroom. 'After the family moved into
          the house, young Emma and Geoffrey Goodman slept here. But in 1665 they became
          very ill, and they both died. Emma was 14 and Geoffrey was 12.' Oh, that's sad.
Kate   Is there a question about it?
Mark   No, but what about this one that I can't answer?
          'What can you see from the west window of the house?'
Kate   No idea. Which way is west?
Mark   Er, that way, I think. *(points to the right)*

76   seventy-six

SKETCH 1

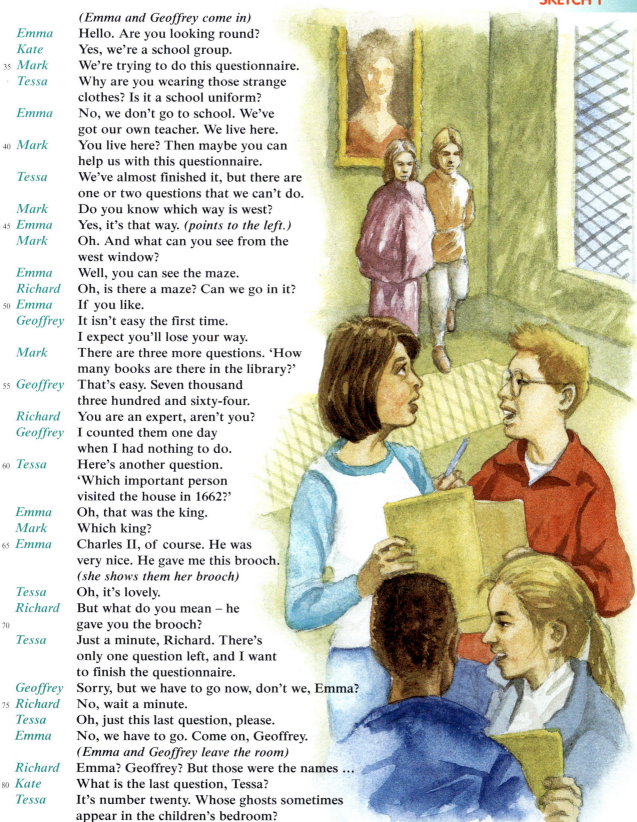

(Emma and Geoffrey come in)

Emma	Hello. Are you looking round?
Kate	Yes, we're a school group.
35 Mark	We're trying to do this questionnaire.
Tessa	Why are you wearing those strange clothes? Is it a school uniform?
Emma	No, we don't go to school. We've got our own teacher. We live here.
40 Mark	You live here? Then maybe you can help us with this questionnaire.
Tessa	We've almost finished it, but there are one or two questions that we can't do.
Mark	Do you know which way is west?
45 Emma	Yes, it's that way. *(points to the left.)*
Mark	Oh. And what can you see from the west window?
Emma	Well, you can see the maze.
Richard	Oh, is there a maze? Can we go in it?
50 Emma	If you like.
Geoffrey	It isn't easy the first time. I expect you'll lose your way.
Mark	There are three more questions. 'How many books are there in the library?'
55 Geoffrey	That's easy. Seven thousand three hundred and sixty-four.
Richard	You are an expert, aren't you?
Geoffrey	I counted them one day when I had nothing to do.
60 Tessa	Here's another question. 'Which important person visited the house in 1662?'
Emma	Oh, that was the king.
Mark	Which king?
65 Emma	Charles II, of course. He was very nice. He gave me this brooch. *(she shows them her brooch)*
Tessa	Oh, it's lovely.
Richard	But what do you mean – he gave you the brooch?
70 Tessa	Just a minute, Richard. There's only one question left, and I want to finish the questionnaire.
Geoffrey	Sorry, but we have to go now, don't we, Emma?
75 Richard	No, wait a minute.
Tessa	Oh, just this last question, please.
Emma	No, we have to go. Come on, Geoffrey. *(Emma and Geoffrey leave the room)*
Richard	Emma? Geoffrey? But those were the names …
80 Kate	What is the last question, Tessa?
Tessa	It's number twenty. Whose ghosts sometimes appear in the children's bedroom?

seventy-seven **77**

SKETCH 2   Robin Hood, the butcher, a play in five scenes

● Scene 1   A road near Sherwood Forest

070 *Robin Hood meets a butcher and Matilda. The butcher is wearing an apron and pushing a cart.*

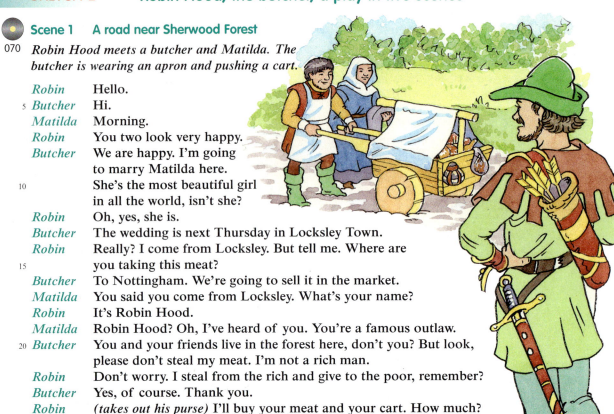

Robin	Hello.
Butcher	Hi.
Matilda	Morning.
Robin	You two look very happy.
Butcher	We are happy. I'm going to marry Matilda here. She's the most beautiful girl in all the world, isn't she?
Robin	Oh, yes, she is.
Butcher	The wedding is next Thursday in Locksley Town.
Robin	Really? I come from Locksley. But tell me. Where are you taking this meat?
Butcher	To Nottingham. We're going to sell it in the market.
Matilda	You said you come from Locksley. What's your name?
Robin	It's Robin Hood.
Matilda	Robin Hood? Oh, I've heard of you. You're a famous outlaw.
Butcher	You and your friends live in the forest here, don't you? But look, please don't steal my meat. I'm not a rich man.
Robin	Don't worry. I steal from the rich and give to the poor, remember?
Butcher	Yes, of course. Thank you.
Robin	*(takes out his purse)* I'll buy your meat and your cart. How much?
Butcher	Oh, erm … ten pounds?
Robin	*(gives him the money)* Here's fifteen and give me your butcher's apron, too.
Butcher	*(takes off his apron)* OK. Thanks.
Matilda	Fifteen pounds is a lot of money.
Robin	It's OK. I stole it from a rich man.
Butcher	Well, we'll go home then. Bye!
Robin	Good luck.

● Scene 2   Nottingham Market

071 *Three butchers are selling meat to several people. Robin Hood comes in wearing his butcher's apron. He takes the meat from the cart and puts it on a table.*

Robin	Come and look at this lovely meat. A pound of meat costs five pence if you're poor. If you're rich, it's twenty pence. If you're a nice young lady who likes butchers, you can just give me a kiss. So come on!
Woman	I'll have some if it's only five pence. I'm not rich.
	(the people all go to his table)
Butcher 1	I don't like this. He's selling that meat very cheaply, and no one's buying ours now.
Butcher 2	Maybe he stole the meat.
Butcher 3	Maybe he's rich and doesn't really need the money.
Butcher 1	I think we should find out. *(He goes to Robin.)* Did you know that the Sheriff of Nottingham has invited all the butchers to a meal at his castle tonight? There'll be lots to eat and drink. Would you like to come?
Robin	Yes, I would. Thank you. I'll see you there later.

SKETCH 2

 Scene 3   Nottingham Castle

072 *The Sheriff and the butchers are standing by the table, where a meal is ready for them.*

Butcher 1	The man was selling his meat very cheaply.
Butcher 2	We think he's a rich man.
Sheriff	That's very strange. But maybe I can get some of his money from him. *(Robin comes in)*
Sheriff	Oh, hello. Come and sit down. We're just going to start the meal.
Robin	Thank you. *(they eat)*
Sheriff	I've heard that you are a rich man.
Robin	Yes, I am. My brothers and sisters are rich, too. We've got a lot of land, and five hundred animals. No one wants to buy them, so I decided to become a butcher and sell the meat in the market.
Sheriff	Who are you? What's your name?
Robin	They call me Robert of Locksley.
Sheriff	Well, Robert, I'll buy your cattle if you like. How much are they?
Robin	Five hundred pounds.
Butcher 1	That's cheap.
Sheriff	That's too much. I'll give you three hundred.
Butcher 2	That's very cheap.
Robin	OK. We can go to my place tomorrow, and I'll show you the animals.
Sheriff	Fine.

 Scene 4   Sherwood Forest

073 *Robin Hood and the Sheriff of Nottingham are walking through the forest.*

Robin	We're in Sherwood Forest now. Oh, look. There are some of my animals.
Sheriff	But those are deer – the King's deer. You said you had cattle.
Robin	I said animals. Those are my animals, and this is my land, the forest.
Sheriff	What! You're crazy. I think I'll go home.
Robin	And look. Here are my brothers and sisters. *(the outlaws come in)*
Will	Hello, Robin.
Marion	Hi, Robin.
Robin	Marion, give me a kiss.
Sheriff	Robin? You mean this is Robin Hood. Oh, my God!
Allan	Come on, there's a nice big meal waiting for all of us.

Scene 5   Sherwood Forest

074 *Robin Hood, the Sheriff and the outlaws are sitting on the grass after their meal.*

Sheriff	*(looking at his watch)* Well, thank you for the meal, but I have to go now.
Robin	Well, if you must. But you've forgotten one thing. Poor people eat with us free, but rich people have to pay.
Sheriff	*(taking out his purse)* But of course. It was a wonderful meal. Here's five pounds.
Robin	That's not enough, I'm afraid. Have you got the bill, Marion?
Marion	*(gives the Sheriff the bill)* Deer and chips and seven beers. That's three hundred pounds, please.
Sheriff	Three hundred pounds for that horrible meal! That's a joke.
Robin	Three hundred pounds, or you'll be sorry. *(the Sheriff gives Marion his purse.)* Now you can go home. Allan here will show you the way, but next time remember. When you buy an animal, look into its mouth first. *(the outlaws laugh and the Sheriff walks angrily away)*

seventy-nine **79**

REVISION

EXERCISE 1

Janet is 15 years old. She's still at school. But she's also a child actor in a soap opera. Copy the sentences and complete them in the simple present.

'Most mornings I … (get up) at half past five. Then I … (go) into the bathroom. After breakfast I … (hurry) to catch the school bus. School … (start) at 9 o'clock. Sometimes my mother … (take) me in the car. I … (not/like) school much. But the pupils in my class … (be) very nice. They always … (help) me when I … (need) them.'

On one or two afternoons Janet's mum … (drive) her to the TV company. Janet … (play) a nice girl in the soap opera. But she … (not/get) a lot of money for her TV job because she … (not be) really famous.

On Sundays she … (not/stay) in bed. She … (go) swimming before breakfast because she … (want) to stay fit. It … (be) sometimes hard for Janet but she … (enjoy) her life.

Now you ask Janet about her life. Write the questions in your exercise book and use the simple present.

1. What time … (get up) ?
2. When … (school/start) ?
3. … (you/walk/to school) ?
4. Who … (take/you/to school) ?
5. … (you/like/school) ?
6. How often … (you/work/for the TV company) ?
7. Where … (you/go swimming) ?
8. What … (your family/do/at weekends) ?

EXERCISE 2

Mike Nolan is a police detective. He's watching two criminals. He's got his mobile and he's telling his partner at the police station what's happening. Use the present progressive.

Mike Now the two men … (leave) the house. They … (go) to the garage. One of them … (carry) something.
Jack What … (he/carry) ?
Mike It looks like a big rubbish bag.
Jack Can you see what's in it?
Mike No, I can't. But the bag looks very heavy. Maybe it's a – Oh, now the other man … (open) the garage door and … (go) inside. He – erm – no, he … (not/go) into the garage. He … (come) out again.
Jack Why … (he/do) that?
Mike I don't know. Ah, yes, he … (take) a mobile from his pocket. But he … (not/talk). He … (just/look) at his mobile. Maybe he … (read) a text message.
Jack What … (happen) now? What … (the other man/do)?
Mike He's near the car. At the moment he … (try) to open the back door. And now he … (put) the bag on the back seat.
Jack … (the men/leave) ?
Mike No, they aren't. They … (walk) back to the front door. Yes, now they … (go) inside again.
Jack OK. That's our chance. We … (come). We'll be with you in a minute to arrest them.

REVISION

EXERCISE 3

Say what these people do in their jobs and what they're doing now.

▶ Mr Batty **teaches** music. He **is washing** his car at the moment.
1 Jane Wilkins drives …   2 The Dexter sisters …

▶ Mr Batty, music teacher
1 Jane Wilkins, taxi driver
2 The Dexter sisters, singers
3 Mike Dooley, footballer
4 Rob Usher, window-cleaner
5 Heather Jones, newspaper seller
6 Greg Nolan, tourist guide

EXERCISE 4

Kirsty and Ben are organizing a garage sale on Saturday afternoon. Some friends are helping. Say what they've done and when they did it, or what they haven't done yet and when they're going to do it.

Name	Job	When
Kirsty	fix sign to gate	Saturday morning
Kirsty, Sam	tidy garage	last week
Amy	bring her old in-line skates	in the morning
Ben	ask his mother for old shoes	two days ago
Lehka	tell all her friends	yesterday
Mr Jewell	repair old radio	last weekend
Sam	carry his toys to the garage	this evening
Mrs Jewell	buy biscuits and lemonade	tomorrow

▶ Kirsty hasn't fixed a sign to the gate yet. She's going to do it on Saturday morning.
▶ Kirsty and Sam have tidied the garage. They tidied it last week.

eighty-one 81

REVISION

EXERCISE 5

This is a report about an air accident on Radio Kent. Copy the text and put in the simple past forms of the verbs in brackets.

There … (be) an air accident near Dartford, Kent, at about 10.30 a.m. yesterday when a hot-air balloon … (fall) about 1,000 ft and … (hit) a tree. The balloon … (land) in a field. The balloon … (belong) to Trevor and Susan Davis from Norwich. An ambulance … (take) both of them to a hospital in Dartford. Later an air ambulance … (fly) the man and his wife to a special hospital in London. Farmer Brian Thompsett, who … (see) the accident, … (arrive) first at the scene. He … (say): 'As we … (get) nearer, we … (see) a young lady. She … (get) out of the basket. I … (be) so glad to see that she … (be) still alive. I … (find) the guy in the basket, and he … (be) alive, too. We … (decide) to leave him there. We … (not try) to move him.'

EXERCISE 6

The people in the village near Dartford are telling a reporter what they were doing at 10.30 when the accident happened.

▶ Mr Trevis was watching TV.
1 Mrs Drabble …
2 Chris …
3 Mrs Wang …
4 Catherine …
5 Mrs MacInnes …
6 Mr Pinman and his son …
7 Mr Jones …

82   eighty-two

REVISION

EXERCISE 7

Can you find out about their plans?

▶ Why is Britta learning English? – Her English friend / come / next month.
Her English friend is going to come next month.
1 Why are you wearing these old clothes? – I / wash / car.
2 Are you staying at home tonight?
– Yes / write / some letters.
3 Does your sister want to come to the cinema with us?
– No / she / watch / game show / TV.
4 Why are you buying the crisps? – We / have / party.
5 Have you read the new Harry Potter book?
– No, but / read / on holiday.

EXERCISE 8

What will the world be like in fifty years from now? Use *will* or *won't* and write sentences.

▶ there – be – a lot more people
There will be a lot more people.
1 computers – do – all the work
2 there – not be – any cars left
3 people – travel – to Mars
4 everyone – have – personal robot
5 people – not fight – any wars
6 cars – not use – petrol
7 telephones – have – colour screens

EXERCISE 9

Fill in the missing tense forms.

Where's Chippy?

Monday April 1st

Chippy the budgie … (disappear). He … (disappear) two days ago on the way to the home of his new owner Alan Dunston. When Alan … (carry) Chippy from the garage into the house, the bottom of his cage … (fall out) and the budgie … (fly off).
Alan … (get) Chippy last Friday as a present for his daughter. He … (do) a job at a house in Burnley and … (become) friendly with the people there. They … (move) to a much smaller house next month. 'Chippy … (be) a friendly bird and everybody … (like) him,' says Alan. But he … (often / use) bad language. His favourite phrases … (be) 'You stupid idiot' and 'Hello Baby'. On Friday Alan … (ask) his neighbours to look for the bird in their gardens. At the moment Alan … (still / look) for the bird. He … (want) to give it to his daughter Adele for her birthday on Wednesday. But if he can't find the bird by Tuesday he … (buy) her a different present. No one in the town of Rishton … (see) Chippy since Friday.

EXERCISE 10

Mr Denton is a millionaire who likes travelling very much. He has been to lots of different countries. And he has lots of beautiful girlfriends. Make sentences.

▶ to Germany / fly / last week / Mr Denton
Mr Denton flew to Germany last week *or*
Last week Mr Denton flew to Germany.
1 not long ago / he and Monica / go / to Fiji
2 on holiday / often / not go / in winter / he
3 travel / ten years ago / through China / and his mother / he
4 stay / next year / he / in Hong Kong / some time / and a Chinese model
5 to the Bahamas / last year / a trip / his girlfriend / take
6 on a safari / twice / be / so far / in Kenya / Mr Denton

eighty-three 83

REVISION

EXERCISE 11

Find the right form.

▶ the boy's budgie
1 the ...
2 the ...
3 the ...
4 the ...

EXERCISE 12

Fiona is in the library. Can you help her to find the titles of some books?

▶ name / game
   The name of the game
▶ driver / mistake
   The driver's mistake
1 singers / voices
2 my aunt / dream
3 star / film
4 end / story
5 colour / dress
6 policeman / report
7 bell / tower
8 teacher / explanation
9 king / castle

EXERCISE 13

Fill in the missing words.

Tessa Are you still looking for your exercise book? I've found this one under my desk.

Sarah Oh, it has got ... name on it. It must be ... . Thank you very much.

Nick Mum, I can't find my football shirt and we've got a match this afternoon.

Mum Let's have a look. There's a football shirt in the wardrobe.

Nick But this is Will's shirt. My shirt is new. ... is old. It must be ... .

Peter Oh damn! I've broken my cup.

Diane No, ... cup is on the table. You haven't broken ... , but you've broken Kate's cup. Look, it has got ... name on it. It must be ... .

Tim I can't find my sandwiches. Whose are you eating? I think they must be ... .

Donna No, of course not. Jane has put ... names on ... sandwiches. Have a look. These are ... .

Julie Vicky and Tom didn't bring any books.

Mrs Cox Yes, they did. ... names are inside these books here. They must be ... .

REVISION

EXERCISE 14

Samantha Willis is collecting information for a tourist guide. She has just been to two guest houses. Look at her notes and compare the two places.

	Grove Farm House	Thorpe House
Are the rooms comfortable?	yes	yes, very comfortable
Are the beds clean?	yes	yes
Is it quiet?	very quiet	OK
Is the landlord friendly?	yes	yes
Is it easy to find?	not really	yes
Is it expensive?	yes	not really
Is it good for children?	not really	yes
Is it a modern guest house?	built 1993	built 1897

▶▶ The rooms at Thorpe House are more comfortable.
The beds at Grove Farm House are as …

EXERCISE 15

Look at the two pictures and say what's different. Use *some* or *any* and these words:
trees, children, elephants, tigers, birds, water on the path, bushes, clouds, flowers

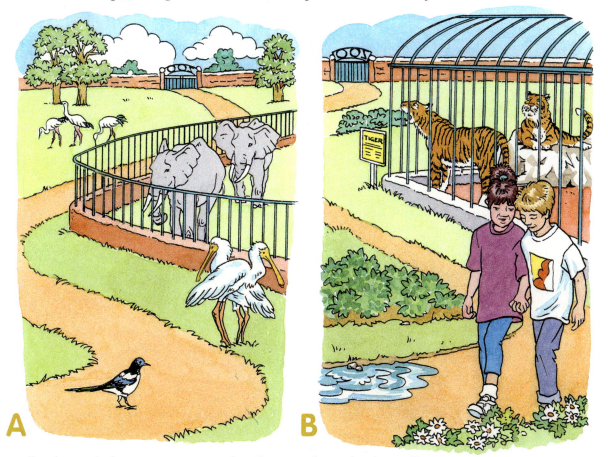

A   B

▶▶ In picture A there are some trees, but there aren't any in picture B.

GUIDED WRITING

1 Textabsätze schreiben

Eine Form des guided writing ist es, wenn du mit Hilfe von clues, wie den folgenden, Sätze eigenständig ausformulierst.

London – capital – United Kingdom / lie – River Thames – have – population – 7 million / lots – things – see and do / look at – waxworks – Madame Tussaud's – old planes – Science Museum / if – tired – city streets – do in-line skating – Hyde Park – visit – zoo – Regent's Park

Wenn du diese clues in vollständige Sätze umformen möchtest, musst du die fehlenden Wörter wie z. B. is und the einfach ergänzen. Achte darauf, ob vielleicht auch Wortendungen verändert werden müssen.

London is the capital of the United Kingdom. It lies on the River Thames and has a population of 7 million. There are lots of things to see and do. You can look at the waxworks in Madame Tussaud's or the old planes in the Science Museum. If you're tired of city streets, you can do in-line skating in Hyde Park or visit the zoo in Regent's Park.

Jetzt schreibe selbst einen kleinen Text über William I of England. Verwende dabei die folgenden clues.

William – conquer – England – 1066 / that – why – call – 'William the Conqueror' / bring – army – Channel – Normandy – defeat – Harold / William – take – land – Anglo-Saxons – give – Norman friends / Normans – build – lot – castles / most famous – White Tower – by – River Thames

2 Hilfreiche Formulierungen

Lies diesen Text über die Band Westlife.

Westlife are a boy band from Ireland. There are five of them – Shane, Bryan, Kian, Nicky and Mark. Their music is full of soulful harmonies. Bryan is the clown of the group, and he tells jokes all the time.

Westlife's first single was 'Swear it again'. It went to number one. Suddenly the band were famous. They had more hits with records like 'If I let you go' and 'My love'. Their album 'Coast to Coast' was also a big hit.

In diesem Text gibt es einige hilfreiche Formulierungen, die du auch in Texten über andere Musikgruppen verwenden kannst, z. B.

… are a … band from … . There are … of them. Their music is … .
… first single was … . It went to number … .
… with records like …
Their album … was …

*Schreibe einen ähnlichen Abschnitt über eine Musikgruppe, die du gut kennst.
Du solltest so viele wie möglich von den Formulierungen verwenden.*

GUIDED WRITING

3 Das Verknüpfen von Ideen

Es ist nicht schön, wenn ein Text ausschließlich aus kurzen Sätzen besteht. Besser ist es, Wörter zu verwenden, die sprachliche Verbindungen schaffen. Die Konjunktionen because *und* but *können z.B. Sätze miteinander knüpfen oder zeigen, wie ein Satz sich auf den vorangehenden bezieht. Dies macht es einfacher, einen Text zu lesen.*

Vervollständige Tims Geschichte über seinen Ausflug nach Disneyland. Füge die folgenden Wörter ein: afterwards, also, because, before, but, if, so, when, where.

Wednesday 18th July
My mum took me and my friend Alex to Disneyland. This was the big day. It was only eight o'clock ... we arrived. We wanted to go on some of the big rides ... the queues got too long. You have to wait hours ... you arrive too late. It was expensive to go in, ... luckily the price includes all the rides, and ... we tried to go on as many as possible. I liked the Indiana Jones Adventure ... the last part of it is really exciting. I ... liked the Star Tours ride. It was a great day, and we had lots of fun. ... my mum drove us back to Los Angeles, ... we were staying in a hotel.

4 Briefe und Mitteilungen beantworten

Wenn du eine Mitteilung (wie z.B. einen Brief, eine Nachricht oder eine SMS) beantwortest, ist es einfacher, wenn du dich in die Person hineinversetzt, an die die Nachricht gerichtet ist.

Lies diese E-Mail von Kate an ihre alte Freundin Zoe.

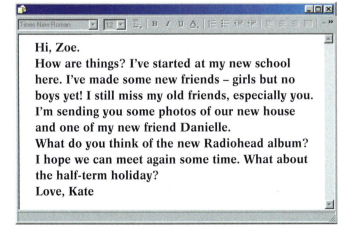

Hi, Zoe.
How are things? I've started at my new school here. I've made some new friends – girls but no boys yet! I still miss my old friends, especially you. I'm sending you some photos of our new house and one of my new friend Danielle.
What do you think of the new Radiohead album? I hope we can meet again some time. What about the half-term holiday?
Love, Kate

Jetzt stell dir vor, du wärest Zoe und beantworte die E-Mail. Falls notwendig, kannst du die fehlenden Details einfach erfinden.

- Say how you are.
- Tell Kate some news, for example about a class trip you made recently and how you enjoyed it.
- Make a friendly comment about Kate's photo.
- Give your opinion on the new album.
- Invite Kate to come and stay at your house at half-term. Explain that your parents have given permission.

eighty-seven **87**

GUIDED WRITING

5 Bildgeschichten

Einkaufszentrum – shopping mall [ˈʃɒpɪŋ mɔːl]
entreißen – snatch [snætʃ]
Wächter/in – security guard [sɪˈkjʊərəti gɑːd]

Look at the picture story.

Wenn du eine Geschichte erzählen möchtest, solltest du dir zuerst überlegen, welche wichtigen Wörter du benötigen wirst. Manchmal sind gerade solche Wörter wichtig, die du noch nicht gelernt hast, sodass du ein Wörterbuch benutzen oder deinen Lehrer/deine Lehrerin fragen musst. Über den Bildern findest du einige Wörter, die vielleicht hilfreich sind.

Natürlich kannst du für diese Geschichte auch viele Wörter verwenden, die du bereits kennst. Wähle aus dieser Liste sechs Wörter aus, die du in deiner Geschichte verwenden möchtest.

airport, arrested, bag, breakfast, caught, clothes, factory, fair-haired, kissed, message, pencil, umbrella

Jetzt kannst du anfangen, die Geschichte zu schreiben. Du solltest beschreiben, was passiert, doch du brauchst dich dabei nicht zu eng an die Bilder zu halten. Benutze deine Fantasie. Wenn du möchtest, kannst du so anfangen:

One day Vicky and Hannah went to the shopping mall together. It was only two days before the end-of-term disco, and they wanted to …

Grammatical terms Grammatikalische Fachausdrücke

adjective ['ædʒɪktɪv]	Eigenschaftswort, Adjektiv	*big, good, bad, dangerous, expensive, …*
adverb ['ædvɜːb]	Adverb	***very** big, **usually**, …*
adverb of frequency [ˌædvɜːb əv 'friːkwənsi]	Adverb der Häufigkeit	*always, often, never, …*
adverb of manner [ˌædvɜːb əv 'mænə]	Adverb der Art und Weise	*carefully, slowly, well, …*
article ['ɑːtɪkl]	Geschlechtswort, Artikel	*a, an, the*
auxiliary verb [ɔːgˌzɪliəri 'vɜːb]	Hilfsverb	***don't** know, **is** swimming, **has** seen*
clause [klɔːz]	Teilsatz	***He was late** because he missed the last bus.*
comparative [kəm'pærətɪv]	Komparativ, erste Steigerungsform	*bi**gger**, **better**, **more** interesting, …*
comparison of adjectives [kəmˌpærɪsn əv 'ædʒɪktɪvz]	Steigerung der Adjektive	*big – bigger – biggest; **as** big **as**, bigger **than***
conditional [kən'dɪʃənl]	Konditional	*I **wouldn't** do that.*
conjunction [kən'dʒʌŋkʃn]	Bindewort, Konjunktion	*and, or, but, after, when, …*
consonant ['kɒnsənənt]	Mitlaut, Konsonant	*b, c, d, f, g, k, …*
contact clause ['kɒntækt klɔːz]	Satz ohne Relativpronomen	*The girl **he met** was Lisa.*
direct object [daɪˌrekt 'ɒbdʒɪkt]	direktes –, Akkusativobjekt	*He drinks **milk**. She gave him **a present**.*
future with *going to* ['fjuːtʃə]	Futur mit *going to*	***I'm going to leave** now.*
future with *will* ['fjuːtʃə]	Futur mit *will*	*I **will come** tomorrow.*
imperative [ɪm'perətɪv]	Befehlsform, Imperativ	*Now **listen**. **Don't talk** to your neighbour.*
indirect object [ˌɪndaɪrekt 'ɒbdʒɪkt]	indirektes –, Dativobjekt	*She gave **her father** a present.*
infinitive [ɪn'fɪnətɪv]	Grundform, Infinitiv	*to go, to see, to eat, to run, to work, …*
***ing*-form** ['ɪŋfɔːm]	-*ing*-Form	*singing, dancing, sitting, …*
irregular verb [ɪˌregjʊlə 'vɜːb]	unregelmäßiges Verb	*do – **did** – **done**, buy – **bought** – **bought**, …*
long form ['lɒŋ fɔːm]	Langform	*He **is** reading. She **does not** work.*
main clause ['meɪn klɔːz]	Hauptsatz	***Peter isn't at school** because he's ill.*
main verb ['meɪn vɜːb]	Vollverb	*work, dance, read, write, play, …*
modal auxiliary [ˌməʊdl ɔːg'zɪliəri]	Modalverb	*can, must, could, might, ought to*
negative statement [ˌnegətɪv 'steɪtmənt]	verneinter Aussagesatz	*Emily does**n't** like tennis.*
noun [naʊn]	Nomen, Substantiv	*house, book, tea, plan, idea, …*
object ['ɒbdʒɪkt]	Satzergänzung, Objekt	*She likes **pop music**.*
***of*-phrase** ['ɒvfreɪz]	Fügung mit *of*	*the name **of** the game*
past progressive [ˌpɑːst prə'gresɪv]	Verlaufsform der Vergangenheit	*She **was reading**. We **were watching** TV.*
personal pronoun [ˌpɜːsənl 'prəʊnaʊn]	persönliches Fürwort, Personalpronomen	*I, you, she, … , me, us, them, …*
phrasal verb [ˌfreɪzl 'vɜːb]	Verbindung Verb–Adverb	*to put on, to take away, …*
plural ['plʊərəl]	Mehrzahl, Plural	*book**s**, letter**s**, dog**s**, wom**e**n, child**ren**, **feet***
positive ['pɒzətɪv]	Positiv, Grundform des Adjektivs	*good – better – best, **interesting** – more interesting – most interesting*
positive statement [ˌpɒzətɪv 'steɪtmənt]	bejahter Aussagesatz, Erzählsatz	*I speak English and French.*

eighty-nine 89

Grammatikalische Fachausdrücke

possessive adjective [pəˌzesɪv ˈædʒɪktɪv]	adjektivisch gebrauchtes, besitzanzeigendes Fürwort, Possessivpronomen	*my, your, his, her, its, our, your, their*
possessive form [pəˌzesɪv ˈfɔːm]	besitzanzeigende Form, *s*-Genitiv	***Adam's*** *computer,* **his friends'** *books*
possessive pronoun [pəˌzesɪv ˈprəʊnaʊn]	nominal gebrauchtes Possessivpronomen	*mine, yours, his, hers, its, ours, yours, theirs*
preposition [prepəˈzɪʃn]	Verhältniswort, Präposition	*in, at, on, with, because of, …*
preposition of direction [prepəˌzɪʃn əv dəˈrekʃn]	Präposition der Richtung	***to*** *school,* **onto** *the table,* **into** *the water, …*
preposition of place [prepəˌzɪʃn əv ˈpleɪs]	Präposition des Ortes	***at*** *the bus stop,* **on** *the wall,* **in** *the house, …*
preposition of time [prepəˌzɪʃn əv ˈtaɪm]	Präposition der Zeit	***at*** *seven o'clock,* **on** *Sunday,* **in** *winter, …*
prepositional verb [prepəˌzɪʃənl ˈvɜːb]	Präpositionalverb, Verbindung Verb–Präposition	*to look* **after** *… , to listen* **to** *… , …*
present perfect [ˌpreznt ˈpɜːfɪkt]	*present perfect* (Perfekt)	*We* **have finished** *the lesson.*
present perfect progressive [ˌpreznt pɜːfɪkt prəˈgresɪv]	Verlaufsform des *present perfect*	*We* **have been reading** *for two hours.*
present progressive [ˌpreznt prəˈgresɪv]	Verlaufsform des Präsens	*I* **am watching** *TV.*
pronoun [ˈprəʊnaʊn]	Fürwort, Pronomen	*I, me, my, this, …*
proper noun [ˌprɒpe ˈnaʊn]	Eigenname	*Mr Smith, Munich, the Thames*
propword [ˈprɒpwɜːd]	Stützwort	*Do you want the red* **one** *or the green* **ones***?*
question [ˈkwestʃn]	Frage, Fragesatz	***Is Adam at school?*** *– No, he isn't. –* **Where is Adam?**
question tag [ˈkwestʃn tæg]	Frageanhängsel	*It's cold today,* **isn't it***?*
question word [ˈkwestʃn wɜːd]	Fragewort	*what, when, where, who, whose, why, which, how*
regular verb [ˌregjʊlə ˈvɜːb]	regelmäßiges Verb	*call – called – called, …*
relative clause [ˌrelətɪv ˈklɔːz]	Relativsatz	*The girl* **who phoned** *was Mary.*
relative pronoun [ˌrelətɪv ˈprəʊnaʊn]	Relativpronomen	*who, that, which, whose*
sentence [ˈsentəns]	Satz, Satzgefüge	*I love Star Trek. Do you speak French?*
short answer [ˈʃɔːt ɑːnsə]	Kurzantwort	*Do you understand? –* **Yes, I do.**
short form [ˈʃɔːt fɔːm]	Kurzform	*I've got a rabbit. She's over there. – I can't see her.*
simple past [ˌsɪmpl ˈpɑːst]	einfache Form der Vergangenheit	*I* **called** *Katie. She* **bought** *a new skirt.*
simple present [ˌsɪmpl ˈpreznt]	einfache Form des Präsens	*She* **reads** *love stories every day.*
singular [ˈsɪŋgjʊlə]	Einzahl, Singular	*book, letter, dog, woman, child, foot*
statement [ˈsteɪtmənt]	Aussage, Aussagesatz	*She likes cats. I don't like dinosaurs.*
subject [ˈsʌbdʒɪkt]	Satzgegenstand, Subjekt	***Jessica*** *likes maths.* **The girl over there** *is Sophie.*
superlative [suːˈpɜːlətɪv]	Superlativ, höchste Steigerungsform	*big**gest**,* **best***,* **most** *interesting, …*
tense [tens]	grammatische Form, Tempus	*present tense, past tense, …*
time [taɪm]	(wirkliche) Zeit	*past, present, future*
verb [vɜːb]	a) Zeitwort, Verb	*be, love, play, get up, … ; can, will, do, …*
	b) Satzaussage, Prädikat	*She* **likes** *yoghurt. We* **can play** *cards.*
vowel [ˈvaʊəl]	Vokal, Selbstlaut	*a, e, i, o, u*
word order [ˈwɜːd ɔːdə]	Wortstellung	*subject – verb – object (S – V – O)*
***yes*/*no* question** [jesˈnəʊ kwestʃən]	Entscheidungsfrage	***Is Adam at home?*** *– Yes, he is. / No, he isn't.*

90 ninety

Classroom phrases

You can say …

What are we going to do today?	Was machen wir heute?
What page are we on?	Auf welcher Seite sind wir?
What do we have to do?	Was müssen wir machen?
I'm sorry. I've forgotten my homework.	Es tut mir leid. Ich habe meine Hausaufgabe vergessen.
What's … in English/German?	Wie heißt … auf Englisch/Deutsch?
What does … mean?	Was bedeutet … ?
How do you spell … , please?	Wie schreibt man bitte … ?
I don't understand this word/sentence.	Ich verstehe dieses Wort/diesen Satz nicht.
Can you explain it, please?	Können Sie das bitte erklären?
Pardon?	Wie bitte?
I've got something different.	Ich habe etwas anderes.
Can I ask a question?	Darf ich eine Frage stellen?
I don't know the answer.	Ich weiß die Antwort nicht.
Can you repeat the answer?	Können Sie die Antwort wiederholen?
Could you write this word/sentence on the board?	Könnten Sie dieses Wort/diesen Satz an die Tafel schreiben?
Can you play the CD again, please?	Können Sie die CD bitte nochmals vorspielen?
It's my turn now.	Jetzt bin ich dran.
What's for homework?	Was haben wir auf?
Can I go to the toilet, please?	Kann ich bitte auf die Toilette gehen?
Can I open/shut the window?	Darf ich das Fenster öffnen/schließen?
I'm not feeling well.	Ich fühle mich nicht wohl.
I've got a headache.	Ich habe Kopfschmerzen.
I must go to the doctor.	Ich muss zum Arzt gehen.
Have a nice weekend.	Schönes Wochenende.

The teacher can say …

Open your books at page … , please.	Öffnet eure Bücher auf Seite … , bitte.
Read the text on page … .	Lies den Text auf Seite … .
Do exercise … for homework.	Macht die Übung … als Hausaufgabe.
Write the answers in your exercise books.	Schreibt die Antworten in eure Hefte.
Look at line … on page … .	Schaut zu Zeile … auf Seite … .
Complete the gaps/table/… .	Füllt die Lücken/die Tabelle/… aus.
Correct the mistakes.	Verbessert die Fehler.
Fill in/Put in the right words.	Setzt die richtigen Wörter ein.
Take notes.	Macht euch Notizen.
Read out your answers.	Lest die Antworten vor.
Have you finished?	Seid ihr fertig?
Do exercise … for homework, please.	Als Hausaufgabe macht bitte Übung … .

UNIT 1

GRAMMATIKANHANG

1 revision of tenses

a simple present and present progressive

Mike **plays** volleyball
(every Tuesday evening).

Mike **is play**ing volleyball
(at the moment/now).

Mr Boyle **works** at Dublin Airport.
Does he **usually work** on Saturdays?
Yes, he **does**. He **often works at the weekends**.
But he **doesn't work at Christmas**.

Mr Boyle **is working** in his office now.
Is he **working** alone?
No, he **isn't**. He**'s working** with a partner **at the moment**.
He **isn't working** alone.

What **does** the word 'burglar' **mean** in German?
– It **means** *Einbrecher*.

He **doesn't like** hamburgers. But he **loves** fish and chips.

Do you **know** his phone number? – No, I **don't**.

Revision: Zeitformen

Simple present und present progressive

Im Deutschen drückt der Satz „Mike spielt Volleyball." zwei unterschiedliche Dinge aus:

Mikes Hobby ist Volleyball.

oder

Mike spielt gerade Volleyball.

Im Gegensatz zum Deutschen steht dafür im Englischen das *simple present* oder das *present progressive*.

Das *simple present* verwenden wir,

◆ um auszudrücken, dass etwas **regelmäßig**, **immer**, **normalerweise**, **oft** oder **nie** passiert.

Signalwörter für das *simple present*:
always, usually, often, sometimes, never, every day, on Saturdays, every year ...

Das *present progressive* verwenden wir,

◆ um auszudrücken, dass etwas **im Augenblick/ jetzt/gerade** passiert. Die Handlung ist gerade im Gange und noch **nicht abgeschlossen**.

Signalwörter für das *present progressive*
at the moment, now, today, just ...

Nicht in der *ing*-Form stehen folgende Verben. Sie beschreiben keine Tätigkeiten, sondern:

◆ **Zustände:** *be* = sein, *belong to* = gehören, *have got* = haben/besitzen, *look* = aussehen, *mean* = bedeuten, *need* = brauchen, *sound* = klingen

◆ **Gefühle:** *hate* = hassen, *like* = mögen, *love* = lieben, *want* = wollen

◆ **Gedanken:** *imagine* = sich vorstellen, *know* = wissen, *remember* = sich erinnern, *think* = glauben

92 ninety-two

Grammatikanhang — UNIT 1

Simple past und present perfect | simple past and present perfect b

Beide Zeitformen werden verwendet, um über die Vergangenheit zu sprechen. Sie sind jedoch **nicht** (wie oft im Deutschen) **austauschbar**.

Criminals **have stolen** all the computers at Computer World.
They **stole** them last night.

Patricks Mutter möchte wissen, **ob** (nicht wann!) er sein Fahrrad repariert hat.
→ *present perfect*

MUM   **Have** you **repaired** your bike?
Hast du dein Fahrrad repariert?

Patrick antwortet, **dass** er es repariert hat. (*Yes, I have.*) → *present perfect*

PATRICK   Yes, I **have**.

Er fügt hinzu, **wann** er es getan hat. (*I repaired it two hours ago.*) → *simple past*

I **repaired** it two hours ago.
Ja. Ich habe es vor zwei Stunden repariert.

Wir drücken mit dem

present perfect	*simple past*
aus, **dass** oder **ob** etwas geschehen ist.	aus, **wann** etwas geschehen ist.
Häufige Zeitangaben sind: *already, ever, just, never, yet*	Häufige Zeitangaben sind: *yesterday, last week, three days ago, in 1998 …, when?*

POLICEMAN   May I see your driving licence?
Führerschein
DRIVER   I haven't got a driving licence. You **took** it from me last month. I hope you **haven't lost** it.

Past progressive und simple past | past progressive and simple past 2

Wir wissen bereits, dass wir mit dem *past progressive* ausdrücken, was zu einem bestimmten Zeitpunkt in der Vergangenheit gerade geschah.

Das kennen wir ja schon vom letzten Schuljahr.

Stimmt. Die *ing*-Form nehmen wir immer dann, wenn etwas im Gange ist – jetzt (*present progressive*) oder in der Vergangenheit (*past progressive*).

Ach so.

At nine o'clock Liz and Kim **were dancing** at the disco.

ninety-three   **93**

UNIT 1   Grammatikanhang

I **was reading** a magazine when you **phoned**.

The bus **was waiting** when we **arrived** at the bus-stop.

When we **heard** the crash we **ran** outside.

Wir verwenden das *past progressive* auch für eine Handlung, die gerade stattfand (*I was reading a magazine*), als eine zweite Handlung begann (*you phoned*).
Die zweite Handlung steht im *simple past*.

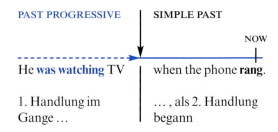

PAST PROGRESSIVE	SIMPLE PAST
He **was watching** TV	when the phone **rang**.
1. Handlung im Gange …	… , als 2. Handlung begann

Das *simple past* beschreibt die kürzere, neue Handlung. Davor steht meist *when*.

Folgen zwei kurze Handlungen aufeinander, so stehen beide im *simple past*.

3   'since' and 'for' with perfect tenses

„since" und „for" mit perfect tenses

Look, I **have cleaned** my shoes.

She**'s always worn** glasses.

Wir verwenden das *present perfect*, um auszudrücken, **dass** etwas oder **ob etwas geschehen ist**, nicht wann. (Vgl. dazu S. 93.)

Das *present perfect* wird auch verwendet, um zu zeigen, dass ein **Zustand in der Vergangenheit begonnen** hat und **jetzt noch andauert**.

Häufige Zeitbestimmungen sind dabei: *always, all day, all week, all my life* und *how long?*

Grammatikanhang UNIT 1/2

Auf eine Frage mit *How long … ?* gibt es zwei Möglichkeiten zu sagen, **seit wann** oder **wie lange** etwas schon andauert:

◆ Wir verwenden *since*, um zu sagen, **wann** ein Zustand oder eine Tätigkeit **begonnen** hat. (Seine Erkrankung hat am Freitag angefangen.)

◆ Wir verwenden *for*, um zu sagen, **wie lange** ein Zustand oder eine Tätigkeit schon andauert. (Seine Krankheit dauert schon drei Tage.)

> MERKE: Im Deutschen verwenden wir „seit" meistens mit dem Präsens:
>
> Ich kenne sie seit fünf Jahren.
> **Falsch:** I ~~know~~ her for five years.
> **Richtig:** I**'ve known** her for five years.
>
> Wie lange bist du schon in Dublin?
> **Falsch:** How long ~~are you~~ in Dublin?
> **Richtig:** How long **have** you **been** in Dublin?

How long has Patrick **been** ill?
Wie lange ist Patrick schon krank?

He**'s been** ill **since** Friday.
seit Freitag

He**'s been** ill **for** 3 days.
seit drei Tagen

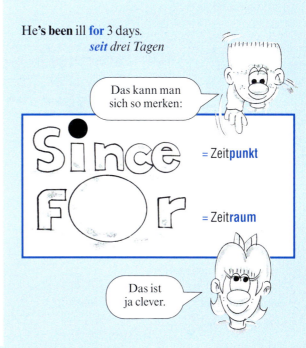

UNIT 2

Frageanhängsel

In der gesprochenen Sprache hängen wir Frageanhängsel an Aussagesätze an, wenn wir eine Bestätigung unserer Aussage erwarten. Im Deutschen verwenden wir „nicht wahr?", „oder?" bzw. „gell?".

Frageanhängsel werden normalerweise mit fallender Intonation gesprochen. Die Stimme geht also am Satzende nach unten, wenn wir etwas eigentlich wissen, es aber bestätigt haben wollen.

Geht die Stimme am Satzende nach oben, so bedeutet dies, dass wir uns nicht sicher oder überrascht sind.

question tags   1

It's a nice day, **isn't it?** (…, *nicht wahr?*)
You aren't waiting for me, **are you?** (…, *nicht?*)
We can go to a café later, **can't we?** (…, *oder?*)

↘
The Jewells have got a German car, **haven't they?**

↗
He can't really speak Japanese, **can he?**

ninety-five 95

UNIT 2 Grammatikanhang

You're German, **aren't you?**
bejaht   verneint

Auf einen **bejahten Aussagesatz** folgt ein **verneintes Frageanhängsel**.

Es besteht aus:
Hilfsverb + *n't* + Pronomen
  are   *n't*   *you?*

Anita **isn't** tired, **is she?**
verneint   bejaht

Auf einen **verneinten Aussagesatz** folgt ein **bejahtes Frageanhängsel**.

Es besteht aus:
Hilfsverb + Pronomen
  is   *she?*

It's a nice evening, **isn't it?**
King Arthur wasn't a real person, **was he?**
You don't want to leave, **do you?**
Lauren doesn't believe those stories, **does she?**
You've got two cats, **haven't you?**
She can't swim, **can she?**
We won't be back before 10 o'clock, **will we?**
King Arthur didn't really live in Cornwall, **did he?**

Steht im Aussagesatz ein Hilfs- oder Modalverb, so benutzt man dieses auch im Frageanhängsel.

Das Pronomen (*he*) bezieht sich auf das Subjekt des Aussagesatzes (*King Arthur*).

I'm doing it right, **aren't I?**

Beachte die Ausnahme: *I'm late, aren't I?*
                        (~~amn't I~~)

You **like** castles, **don't you?**
He always **reads** history books, **doesn't he?**
She **came** here last year, **didn't she?**

Enthält der Aussagesatz kein Hilfs- oder Modalverb, so benutzt man im Frageanhängsel *don't, doesn't, didn't*.

You can speak French, **can't you?**

Aussagen mit Frageanhängseln kann man entweder zustimmen oder widersprechen.

ZUSTIMMUNG	WIDERSPRUCH
Yes, I can. / **Yes, that's right.** (*Ja, stimmt.*)	**No, I can't.** (*Nein.*)

You aren't from London, **are you?**

ZUSTIMMUNG	WIDERSPRUCH
No, I'm not. (*Nein.*) **That's right.** (*Stimmt.*)	**I am!** (*Doch.*) **Oh yes, I am!**

ninety-six

Grammatikanhang   UNIT 2

„have to"   'have to'   **2**

a

Du weißt bereits, dass wir *must* benutzen, wenn etwas notwendig ist oder gemacht werden muss.

> You must tidy your room.

> Yes, but I have to finish my homework first.

Während *must* nur im *present tense* benutzt werden darf, kann man das gleichbedeutende *have to* auch in anderen Zeitstufen verwenden.

must verwenden wir bei **Befehlen** oder wenn man seine **innere Überzeugung** ausdrückt.

Mit *have to* berichtet man, was **von anderen angeordnet** wurde.

I **had to** go to the doctor this morning.

You **must** be there at 2 o'clock.
I **must** find a birthday present for Kirsty.

I **have to** do my homework first. Then we can go in-line skating.

Gegenwart   present   **b**

Auf *must* und *have to/has to* folgt immer die Grundform des Verbs.

We **must meet** more often.
Ben **has to go** and see Mrs Jenkins first.
We **have to leave** now.

In verneinten Sätzen wird das Hilfsverb *don't/ doesn't* + *have to* verwendet.

You **don't have to hurry**.
She **doesn't have to wait**.

Beachte:
You **mustn't** go. = Du **darfst nicht** gehen.

Auch bei Fragen ist eine Umschreibung mit *do* oder *does* notwendig.
do/does wird vorangestellt, dann folgt das Subjekt und *have to* + Grundform des Verbs.

Does she **have to work** today?   – Yes, she **does**.
    – No, she **doesn't**.

Bei Fragen mit Fragewörtern stehen diese (*where/when/why/*…) am Satzanfang.

Where do you **have to** go?

ninety-seven   **97**

UNIT 2   Grammatikanhang

c   **past**

We **had to hurry** because we were late.
He **had to leave** early.

We **didn't have to wait** long.
Did he **have to help** his dad?   – Yes, he **did**.
                                      – No, he **didn't**.
What did he **have to do** there?

Vergangenheit

In der Vergangenheit steht bei allen Personen *had to* und die Grundform des Verbs, nicht *must*.

Fragen, Verneinungen und Kurzantworten werden mit *did* gebildet.

d   **future**

She **will have to wait**.

Zukunft

On Sunday we **won't have to get up** early.
When will they **have to be** back?
Die Zukunft wird mit *will/won't* + *have to* gebildet.

3   propword 'one/ones'   Stützwort „one/ones"

He has got three **baseball caps** – a big **one** and two small **ones**.

I need some T-shirts, some **yellow ones**.
This shop isn't very good. **The one** in Archer Street is better.

I need some socks. **These** (**ones**) look all right.
What about **that** (**one**)?
We've got four different sizes. **Which** (**one**) do you want?
I'd like to see **another** (**one**).

I'd like the red **one** and the **one** on the table.
Ich möchte das Rote und das auf dem Tisch.

Um die Wiederholung von bereits genannten, zählbaren Nomen zu vermeiden, ersetzt man sie in der Einzahl durch *one*, in der Mehrzahl durch *ones*.

Dabei muss *one* bzw. *ones* nach einem
◆ Adjektiv und nach
◆ *the* stehen.

one/ones kann nach
◆ *this, that, these, those*
◆ *which?*

◆ *another* stehen.

Beachte: Im Deutschen wird *one* oft nicht übersetzt!

98   ninety-eight

Bedingungssätze

Ein Bedingungssatz besteht aus zwei Teilen: einem Nebensatz mit *if* und einem Hauptsatz.

Ein Bedingungssatz gibt die Bedingung an (Wenn es regnet, …), unter der ein bestimmtes Ereignis (… bleiben wir zu Hause) stattfindet.

Offene, erfüllbare Bedingung

Wir verwenden im:

if-Satz	Hauptsatz
	will-future
	Modalverb *can* + Infinitiv
simple present	Modalverb *must* + Infinitiv
	Modalverb *should* + Infinitiv
	Befehlsform

Was kann man sich da merken?

Ah ja!

Steht der Hauptsatz am Anfang, so steht vor *if* kein Komma.

Auch Nebensätze mit *when* stehen im *simple present*, obwohl sie sich auf die Zukunft beziehen. Beachte jedoch den Bedeutungsunterschied zwischen *if* und *when*.

Es ist nicht sicher, ob ich ihn sehe.

Ich weiß bereits, dass ich ihn wieder sehen werde.

conditional clauses

1

a

If it **rains**, we **will** stay at home.

open condition

b

IF-CLAUSE	MAIN CLAUSE
If we **travel** in September,	it**'ll** be cheaper.
If we **go** to London,	I **can** practise my English.
If you **climb** a mountain,	you **must** be careful.
If you **don't understand**,	you **should** ask me.
If you **want** to come,	please **tell** us.

Willst du nicht die Briten schrecken, darf kein *will* im *if*-Satz stecken!

You **must** be careful **if** you **do** in-line skating.
It**'ll** be cheaper **if** we **travel** in September.

If I see him, I'll ask him about it.
Wenn (= Falls) ich ihn sehe, frage ich ihn danach.

When I see him, I'll ask him.
Wenn (= Sobald) ich ihn sehe, frage ich ihn.

UNIT 3   Grammatikanhang

c   **automatic result**

If you **add** blue to yellow, you **get** green.
If it**'s** hot, people **drink** a lot.

Logische Folge

Wir verwenden im *if*-Satz und im Hauptsatz das *simple present*, um auszudrücken, dass etwas als logische Folge von etwas anderem passiert.

2   verbs with two objects

Her mum gave **Chloe a new guitar**.

He	gave	**Jodie**	**the poster**.
S	V	Indir. Obj.	Dir. Obj.
He	gave	**the poster**	**to Jodie**.
S	V	Dir. Obj.	Indir. Obj.

I	sent	**him**	a postcard.
I	sent	it	**to my brother**.
I	sent	it	**to him**.

| She | gave | **Phil** | **a ticket for the new musical**. |
| He | gave | the ticket | **to another boy in his class**. |

| We | cooked | a meal | **for our friends**. |
| Kate | bought | a magazine | **for her father**. |

He explained	the sentence	**to the pupils**.
Can you describe	the problem	**to me**?
She didn't say	anything	**to the others**.

Verben mit zwei Objekten

Nach einigen Verben (z.B. *give*) können zwei Objekte stehen. Normalerweise ist das indirekte Objekt eine Person (*Chloe*), das direkte Objekt eine Sache (*a new guitar*).

Das indirekte Objekt (*Jodie*) steht normalerweise vor dem direkten Objekt (*the poster*).

Es kann auch nach dem direkten Objekt kommen, dann muss es mit *to* angeschlossen werden (*the poster to Jodie*).

Wenn eines der Objekte ein Pronomen ist, so kommt dieses immer zuerst.

Sind beide Objekte Pronomen, so verwenden wir *to*.

Ist ein Objekt sehr lang, so stellen wir es an das Satzende.

Anstelle von *to* steht bei einigen Verben *for*. Beispiele sind: *buy, cook, fetch, get, make*.

Bei den Verben *explain* (erklären), *describe* (beschreiben), *say* (sagen) muss die Person immer mit *to* nachgestellt werden.

100   one hundred

Grammatikanhang UNIT 4

Relativsätze / relative clauses 1

Relativsätze erläutern **ein Nomen**. Ohne den Relativsatz bliebe unklar, **wer** oder **was** gemeint ist.

a

Welche Leute lebten vor langer Zeit?

The **people who built Stonehenge** lived a long time ago.

Was für ein Poster?

Here is a **poster which tells you all about the Vikings**.

Beachte: Relativsätze haben die Wortstellung S – V – O.
Vor dieser Form des Relativsatzes steht im Englischen **kein** Komma.

These are the people **who invaded England**.
Das sind die Leute, die England überfielen.

Relativpronomen: „who, which, that" / relative pronouns: 'who, which, that' b

Wir verwenden:

◆ *who* für Personen

The **soldiers who** conquered the country were Normans.

◆ *which* für Dinge

The **land which** belonged to the Anglo-Saxons fell into the hands of the Norman knights.

◆ *that* für Dinge und Personen

The **sword that** they found last week was Norman.
The Anglo-Saxons were **people that** already lived in England.

Alle Relativpronomen können sich auf Nomen im Singular oder Plural beziehen.

Kennst du dazu eine Merkhilfe?

Und *that* geht im Zweifelsfall immer?

Klar! *who* für *person*
which für *thing*.

Stimmt!

one hundred and one 101

UNIT 4   Grammatikanhang

c   **relative pronouns: 'whose'**

Who's the **king whose** soldiers conquered England in 1066? (… *der König, dessen Soldaten …*)

That's the **club whose** members are interested in Anglo-Saxon history.
(… *der Club, dessen Mitglieder …*)

Relativpronomen: „whose"

Man verwendet:
◆ *whose* (= deren/dessen) für Personen (und Dinge), um auszudrücken, dass jemand oder etwas zusammengehört. Auf *whose* muss immer ein Nomen folgen.

Beachte:
Whose *car is this?* (Wessen?)
This is the girl **whose** *car is over there.* (deren)
This is the girl **who's** *in my class.* (… die … ist)

d   **'who, which, that' as subject**

	S	V	O
He's the **guide**	who/that	told	Nick about Jorvik.
	(He	told	Nick about Jorvik.)
The museum has got **cars**	which/that	take	you back in time.
	(They	take	you back in time.)

„who, which, that" als Subjekt

Werden *who*, *which* oder *that* als **Subjekt** verwendet, so folgt ein Verb (*told, take*).

e   **'who, which, that' as object**

„who, which, that" als Objekt

	O	S	V	
The girl	who	we	met at the museum was from York.
	(We	met **her** at the museum.)
The book	which/that	the boy	read was about Guy Fawkes.
	(The boy	read **it**.)

Werden *who*, *which* oder *that* als **Objekt** verwendet, so folgt ein Subjekt (*you, the boy*).

Grammatikanhang UNIT 4

Relativsätze ohne Relativpronomen

Die Relativpronomen *who*, *which* und *that* können **weggelassen** werden, wenn sie **Objekt des Relativsatzes** sind.

Wie soll ich mir das alles merken?

Ganz einfach: Wenn auf *who*, *which* oder *that* ein Verb folgt, dann darf man sie nicht weglassen.

Es muss also zwischen Relativpronomen und Verb noch etwas dazwischen stehen, damit man das Pronomen weglassen kann.

Du hast es erfasst.

Die Relativpronomen können auch weggelassen werden, wenn sie Präpositionalobjekt sind.

Präpositionen in Relativsätzen

Die Relativpronomen können auch als Präpositionalobjekt stehen. Die Präposition bleibt dabei aber hinter dem Verb (*looked at*).

Beachte:
Im formellen Englisch kann *whom* statt *who* als Objekt stehen.

Nach einer Präposition (*to, for …*) kann nur *whom* (oder *which*) stehen, nicht ~~who~~ oder ~~that~~.

contact clauses f

	O	S	V
He's the teacher	**who/that**	**you**	met at the museum.
He's the teacher		**you**	met at the museum.
	den	*du*	*getroffen hast*

who/that ist Objekt und kann weggelassen werden.

	S	V
Was William the man	**who/that**	conquered England?
	der	*England eroberte*

Beachte: who/that ist Subjekt und darf nicht weggelassen werden.

	O	S	V
The weapons	**which/that**	**we**	saw were old.
The weapons		**we**	saw were old.
	die	*wir*	*sahen*

which/that ist Objekt und kann weggelassen werden.

	O	S	V
The boy	**who/that**	**you**	spoke **to** was Luke.
The boy		**you**	spoke **to** was Luke.
		mit dem	*du sprachst*

who/that ist Objekt und kann weggelassen werden.

prepositions in relative clauses g

	O	S	V
The man	**who/that**	you	looked **at** was a Viking.
		(You	looked **at him**.)
The weapons	**which/that**	the Vikings	fought **with** were there.
		(The Vikings	fought **with them**.)

The girl **who** I was waiting **for** was late.
*Das Mädchen, **auf das** ich wartete, kam zu spät.*

The girl **whom** we met was in my class.

The guide **to whom** we talked was very nice.

one hundred and three **103**

UNIT 5   Grammatikanhang

1 adverbs

a

Alex **spoke quietly**.
They **walked slowly** around the fairground.

Adverbien

Wir wissen bereits, dass Adverbien die Art und Weise (*adverbs of manner*) angeben

◆ **wie** eine Handlung geschieht.

Sie beziehen sich daher oft auf ein Verb.

b revision: the formation of adverbs from adjectives

ADJECTIVE	ADVERB
cheap	cheap**ly**
exact	exact**ly**
polite	polit**ely**
safe	saf**ely**
possib**le**	possib**ly**
hungr**y**	hungr**ily**
fantast**ic**	fantastic**ally**
full	**fully**
whole	**wholly**
true	**truly**

Revision: Die Bildung von Adverbien aus Adjektiven

Die von Adjektiven abgeleiteten Adverbien bildet man, indem man *-ly* an das Adjektiv anhängt.

Beachte: Stummes *-e* entfällt bei der Bildung von Adverbien **nicht**. (*polite* ➔ *politely*)

Besonderheiten bei der Schreibung der Adverbien

◆ *-le* fällt vor *-ly* weg
◆ *-y* wird vor *-ly* zu *-i-*.

Ausnahme: *shy* (schüchtern) ➔ *shyly*

◆ Bei Adjektiven auf *-ic* hängt man *-ally* an.
Ausnahme: *public* (öffentlich) ➔ *publicly*

◆ Die Adjektive *full*, *whole* und *true* bilden die Gradadverbien
fully (völlig),
wholly (ganz) und
truly (wirklich).

c special forms

The girl is **friendly**. She answers **in a friendly way**.

Scot ran a **good** race. Scott ran **well**.

She's **well** again. (*Sie ist wieder gesund.*)

Sonderformen

◆ Bei Adjektiven auf *-ly* (*friendly*, *silly*, *lively*, *lovely*) verwendet man die Umschreibung *in a … way*.

◆ *good* bildet die Adverbform *well*.

Beachte: *well* kann auch ein Adjektiv sein.

Grammatikanhang   UNIT 5

Revision: Adverbien, die die gleiche Form wie Adjektive haben

Einige Adverbien haben die gleiche Form wie Adjektive.

Dies sind:
daily (täglich)   *deep* (tief)
early (früh)   *far* (weit)
fast (schnell)   *free* (frei, kostenlos)
hard (hart, schwer)   *high* (hoch)
late (spät)   *left* (links)
long (lang)   *near* (nahe)
right (richtig, rechts) *straight* (geradeaus)
wrong (falsch)

Zu einigen dieser Adverbien gibt es eine weitere Adverbform auf *-ly*. Diese Adverbien haben aber eine völlig andere Bedeutung:

deeply (sehr, zutiefst)   *hardly* (kaum)
highly (sehr, höchst)   *nearly* (fast, beinahe)
lately (in letzter Zeit)

Adjektive nach „be, get, seem" usw.

Nach Verben, die einen **Zustand** oder eine **Eigenschaft** ausdrücken:
be, seem (scheinen), *become/get* (werden), *stay* (bleiben), *look* (aussehen), *smell* (riechen), *feel* (sich anfühlen), *taste* (schmecken), *sound* (klingen)
stehen **Adjektive**, keine Adverbien, da es sich nicht um eine Tätigkeit handelt.

Beachte:
*He looked **angry**.*   *He looked at us **angrily**.*
sah ... aus   **sah** uns **an**
(Zustand)   (Tätigkeit)

revision: adverbs with the same form as adjectives   d

ADJECTIVE	ADVERB
They had a **fast** car.	They all drove **fast**.
I had to do some **hard** work.	I had to work **hard**.
Peter is **late** again.	He always arrives **late**.

The pupils had to work **hard**. (*schwer, hart*)
I can **hardly** understand the teacher. (*kaum*)

He lives **near** his school. (*in der Nähe*)
Nearly 500 pupils go there. (*fast*)

Don't stay out **late**. (*spät*)
I haven't met her **lately**. (*in letzter Zeit*)

adjectives after 'be, get, seem', etc   e

Everyone **is excited** about the party.
I have to **get ready**.
Richard **seemed tired**.
Louise **felt nervous** about her exam.
Jeff **looked happy**.

one hundred and five   **105**

UNIT 5   **Grammatikanhang**

2   the present perfect progressive | Das present perfect progressive

a

Wir verwenden das *present perfect progressive*, wenn eine Handlung in der Vergangenheit begann und sich bis jetzt erstreckt.

I've been waiting for you since seven o'clock.
Matthew **has been waiting** for two hours now.

Dabei wird besonders die **Dauer des Vorgangs** hervorgehoben.

b   positive statements

I	have	been waiting
You	've	been waiting
He/She/It	has	been waiting for a long time.
	's	been waiting
We		
You	have	been waiting
They	've	been waiting

I've known him for a long time.

Bejahte Aussagesätze

Das *present perfect progressive* bildet man mit *have been/has been* und der *-ing*-Form des Verbs.

Beachte:
Man gebraucht diese Zeitform nicht bei Verben, die
◆ Zustände (*be, have, belong to, cost, own …*)
◆ Gefühle (*like, love …*)
◆ Gedanken (*know, understand …*)
ausdrücken.

c   negative statements

I	have not	been waiting
You	haven't	been waiting
He/She/It	has not	been waiting for an hour.
	hasn't	been waiting
We		
You	have not	been waiting
They	haven't	been waiting

Verneinte Aussagesätze

Verneinungen werden mit *have not* (*haven't*) *been* oder *has not* (*hasn't*) *been* und der *-ing*-Form des Verbs gebildet.

106   one hundred and six

Grammatikanhang **UNIT 5**

Fragen

Bei Fragen steht *have* oder *has* vor dem Subjekt.

Questions **d**

Have	I you	
Has	he/she/it	**been working**?
Have	we you they	

Bei Fragen mit Fragewörtern stehen diese am Anfang des Satzes.

| **Where** | **have** | you | **been working**? |
| **How long** | **has** | she | **been waiting**? |

Kurzantworten werden mit Subjekt + *have* oder *has* gebildet.

Yes,	I/you/we/you/they	**have**.
	he/she/it	**has**.
No,	I/you/we/you/they	**haven't**.
	he/she/it	**hasn't**.

„must, mustn't, needn't"

must und *have/has to* (müssen) drücken aus, dass etwas jetzt **notwendig** ist.

need not und *do not/does not have to* verwendet man, wenn etwas **nicht notwendig** ist.

Beachte:

must not/mustn't bedeutet, dass etwas **verboten** ist:

'must, mustn't, needn't' **3**

We **must** / **have to** call a doctor. (*müssen*)

They **need not** / **needn't** / **don't have to** help us. (*brauchen nicht / müssen nicht*)

You **needn't/don't have to** tell me. I already know.
*Du **brauchst** es mir **nicht** zu sagen. /*
*Du **musst** es mir **nicht** sagen.*

We **mustn't** forget his birthday.
*Wir **dürfen** seinen Geburtstag **nicht** vergessen.*

You **mustn't** tell anybody. It's a secret.
*Du **darfst** es **nicht** weitersagen.*

one hundred and seven **107**

English sounds Erklärung der Lautschriftzeichen

Vowels
Selbstlaute, Vokale

[iː]	**ea**t, w**ee**k, h**e**
[i]	part**y**, ver**y**, read**y**
[ɪ]	**i**n, g**i**ve, f**i**lm
[e]	**e**nd, g**e**t, m**a**ny
[æ]	**a**dd, m**a**n, bl**a**ck
[ʌ]	**u**nder, c**o**me
[ɑː]	**a**sk, h**a**lf, c**a**r
[ɒ]	**o**ften, wh**a**t, c**o**ffee
[ɔː]	**a**ll, f**ou**r, d**oo**r
[ʊ]	p**u**t, g**oo**d, w**o**man
[uː]	wh**o**, J**u**ne, bl**ue**
[ɜː]	l**ear**n, g**i**rl, w**o**rk
[ə]	**a**gain, policem**a**n, sist**er**
[eɪ]	**eigh**t, t**a**ble, pl**ay**
[aɪ]	**I**, n**i**ce, b**y**
[ɔɪ]	b**oy**, t**oi**let
[əʊ]	**o**ld, r**oa**d, kn**ow**
[aʊ]	**ou**t, h**ou**se, n**ow**
[ɪə]	w**e're**, h**ere**, n**ear**
[eə]	w**ear**, ch**air**, th**ere**
[ʊə]	y**our**, p**ure**, s**ure**

Consonants
Mitlaute, Konsonanten

[p]	**p**en, s**p**eak, ma**p**
[b]	**b**ook, ra**bb**it, jo**b**
[t]	**t**able, le**tt**er, si**t**
[d]	**d**esk, ra**d**io, ol**d**
[k]	**c**ar, bas**k**etball, ba**ck**
[g]	**g**et, bi**gg**er, ba**g**
[f]	**f**ather, le**f**t, cli**ff**
[v]	**v**ery, e**v**ery, ha**v**e
[θ]	**th**ank, bir**th**day, ba**th**
[ð]	**th**is, fa**th**er, wi**th**
[s]	**s**ee, cla**ss**es, dan**ce**
[z]	**z**oo, thou**s**and, plea**s**e
[ʃ]	**sh**op, **s**ugar, Engli**sh**
[ʒ]	televi**s**ion, u**s**ually
[tʃ]	**ch**ild, ki**tch**en, wa**tch**
[h]	**h**elp, **wh**o, **h**ome
[m]	**m**ouse, nu**m**ber, fil**m**
[n]	**n**ame, wi**n**dow, pe**n**
[ŋ]	si**ng**, mor**n**ing, lo**ng**
[l]	**l**ike, b**l**ue, a**ll**
[r]	**r**ead, bo**rr**ow, ve**r**y
[j]	**y**es, **y**ou, **y**ear
[w]	**w**alk, **wh**ere, q**u**iz

The English alphabet
Das englische Alphabet

a	[eɪ]
b	[biː]
c	[siː]
d	[diː]
e	[iː]
f	[ef]
g	[dʒiː]
h	[eɪtʃ]
i	[aɪ]
j	[dʒeɪ]
k	[keɪ]
l	[el]
m	[em]
n	[en]
o	[əʊ]
p	[piː]
q	[kjuː]
r	[ɑː]
s	[es]
t	[tiː]
u	[juː]
v	[viː]
w	['dʌbl juː]
x	[eks]
y	[waɪ]
z	[zed]

Erklärung der Symbole im Wörterverzeichnis

Act	=	Activities	Read	=	Reading	W&P	=	Words and Pictures
Com	=	Communication	Rev	=	Revision	›	=	definition
Ex	=	Exercise	Sit	=	Situation	››	=	synonym
Intro	=	Introduction	Sket	=	Sketch	›‹	=	opposite
List	=	Listening	TYE	=	Test your English	≠	=	false friend

Wörter, die nicht **fett** gedruckt sind, sind rezeptiv, d.h. sie müssen nicht gelernt werden.

Wörterverzeichnis

Unit 1

WP **country** ['kʌntri]   Land, Staat
field [fi:ld]   Feld
traditional [trə'dɪʃənl]   traditionell
still [stɪl]   (immer) noch

≫ *state*   *Italy, France and Germany are **countries**.*
*in the field = **auf** dem Feld*

*Where is Dad? – He's **still** in his office.*

MERKE: still   Do you **still** live in Dublin? (immer noch)
              Can't you sit **still**? (ruhig)

---

to **change** [tʃeɪndʒ]   ändern, verändern
block [blɒk]   Block
office block ['ɒfɪs blɒk]   Bürogebäude, Bürokomplex
smart [smɑ:t]   schick, elegant, flott
to **export** [ɪk'spɔ:t]   ausführen, exportieren
software ['sɒftweə]   Software
except [ɪk'sept]   außer

kingdom ['kɪŋdəm]   Königreich
United Kingdom   Vereinigtes Königreich, UK
   [ju,naɪtɪd 'kɪŋdəm]
republic [rɪ'pʌblɪk]   Republik

separate ['seprət]   getrennt
northern ['nɔ:ðən]   nördlich, Nord-
to **start** do**ing** sth   anfangen, etw. zu tun
   [stɑ:t 'du:ɪŋ]
Irish ['aɪrɪʃ]   irisch
board [bɔ:d]   Kommission, Behörde, Aufsichtsrat
Irish Tourist Board   das irische Fremden-
   [,aɪrɪʃ 'tʊərɪst bɔ:d]   verkehrsamt
Sit1   **top** [tɒp]   Oberteil, Top
to **like** do**ing** sth   etwas gerne tun
   [laɪk 'du:ɪŋ]

❯ *to become/make different*

❯ *to sell things to another country*

≫ *but not*

United Kingdom

Republic of Ireland

✕ *together*

*She **started** laugh**ing**.*
(vgl. Kasten bei like doing sth*)*

*He has never **liked** danc**ing**.*

MERKE: Verb + Verb-ing

Bestimmte Verben können als Ergänzung auch eine **-ing**-Form haben. Vergleiche:

Do you **like** | books?   He **start**ed a | new job | yesterday.
Do you **like** | read**ing**?   He **start**ed | work**ing** | yesterday.

Im Wörterverzeichnis werden diese Verben so aufgeführt: to **like** do**ing** sth
                                                  to **start** do**ing** sth

---

guest house ['gesthaʊs]   Gästehaus, Pension
to **run** [rʌn]   leiten, führen
ran, run [ræn, rʌn]

❯ *a small hotel*
*I was late so I **ran** to the bus-stop.* (laufen, rennen)
*Who **runs** this company?* (leiten, führen)

one hundred and nine   **109**

UNIT 1 Wörterverzeichnis

> **MERKE: a/an**
>
> Im Gegensatz zum Deutschen verwenden wir **a/an** …
>
> - bei Berufsbezeichnungen   He is **a** technician. (… ist Techniker)
>   She's **an** ambulance driver. (… ist Krankenwagenfahrerin)
> - bei Nationalitätsangaben   Sean Connery is **a** Scotsman. (… ist Schotte.)
> - Konfessionsangaben   She is **a** Catholic. (… ist Katholikin)

	technician [tek'nɪʃn]	Techniker/in	› someone who works with machines
Sit2	**tidy** ['taɪdi]	ordentlich	Her room is always **tidy**.
	raven ['reɪvn]	Rabe	
Sit3	to **spill** [spɪl] **spilt/spilled, spilt/spilled** [spɪlt, spɪld]	verschütten, vergießen	
	strawberry ['strɔːbəri]	Erdbeere	
Ex3	**forward(s)** ['fɔːwəd(z)]	vorwärts	
	to **try to** do sth [traɪ]	versuchen, etwas zu tun	(vgl. Kasten bei *need to do sth*)
	title ['taɪtl]	Titel	› the name of a book, film, piece of music, etc.
	start [stɑːt]	Start, Anfang, Beginn	
T1	**musical** ['mjuːzɪkl]	Musical	'Cats' is a **musical** by Andrew Lloyd Webber.
	to **relax** [rɪ'læks]	sich erholen	Just **relax** and enjoy the movie.
	to **shut up** [ʃʌt 'ʌp] **shut, shut** [ʃʌt, ʃʌt]	den Mund halten	›› to stop talking
	somewhere ['sʌmweə]	irgendwo	I've seen him **somewhere** before.
	county ['kaʊnti]	Verwaltungsbezirk, Grafschaft	
	Gaeltacht ['geɪltæxt]	Gebiet, in dem Gälisch gesprochen wird	Der Begriff *Gaeltacht* bezeichnet ein ländliches Gebiet im Westen Irlands, in dem Gälisch (die keltische Sprache Irlands) besonders stark verbreitet ist.
	college ['kɒlɪdʒ]	College	She's going to **college** next year.
	céilí ['keɪli]	Tanzveranstaltung auf Gälisch	
	to **mean** [miːn] **meant, meant** [ment, ment]	bedeuten	What does the word 'céilí' **mean**? – It **means** 'dance'.
	to **break** [breɪk] **broke, broken** [brəʊk, 'brəʊkən]	(zer)brechen	
	to **break in** [ˌbreɪk 'ɪn] **broke, broken** [brəʊk, 'brəʊkən]	einbrechen	They **broke in** through the window.
	else [els]	sonst	What **else** do you know about Ireland?

> **MERKE: else**
> I don't like tennis. Let's play **something else**.   (etwas anderes)
> **Where else** did you go?   (Wohin … sonst noch?)
> I'm busy. Perhaps **someone else** can help you.   (jemand anders)
> **Who else** came to your party?   (Wer … sonst noch?)
> Please wait like **everyone else**.   (alle anderen)
> **What else** did you get for Christmas?   (Was … sonst noch?)

Wörterverzeichnis UNIT 1

	community [kə'mjuːnəti]	Bevölkerungsgruppe; Gemeinde
	community centre [kə'mjuːnəti sentə]	Gemeindezentrum
	type [taɪp]	Typ
Ex4	**speaker** ['spiːkə]	Sprecher/in, Redner/in
Ex6	to **rewrite** [ˌriː'raɪt] **rewrote, rewritten** [ˌriː'rəʊt, ˌriː'rɪtn]	umschreiben, neu schreiben
	italics [ɪ'tælɪks]	Kursivdruck
Sit4	**for** [fɔː]	seit
	since [sɪns]	seit

> *a group of people who live in one place*

> *an Irish speaker* = jemand, der Irisch spricht

> *to write something again in a different way*

*This sentence is in **italics**.*

MERKE: since / for

Beide Wörter bedeuten im Deutschen „seit".

Patrick has been at the computer shop **since** 9 o'clock.
Patrick has been at the computer shop **for** 3 hours.

Wir verwenden …
… **since** mit **Zeitpunkten**, zu denen etwas begann:
since ten o'clock, **since** Monday, **since** May 6th, **since** we arrived, **since** 1953
… **for** mit **Zeitspannen**, die angeben, wie lange etwas schon andauert: **for** three days, **for** some years, **for** three hours, **for** a long time

---

Ex10	to **answer** ['ɑːnsə]	(be)antworten
Sit5	to **bring out** [ˌbrɪŋ 'aʊt] **brought, brought** [brɔːt, brɔːt]	herausbringen
	CD player [ˌsiː 'diː 'pleɪə]	CD-Spieler
	to **put on** [ˌpʊt 'ɒn] **put, put** [pʊt, pʊt]	anmachen, auflegen (CD)
	to **take out** [ˌteɪk 'aʊt] **took, taken** [tʊk, 'teɪkən]	herausnehmen, herausziehen
	plug [plʌg]	Stecker, Stöpsel
	to **put in** [ˌpʊt 'ɪn] **put, put** [pʊt, pʊt]	einstecken, einlegen

*The pop group have just **brought out** their new CD.*

*Can you **put** some music **on**?*

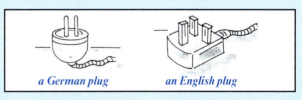

a German plug   *an English plug*

MERKE: verbs and adverbs / prepositions

Viele englische Verben bestehen aus zwei Teilen: einem **Verb** und einem (kurzen) **Adverb** bzw. einer **Präposition**, z.B.: **to take away** (wegnehmen).
Eine solche Verb-Adverb bzw. Verb-Präposition Kombination heißt *phrasal verb*:

Ben **put on** the CD player.

Ben **put** the CD player **on**.

The CD player is over there. **Put** it **on**.

Ist das Objekt eines *phrasal verbs* ein Nomen (*the CD player*), so kann das Adverb (*on*) **vor** oder **nach** dem Objekt stehen.

Ist das Objekt ein Pronomen (*it*), so steht das Adverb (*on*) **dahinter**.

UNIT 1 Wörterverzeichnis

T2	**urgent** [ˈɜːdʒənt]	dringend	There was an **urgent call** and the doctor had to leave.
	call [kɔːl]	Ruf, Anruf	
	lane [leɪn]	Feldweg, Gasse	
	no one [ˈnəʊ wʌn]	niemand	❯❮ *everyone*
	to **kick** [kɪk]	(mit dem Fuß) treten	❯ *to hit something or someone with your foot*
	secret [ˈsiːkrɪt]	geheim	**secret** information/talks/meetings
	stolen [ˈstəʊlən]	gestohlen	
	break-in [ˈbreɪkɪn]	Einbruch	There were three **break-ins** in our street last night.
	guard [gɑːd]	Polizist/in (in Irland)	❯❯ *policeman*
	hurry [ˈhʌri]	Eile	Take your time – there's no **hurry**.
	in a hurry [ɪn ə ˈhʌri]	in Eile	❯❯ *very quickly*
	police [pəˈliːs]	Polizei	The **police** are coming. = Die Polizei kommt.
	crash [kræʃ]	Krach(en)	a car **crash** = ein Autounfall
	van [væn]	Lieferwagen	
	(tele)phone box [ˈtelɪfəʊn bɒks]	Telefonzelle	
	while [waɪl]	während	
	over [ˈəʊvə]	zu Ende	
	to **get out (of)** [ˌget ˈaʊt əv]	aussteigen, herauskommen	❯ *to leave a place* You can **get out** of the car now.
	got, got [gɒt, gɒt]		
	to **arrest** [əˈrest]	festnehmen	
Ex14	**headache** [ˈhedeɪk]	Kopfschmerzen	
Proj	**display** [dɪˈspleɪ]	Ausstellung, Vorführung	a firework **display** = ein Feuerwerk
	mixture [ˈmɪkstʃə]	Mischung, Gemisch	❯ *a group of different things*
	sweet talk [ˈswiːt tɔːk]	Schmeicheleien, schöne Worte	
	to **sweet-talk** [ˈswiːt tɔːk]	jemandem schmeicheln	
Com	**invitation** [ˌɪnvɪˈteɪʃn]	Einladung	
	would like/love to do sth [wʊd ˈlaɪk / lʌv tə]	etwas gerne tun wollen	
	I'm afraid [aɪm əˈfreɪd]	ich fürchte, leider	**I'm afraid** we can't come.
	to **need to** do sth [ˈniːd tə]	etwas tun müssen	He's ill. He **needs to** go to the doctor.

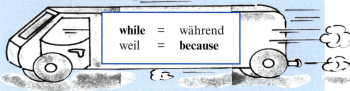

MERKE: Verb + to +infinitive

Bestimmte Verben können als Ergänzung ein weiteres Verb in der Grundform haben. Vergleiche:

I need	some help.		He tried	a new computer game	yesterday.
I need	**to do** my homework.		He tried	**to play**	it yesterday.

Im Wörterverzeichnis werden diese Verben so aufgeführt: to **try to** do sth
                                                            to **need to** do sth

---

Ex16	to **act out** [ˌækt ˈaʊt]	durchspielen, aufführen	
TYE	**cricket** [ˈkrɪkɪt]	Cricket	*cricket*
	polo, *no pl.* [ˈpəʊləʊ]	Polo	*polo*
	residence [ˈrezɪdəns]	Residenz, Amtssitz	
	ambassador [æmˈbæsədə]	Botschafter/in	the British **ambassador** to Italy

Wörterverzeichnis   UNIT 1

open ['əʊpən] offen, geöffnet ✕ *closed*   *Is the museum open on Sundays?*
over ['əʊvə] über, mehr als ✕ *more than*
lion ['laɪən] Löwe
to **be born** [bi 'bɔːn] geboren werden *He was born in a small village.*
TYE1 to **name** [neɪm] nennen
TYE4 **bracket** ['brækɪt] Klammer
TYE5 **visit** ['vɪzɪt] Besuch *It's my first visit to Dublin.*
wax [wæks] Wachs
Read **urban** ['ɜːbən] städtisch
cowboy ['kaʊbɔɪ] Cowboy
cowgirl ['kaʊgɜːl] Cowgirl
bareback ['beəbæk] ohne Sattel
drug [drʌg] Droge; Medikament *Heroin and LSD are dangerous drugs.*
proud (of) ['praʊd əv] stolz (auf) *He's very proud of his new car.*
what for? [wɒt 'fɔː] wozu?
two out of three zwei von dreien *She got two out of three answers right.*
  [ˌtuː aʊt əv 'θriː]
to **hang around** herumlungern, ❯ *to stand around doing nothing*
  [ˌhæŋ ə'raʊnd] herumhängen
  hung, hung [hʌŋ, hʌŋ]
to **forbid** [fə'bɪd] verbieten,
  forbade, forbidden untersagen
  [fə'bæd, fə'bɪdn]
to **hide** [haɪd] (sich) verstecken ❯ *to be in a secret place, to put in a secret place*
  hid, hidden [hɪd, 'hɪdn]
crazy ['kreɪzi] verrückt; wütend
jockey ['dʒɒki] Jockey
fresh [freʃ] frisch *fresh milk / air / colours / ideas*
foreleg ['fɔːleg] Vorderbein
to **step** [step] gehen, treten *Careful! Don't step on my CD.*
beer [bɪə] Bier
can [kæn] Dose
heroin ['herəʊɪn] Heroin *Heroin is a drug.*
needle ['niːdl] Nadel
anything ['eniθɪŋ] irgendetwas
proper ['prɒpə] hinreichend,
  gebührend, richtig
ghetto ['getəʊ] Getto, abgesondertes
  pl. **ghettos** Wohnviertel
backyard [ˌbæk'jɑːd] Hinterhof
to **shoot** [ʃuːt] schießen, erschießen
  shot, shot [ʃɒt, ʃɒt] *needles*
to **save** [seɪv] retten ❯ *to take someone away from danger*

MERKE: to save	The little boy **saved** the man's life.	(retten)
	I'm **saving** for a new bike.	(sparen)
	Save the text on a disk.	(speichern)

---

disease [dɪ'ziːz] Krankheit *Malaria is a disease.*
the **slums** [slʌmz] Elendsviertel
law [lɔː] Gesetz, Recht ❯ *rules for all the people in a country*

one hundred and thirteen   113

UNIT 2   Wörterverzeichnis

Unit 2

WP	Celt [kelt]	Kelte, Keltin
	Briton ['brɪtn]	Brite, Britin
	chalk [tʃɔːk]	Kreide
	Roman ['rəʊmən]	römisch; Römer, Römerin

	to conquer ['kɒŋkə]	erobern
	bath [bɑːθ]	Bad
	emperor ['empərə]	Kaiser
	to decide to do sth [dɪ'saɪd]	sich entschließen, etwas zu tun
	to keep out [ˌkiːp 'aʊt] kept, kept [kept, kept]	fernhalten, nicht hereinlassen
	the Angles [ðɪ 'æŋglz]	die Angeln
	Saxon ['sæksn]	sächsisch; Sachse, Sächsin
	to fight [faɪt] fought, fought [fɔːt, fɔːt]	kämpfen

*2000 years ago the Romans **conquered** Britain.*

*We **decided to** visit the Roman museum.*

❯ *to stop someone from coming in*

❯ *to use hands, guns, etc against another person*

	knight [naɪt]	Ritter
	church [tʃɜːtʃ]	Kirche
Sit1	ruin ['ruːɪn]	Ruine

	true [truː]	wahr
	positive ['pɒzətɪv]	positiv
	negative ['negətɪv]	negativ
Sit2	to believe (in) [bɪ'liːv]	glauben (an)

	perhaps [pə'hæps]	vielleicht
Sit3	afterwards ['ɑːftəwədz]	danach
Ex3	excuse [ɪk'skjuːs]	Entschuldigung

	spaceship ['speɪsʃɪp]	Raumschiff
	reporter [rɪ'pɔːtə]	Reporter/in
T1	sword [sɔːd]	Schwert
	magician [mə'dʒɪʃn]	Zauberer, Magier

	clever ['klevə]	klug
	duke [djuːk]	Herzog
	battle ['bætl]	Schlacht
	to kill [kɪl]	töten, umbringen
	beautiful ['bjuːtɪfl]	schön, hübsch
	magic ['mædʒɪk]	Magie, Zauberkunst
	to fall in love (with) [fɔːl ɪn 'lʌv wɪð] fell, fallen [fel, 'fɔːlən]	sich verlieben (in)

❯❯ *correct, right*

❯ *to think that something is true*
*Do you **believe** in ghosts?*
❯❯ *maybe*
❯❯ *later*

❯❯ *stupid*

❯ *to make a person or animal die*
❯❯ *lovely*

❯ *to start to love someone*

114   one hundred and fourteen

Wörterverzeichnis UNIT 2

	to **marry** ['mæri]	heiraten
	if [ɪf]	ob
	safe [seɪf]	sicher
	to **call** [kɔːl]	rufen, anrufen; (be)nennen
	to **die** [daɪ]	sterben
	important [ɪm'pɔːtnt]	wichtig, bedeutend
	archery ['ɑːtʃəri]	Bogenschießen
	to **pull** [pʊl]	ziehen
	strong [strɒŋ]	stark
Ex6	**outside** [ˌaʊt'saɪd]	außerhalb
Ex7	**times** [taɪmz]	mal

>< *dangerous*

>< *to be born*

Is he **strong** enough to carry this box?
>< *inside*
I've already seen this film three **times**.

MERKE: How often?	once a week	einmal pro / in der Woche
	twice a day	zweimal pro / am Tag
	three times a month	dreimal pro / im Monat
	four times a year …	viermal pro / im Jahr

Sit4	**part** [pɑːt]	Rolle
	to **join** [dʒɔɪn]	verbinden; sich anschließen
	costume ['kɒstjuːm]	Kostüm
Ex8	**whole** [həʊl]	ganz
Sit5	**shield** [ʃiːld]	(Schutz-)Schild
	one [wʌn]	
	pl. **ones**	

> *the character you play in a film.*

> *to become a member of a club, group, etc*

I read the **whole** book in a day.

Wort, das anstelle eines Substantivs stehen kann

MERKE: one / ones	
This bookshop is better than the **one** in Baker Street.	… als **der** in der Baker Street.
We've got two cars – a white **one** and a blue **one**.	… ein **weißes** und ein **blaues**.
The blue **one** is three years old.	Das **Blaue** ist … .
I like most cars but I like the little **ones** best.	… die **kleinen** … .

Ex9	**sock** [sɒk]	Socke
T2	**weapon** ['wepən]	Waffe
	inn [ɪn]	Gasthaus
	armour ['ɑːmə]	Rüstung
	excited [ɪk'saɪtɪd]	aufgeregt, begeistert
	to **notice** ['nəʊtɪs]	bemerken
	locked [lɒkt]	verschlossen
	feeling ['fiːlɪŋ]	Gefühl
	to **admit** [əd'mɪt]	zugeben, eingestehen
	crowd [kraʊd]	Menge
	knife [naɪf]	Messer
	pl. **knives** [naɪvz]	
	round [raʊnd]	rund
	adventure [əd'ventʃə]	Abenteuer
	marvellous ['mɑːvələs]	fabelhaft

Guns and swords are **weapons**.

guest house	=	Pension
Gasthaus	=	**inn**

> *to see something or someone*
a **locked** door/room
I have a **feeling** that he doesn't like me.
> *to say that you've done something wrong*
> *a large number of people together*

>> *wonderful*

one hundred and fifteen **115**

UNIT 2   Wörterverzeichnis

	to **enjoy** do**ing** sth [ɪn'dʒɔɪ 'duːɪŋ]	gerne etwas tun	*She **enjoys** reading detective stories.*
Com	**interest** ['ɪntrəst]	Interesse	

> **MERKE:**   He showed **interest in** my problems.   Interesse an
>   Are you **interested in** sports?   interessiert an
>   I've read an **interesting** book.   interessant

	detective [dɪ'tektɪv]	Detektiv/in	*Famous **detectives**: Sherlock Holmes, Hercule Poirot*
	play [pleɪ]	(Schau)spiel	*'Hamlet' is a **play** by Shakespeare.*
Proj	**enemy** ['enəmi]	Feind	✗ *friend*
	to **choose** [tʃuːz]	wählen	❯ *to decide which thing or person you want*
	chose, chosen [tʃəʊz, 'tʃəʊzn]		
	as [əz]	als	
TYE	**gown** [gaʊn]	Robe, Talar	
	torch [tɔːtʃ]	Fackel	
	priest [priːst]	Priester/in	

priest   *druid*

	Druid ['druːɪd]	Druide	
	heavy ['hevi]	schwer	❯ *difficult to lift or move*
	observatory [əb'zɜːvətri]	Sternwarte, Observatorium	❯ *a building where you can watch the sun, the stars, etc*
	ramp [ræmp]	Rampe	
	rope [rəʊp]	Seil, Tau	
	to **weigh** [weɪ]	wiegen	*How much do you **weigh**? = How heavy are you?*
	ton [tʌn]	Tonne	
TYE6	to **hope to** do sth [həʊp]	hoffen, etwas zu tun	*I **hope to** meet him soon.*
Read	**witch** [wɪtʃ]	Hexe	*a witch on her **broomstick***
	broomstick ['bruːmstɪk]	Besen(stiel)	
	nobody ['nəʊbədi]	niemand	❯❯ *no one*
	sadist ['seɪdɪst]	Sadist	
	owl [aʊl]	Eule	
	to **hoot** [huːt]	hupen (*Auto*); rufen (*Eule*)	*The bus driver **hooted** angrily at the car in front.*
	spell [spel]	Zauber, Zauberspruch	
	snake [sneɪk]	Schlange	

⚠ *a queue*

	code [kəʊd]	Kode, Chiffre	*I can't read the message because it's in **code**.*
	key [kiː]	Schlüssel	*Mrs Preston opened the door with a **key**.*
	wing [wɪŋ]	Flügel	*A bird uses its **wings** when it flies.*
	to **cry** [kraɪ]	weinen, schreien	*He **cried** 'Help!' when he fell off the horse.* (schrie) *Ann **cried** when her budgie died.* (weinte)
	what's the matter? ['wɒts ðə 'mætə]	was ist los?	*What's the **matter**? Are you all right?*
	truth [truːθ]	Wahrheit	*It's the **truth**. = It's true.*

116   one hundred and sixteen

Wörterverzeichnis   UNIT 2/3

MERKE: Arten der Wortbildung

Es gibt im Wesentlichen vier Möglichkeiten, aus bekannten Wörtern neue zu bilden:

happy	**un**happy	**Hinzufügen von Vorsilben**
walk	walk**er**	**Hinzufügen von Nachsilben**
post + man	**postman**	**Zusammensetzung**
tidy (Adjektiv)	**to** tidy (Verb)	**Übernahme in eine andere Wortart (Konversion)**

Oft wirken mehrere Wortbildungstypen zusammen:

friend	**(Grundwort)**
friend**ly**	(Grundwort + **Nachsilbe**)
unfriendly	(**Vorsilbe** + Grundwort+ Nachsilbe)
unfriendli**ness**	(Vorsilbe+Grundwort+Nachsilbe+**Nachsilbe**)

ball	(Grundwort)
football	**(Zusammensetzung)**
football**er**	(Zusammensetzung + **Nachsilbe**)

Unit 3

| to **hit/be the big time** | ganz groß |
| [hɪt, bi ðə 'bɪg taɪm] | 'rauskommen, ganz oben sein |

MERKE: unregelmäßige Verben

| to **hit, hit, hit** | schlagen, treffen | to **meet, met, met** | treffen |
| to **sing, sang, sung** | singen | to **make, made, made** | machen |

Alle unregelmäßigen Verben findest du auf Seite 130–131.

WP | **all over** [ɔːl 'əʊvə] | überall in, auf | ❯❯ *everywhere*
| **posh** [pɒʃ] | chic, vornehm, nobel | *We went for a meal in a **posh** hotel.*

| **ordinary** | = | normal, gewöhnlich |
| ordinär | = | **vulgar** |

| **ordinary** ['ɔːdnri] | normal, gewöhnlich |

to **star (in)** ['staːr ɪn]	eine Hauptrolle spielen (in)	❯ *to be one of the main actors in a film, etc*
ship [ʃɪp]	Schiff	*A boat is smaller than a **ship**.*
iceberg ['aɪsbɜːg]	Eisberg	
to **sink** [sɪŋk]	sinken, untergehen	❯ *to go down*
sank, sunk [sæŋk, sʌŋk]		

| **at least** [ət 'liːst] | zumindest, mindestens |

| **at last** | = | schließlich |
| **at least** | = | mindestens |

Sit1 | to **succeed (in)** [sək'siːd ɪn] | gelingen, Erfolg haben (mit) | *Did your plan **succeed**?* |
| **chance** [tʃɑːns] | Chance | |
| **tip** [tɪp] | Tipp, nützlicher Hinweis | *She gave me some **tips** on how to save money.* |

one hundred and seventeen   **117**

UNIT 3   Wörterverzeichnis

	overnight [ˌəʊvə'naɪt]	über Nacht, ganz plötzlich	› during the night; suddenly
	to **organize** ['ɔːgənaɪz]	organisieren	to **organize** a meeting/party/trip
	to **be left** [bi 'left]	übrig sein	**Is** there any tea **left**?
	gig [gɪg]	Konzert, Auftritt	
	somebody ['sʌmbədi]	jemand	›› someone
	audience ['ɔːdiəns]	Zuschauer, Publikum	› a group of people who listen to a singer, speaker
	contract ['kɒntrækt]	Vertrag	
	in trouble [ɪn 'trʌbl]	in Schwierigkeiten	› in a difficult situation
Ex1	**beginning** [bɪ'gɪnɪŋ]	Anfang, Beginn	›‹ end
	to **occur** [ə'kɜː]	geschehen, vorkommen	›› to happen
Sit2	**video recorder** ['vɪdiəʊ rɪkɔːdə]	Videorekorder	

	nuisance ['njuːsns]	Ärgernis, Quälgeist	
T1	**stepbrother** ['stepbrʌðə]	Stiefbruder	
	to **rhyme** [raɪm]	(sich) reimen	'Tip' **rhymes** with 'ship'.
	annoying [ə'nɔɪɪŋ]	ärgerlich	
	to **agree** [ə'griː]	zustimmen, einwilligen	› to say that something is true
	especially [ɪ'speʃəli]	besonders	› more with one person/thing, etc than with others
	to **cheer** [tʃɪə]	zujubeln, bejubeln, anfeuern	› to shout to show that you like someone
	fashion ['fæʃn]	Mode	Jeans are still **in fashion**.
	hit [hɪt]	Hit	
	demo tape ['deməʊ teɪp]	Demoband	
	might [maɪt]	könnte (vielleicht)	She **might** come. = Perhaps she will come.
	to **remind** [rɪ'maɪnd]	erinnern	› to tell someone to remember something
	prince [prɪns]	Prinz; Fürst	
	so what? [səʊ 'wɒt]	na und?	
	actually ['æktʃuəli]	tatsächlich, in Wirklichkeit	›› really
	drums [drʌmz]	Schlagzeug	
	bin [bɪn]	Mülleimer, Abfalleimer	

	break [breɪk]	Durchbruch, Chance	›› chance
Sit3	to **perform** [pə'fɔːm]	spielen, vorführen	› to act in a film, play, etc
	language ['læŋgwɪdʒ]	Sprache	How many **languages** do you speak? – Two, English and German.
	bad language [ˌbæd 'læŋgwɪdʒ]	Kraftausdrücke, unanständige Ausdrücke	
Sit4	**surprised** [sə'praɪzd]	überrascht	
	amazed [ə'meɪzd]	erstaunt	›› very surprised
Ex11	**course** [kɔːs]	Kurs, Lehrgang	a language **cours**e, a **course** in information technology
	to **learn to** do sth [lɜːn] **learnt/learned** [lɜːnt, lɜːnd], **learnt/learned** [lɜːnt, lɜːnd]	lernen, etwas zu tun	He's **learning** to dance.
	flute [fluːt]	Flöte	

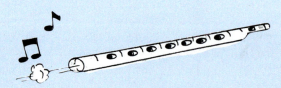

118   one hundred and eighteen

Wörterverzeichnis   UNIT 3

T2	**absolute** ['æbsəluːt]	absolut, vollständig	I'm an **absolute** beginner at chess.
	absolutely ['æbsəluːtli]	absolut, völlig	You're **absolutely** right.
	to **appear** [ə'pɪə]	erscheinen, scheinen	
	aged [eɪdʒd]	im Alter von	❯ at the age of
	to **make a mess of sth**	verkorksen, Mist	
	[meɪk ə 'mes əv]	bauen, verpfuschen	I feel I've **made a mess** of things.
	to **seem** [siːm]	scheinen	
	to **seem to** do [siːm]	etwas zu tun scheinen	What's wrong? You **seem to** be unhappy.
	to **stamp** [stæmp]	stampfen	❯ to put your foot down hard
	clear [klɪə]	klar	
	grandson ['grændsʌn]	Enkel(sohn)	❯ a son of your son or daughter
	hopeful ['həʊpfl]	optimistisch, voller Hoffnung	
	cheeky ['tʃiːki]	frech	❯❰ polite
	to **wake up** [ˌweɪk 'ʌp]	aufwachen;	❯ to (make someone) stop sleeping
	woke, woken	aufwecken	
	[wəʊk, 'wəʊkən]		
	to **complain** [kəm'pleɪn]	sich beschweren	❯ to say angrily that you don't like something
	nowhere ['nəʊweə]	nirgendwo	We looked for the hamster but found him **nowhere**.
	bar mitzvah	Bar-Mizwa	Jüdische Zeremonie, bei der Jungen im Alter von 13
	[ˌbɑː 'mɪtsvə]		Jahren in die Gemeinde aufgenommen werden und aus
			der Tora lesen.
	opinion [ə'pɪnɪən]	Meinung	What's your **opinion** of our work?
	keyboard ['kiːbɔːd]	Keyboard (Musik-instrument)	
	to **get on with**	auskommen mit	We **get on** well **with** our neighbours.
	[ˌget 'ɒn wɪð]		
	got, got [gɒt, gɒt]		
	to **offer** ['ɒfə]	anbieten	
Ex12	**mistake** [mɪ'steɪk]	Fehler	❯ something that is not correct

note	=	Notiz
Note	=	**mark**

Ex14	**note** [nəʊt]	Notiz	
Proj	**sporting** ['spɔːtɪŋ]	Sport(s)-, sportlich	
	hero ['hɪərəʊ] *pl.* **heroes**	Held	❯ a very important or brave (mutig) man
Com	**star** [stɑː]	Stern	
	war [wɔː]	Krieg	❯ two or more countries fighting against each other
	everybody ['evribɒdi]	jede(r), alle	❯❰ no one
TYE	**British** ['brɪtɪʃ]	britisch	
	to **burn down**	niederbrennen	The house **burned down** last year.
	[ˌbɜːn 'daʊn]		The Vikings **burned down** the village.
	supermodel	Supermodel	❯ a very famous fashion model
	['suːpəmɒdl]		
	art [ɑːt]	Kunst, Kunsterziehung	

art	=	Kunst
Art	=	**kind, way**

	the **media** ['miːdɪə]	die Medien	Television, radio and newspapers are **the media**.
	attention [ə'tenʃn]	Aufmerksamkeit	Please pay **attention**. = Bitte pass auf!
	shy [ʃaɪ]	schüchtern, scheu	
	to **be alone** [bi ə'ləʊn]	allein sein	
TYE4	to **translate** [træns'leɪt]	übersetzen	Can you **translate** this French letter for me?
Read	**soccer** ['sɒkə] (AE)	Fußball	❯❯ football (BE)

one hundred and nineteen   119

UNIT 3/4   Wörterverzeichnis

female ['fiːmeɪl]	weiblich	
athlete ['æθliːt]	(Leicht)athlet/in, Sportler/in	❯ *a person who takes part in sports competitions*
air force ['eə fɔːs]	Luftwaffe	
to **score** [skɔː]	erzielen	
goal [gəʊl]	Tor	
foundation [faʊn'deɪʃn]	Stiftung; Gründung	
motor-racing ['məʊtəreɪsɪŋ]	Autorennen	
pub [pʌb]	Kneipe, Pub	❯ *a building where people go to drink and meet their friends*
to **fail** [feɪl]	scheitern, keinen Erfolg haben	❳ *to succeed*

MERKE: Wortbildung mit Vorsilben

Durch **Vorsilben** ändert sich zwar die **Wortbedeutung**, die Wortart bleibt jedoch meist erhalten.

un-	**un**fair, **un**lucky, **un**happy	Durch diese Vorsilben wird das Gegenteil
dis-	**dis**like, **dis**agree	der ursprünglichen Wortbedeutung
in- (**im-**, **il-**, **ir-**)	**in**correct, **im**possible, **il**legal, **ir**regular	ausgedrückt.
non-	**non**sense, **non**-smoker, **non**-stop	

Unit 4

WP	**early** ['ɜːli]	früh	❳ *late*
	Norman ['nɔːmən]	normannisch; Normanne, Normannin	
	army ['ɑːmi]	Armee	❯ *all the soldiers of a country*
	invader [ɪn'veɪdə]	Eindringling, Angreifer/in	
	couple ['kʌpl]	Paar, Ehepaar	
	a couple of [ə 'kʌpl əv]	ein paar	❱ *a few*
	to **defeat** [dɪ'fiːt]	(völlig) besiegen, eine Niederlage zufügen	❯ *to win against somebody in a war, game, etc.*
	to **make sure** [ˌmeɪk 'ʃʊə]	sicherstellen, sorgen für	
	stranger ['streɪndʒə]	Fremder, Fremde	❯ *someone who doesn't know anybody*
	century ['sentʃəri]	Jahrhundert	❯ *a hundred years*
	pope [pəʊp]	Papst	
	to **invade** [ɪn'veɪd]	einmarschieren in, eindringen in	❯ *to enter a country to conquer it*
	storm [stɔːm]	Sturm	❯ *very bad weather, with strong winds and rain*
	theatre ['θɪətə]	Theater	⚠ Aussprache: erste Silbe wird betont!
	to **begin** [bɪ'gɪn] **began, begun** [bɪ'gæn, bɪ'gʌn]	anfangen	❳ *to stop*

120   one hundred and twenty

Wörterverzeichnis UNIT 4

to **begin to** do sth [bɪˈgɪn] **began, begun** [bɪˈgæn, bɪˈgʌn]	anfangen, etwas zu tun
tapestry [ˈtæpəstri]	Wandbehang, Wandteppich
Sit1 **Viking** [ˈvaɪkɪŋ]	Wikinger/in
to **sail** [seɪl]	segeln
which [wɪtʃ]	der, die, das, welcher, welche, welches
Sit3 **whose** [huːz]	deren, dessen

*Our guests **began** to arrive.*

> *to travel on water*

*Mike is the boy **whose** father sells computers.*

MERKE: who/which/whose/where als …

Fragewort	**Relativpronomen**
Who's got his address? (Wer?)	The man **who** asked the way to Stratford was French. (… der …)
Which CD do you want? (Welche?)	The story **which** he told me was strange. (… die …)
Whose house is it? (Wessen?)	The boy **whose** mother drives a BMW is Kevin. (… dessen …)
Where do you live? (Wo?)	The place **where** he lives is called Pimlico. (… wo …)

---

lift [lɪft]	Mitfahrgelegenheit
to **give somebody a lift** [gɪv ə ˈlɪft]	jemanden im Auto mitnehmen
T1 **battlefield** [ˈbætlfiːld]	Schlachtfeld
berry [ˈberi]	Beere
to **pick** [pɪk]	pflücken, auswählen
distance [ˈdɪstəns]	Entfernung
kind (of) [kaɪnd]	Art, Sorte (von)
iron [ˈaɪən]	Eisen
axe [æks]	Axt
slope [sləʊp]	Gefälle, Hang
to **attack** [əˈtæk]	angreifen
to **charge** [tʃɑːdʒ]	anstürmen, angreifen

*I need a **lift** to the airport.*

*Can you **give** me a **lift**?*
> *the place where soldiers fight a battle*

*The **distance** from my flat to my school is one mile.*
*What **kind of** horse is that? – It's a pony.*

> *to start fighting a country/a person*

MERKE: Unregelmäßige Verben

to **begin, began, begun**	beginnen	to **swim, swam, swum**	schwimmen
to **drink, drank, drunk**	trinken	to **stand, stood, stood**	stehen
to **spend, spent, spent**	ausgeben	to **wear, wore, worn**	tragen (Kleidung)
to **sleep, slept, slept**	schlafen	Alle unregelmäßigen Verben findest du auf Seite 130–131.

---

to **swing** [swɪŋ] **swung, swung** [swʌŋ, swʌŋ]	schwingen
horror [ˈhɒrə]	Horror
dead [ded]	tot
body [ˈbɒdi]	Leiche; Körper

UNIT 4   Wörterverzeichnis

	rest [rest]	Ruhe	to **have a rest** = sich ausruhen 》 to be afraid
	to **be scared (of)** [bɪ 'skeəd əv]	Angst haben vor	
	ought to ['ɔːt tə]	sollte	I **ought to** go home now. It's late.
	arrow ['ærəʊ]	Pfeil	
Ex5	to **match** [mætʃ]	passend zusammen- fügen, zusammen- passen	*arrows*
Ex7	**abbey** ['æbi]	Abtei, Kloster, Klosterkirche	
Proj	to **photocopy** ['fəʊtəʊkɒpi]	fotokopieren	
Sit5	**prisoner** ['prɪznə]	Gefangene/r, Häftling	› someone who is in prison
	to **cut** [kʌt] **cut, cut** [kʌt, kʌt]	schneiden, zerschneiden	
	to **cut off** [ˌkʌt 'ɒf]	abschneiden	
Ex10	**attraction** [ə'trækʃn]	Attraktion, Anziehung	Madame Tussaud's is a great tourist **attraction**. 》 real, true
	genuine ['dʒenjuɪn]	echt, unverfälscht	
Ex11	**definition** [ˌdefɪ'nɪʃn]	Definition	› a group of words that tell what another word means
T2	**monster** ['mɒnstə]	Ungeheuer, Monster, Scheusal	
	several ['sevrəl]	mehrere, einige	› some, but not many
	to **spend, spent, spent** [spend, spent, spent]	ausgeben (Geld)	
	for example [fər ɪg'zɑːmpl]	zum Beispiel	to **spend** = (Geld) ausgeben; (Zeit) verbringen spenden = **to donate**
	minister ['mɪnɪstə]	Minister/in	
	marriage ['mærɪdʒ]	Ehe, Hochzeit	
	affair [ə'feə]	Affäre; Angelegenheit	
	to **divorce** [dɪ'vɔːs]	sich scheiden lassen	She **divorced** her husband. › very angry
	furious ['fjʊəriəs]	wütend	
	to **execute** ['eksɪkjuːt]	hinrichten, exekutieren	
	final ['faɪnl]	letzte(r, s), endgültig	》 last 》 at last
	finally ['faɪnəli]	schließlich	
	widow ['wɪdəʊ]	Witwe	› a woman whose husband has died
	fat [fæt]	dick, fett	He's **fat** because he always eats too much.
	temper ['tempə]	Laune, Stimmung, Wesensart	in a **bad temper** = schlecht gelaunt 》 fat
Com	**thin** [θɪn]	dünn	
	quite [kwaɪt]	ziemlich	
	fair(-haired) [ˌfeə'heəd]	blond	
	beard [bɪəd]	Bart	
	glasses ['glɑːsɪz]	Brille	
	grey [greɪ]	grau	
	plastic ['plæstɪk]	Plastik, Kunststoff	
TYE	**shore** [ʃɔː]	Strand, Ufer	› land by the sea or a lake
	fleet [fliːt]	Flotte	› a big group of ships
	crane [kreɪn]	Kran	

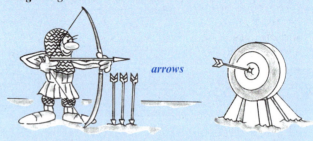
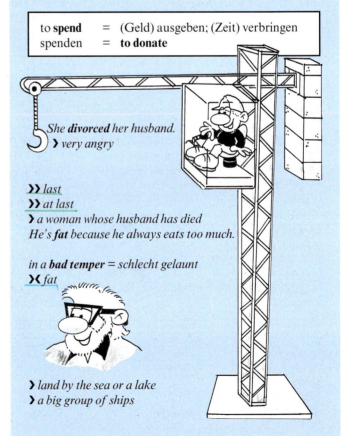

Wörterverzeichnis   UNIT 4/5

	wet [wet]	nass, feucht	
	to **spray** [spreɪ]	(be)sprühen	
	even ['iːvn]	sogar	
TYE4	**painter** ['peɪntə]	Maler/in	*Picasso was a famous **painter**.*
Read	**haunted** ['hɔːntɪd]	Spuk-	
	or so [ɔː 'səʊ]	ungefähr	≫ *about*
	landlord ['lændlɔːd]	Wirt; Vermieter	
	although [ɔːl'ðəʊ]	obwohl	*She didn't have a rest **although** she was tired.*
	meeow [miˈaʊ]	Miau	
	to **knock** [nɒk]	klopfen	*Somebody **knocked** on the door.*
	creaking ['kriːkɪŋ]	knarrend, quietschend	
	doorway ['dɔːweɪ]	Eingang	› *the entrance into a building*
	to **disturb** [dɪ'stɜːb]	stören	
	for sale [fə 'seɪl]	zu verkaufen	*Is this car **for sale**?*

MERKE: Wortbildung mit Nachsilben

Durch Nachsilben lassen sich **Nomen**, aber auch Adjektive und Verben aus anderen Wortarten bilden.

Nomen: Diese Nomen **bezeichnen** oft

- **-er, -or** driv**er**, report**er**, conquer**or**, act**or**, sing**er**, teach**er**, swimm**er** • einen **Beruf** oder eine **Person**, die eine **Tätigkeit** ausübt.
- **-ist** tour**ist**, motor**ist** (Autofahrer) • einen **Beruf** oder eine **Gruppenzugehörigkeit**
- **-ess** actr**ess** (Schauspielerin), host**ess** (Gastgeberin) • **weibliche** Personen
- **-er** comput**er**, CD-play**er**, print**er** • ein **Gerät** für eine bestimmte Funktion

---

Unit 5

WP	**award** [ə'wɔːd]	Auszeichnung, Preis	› *a prize that you give to somebody who has done sth well*
	expedition [ˌekspə'dɪʃn]	Expedition, Forschungsreise	› *a journey to find out about sth*
	to **cycle** ['saɪkl]	Rad fahren	≫ *to ride a bike*
	possible ['pɒsəbl]	möglich	*Is it **possible** to go to the club on foot? – No, it's too far.*
	useful ['juːsfl]	nützlich	› *good for the job*
	aid [eɪd]	Hilfe	≫ *help*
	first aid [ˌfɜːst 'eɪd]	erste Hilfe	
	paragliding ['pærəglaɪdɪŋ]	Drachenfliegen, Paragliding	
	bronze [brɒnz]	Bronze	
	silver ['sɪlvə]	Silber	
	gold [gəʊld]	Gold	
Sit1	**disabled** [dɪs'eɪbld]	behindert	*Jessica is **disabled** – she's in a wheelchair.*

UNIT 5   Wörterverzeichnis

	thick [θɪk]	dick, dicht

> **MERKE: dick** fat, thick

	smoke [sməʊk]	Rauch
	to **pour** [pɔː]	gießen, sich ergießen
	chimney ['tʃɪmni]	Schornstein
	tram [træm]	Tram, Straßenbahn
	fairground ['feəgraʊnd]	Rummelplatz
	to **taste** [teɪst]	schmecken
T1	to **climb** [klaɪm]	klettern
	cloudy ['klaʊdi]	bewölkt
	uncomfortable [ʌn'kʌmftəbl]	unbequem
	minibus ['mɪnɪbʌs]	Kleinbus
	ham [hæm]	Schinken
	roll [rəʊl]	Brötchen
	tomato, *pl.* **tomatoes** [tə'mɑːtəʊ, tə'mɑːtəʊz]	Tomate
	soup [suːp]	Suppe
	to **cook** [kʊk]	kochen
	tent [tent]	Zelt
	hardly ['hɑːdli]	kaum
	backpack ['bækpæk]	Rucksack
	blister ['blɪstə]	Blase
	freezing ['friːzɪŋ]	kalt, frierend
	sleeping bag ['sliːpɪŋbæg]	Schlafsack
	sunny ['sʌni]	sonnig
	thirsty ['θɜːsti]	durstig
	practice ['præktɪs]	Training, Übung
	walk [wɔːk]	Wanderung
	frozen ['frəʊzn]	gefroren, tiefgefroren
	knee [niː]	Knie
	filthy ['fɪlθi]	dreckig
	exhausted [ɪg'zɔːstɪd]	erschöpft
	pain [peɪn]	Schmerz
Ex4	**meaning** ['miːnɪŋ]	Bedeutung
Ex6	**adult** ['ædʌlt]	Erwachsene/r; erwachsen
	fish [fɪʃ]	Fisch
	picnic ['pɪknɪk]	Picknick
Sit2	**anyway** ['eniweɪ]	jedenfalls
Ex7	to **surf** [sɜːf]	surfen
Sit3	**on foot** [ɒn 'fʊt]	zu Fuß
	mustn't ['mʌsnt]	nicht dürfen
	weight [weɪt]	Gewicht

❯❯ *thin*

a thick book   a fat boy

❯ *a place where you can have rides*
This tea **tastes** awful.
⚠ Aussprache: [klaɪm] She **climbed** out of the window.

❯ *a small bus*

to **cook** a meal   Tee/Kaffee kochen: *to* **make** *tea/coffee*

to **go for a walk** = spazieren gehen

❯❯ *very dirty*
❯❯ *very tired*

meaning	=	Bedeutung
Meinung	=	**opinion**

❯❯ *child*

fish and chips

to **go on foot** = to walk
⚠ Aussprache.   Hurry up! We **mustn't be** late.

Wörterverzeichnis   UNIT 5

needn't ['niːdnt]   nicht müssen, nicht brauchen

*I think we ought to go now. –No, we **needn't** go now.*

T2   to **share** [ʃeə]   (sich) teilen, gemeinsam haben

❭ *to use sth with another person*

anybody ['enibɒdi]   irgendeiner
upset [ˌʌp'set]   aufgebracht
mess [mes]   Durcheinander

*There was a terrible **mess** after the party.*

in a mess [ɪn ə 'mes]   durcheinander, in Unordnung

pardon? ['pɑːdn]   Verzeihung

***Pardon**? What did you say?*
❭ *someone who steals*

thief, *pl.* **thieves** [θiːf, θiːvz]   Dieb/in

to **fetch** [fetʃ]   holen

❭ *to go and get something*

spoon [spuːn]   Löffel
anyone ['eniwʌn]   irgendeiner

❭ *any person*

to **argue** ['ɑːgjuː]   streiten, argumentieren

❭ *to talk angrily with someone because you don't agree*

worried ['wʌrid]   besorgt
right [raɪt]   genau

❭❭ *exactly*

awake [ə'weɪk]   wach
to **pack** [pæk]   (ver)packen, einpacken

❭ *to put things into a bag, box, etc*

anywhere ['eniweə]   irgendwo

*He didn't go **anywhere**.*

MERKE:	every-	some-	any-	not … any-	no-
Person	**every**one	**some**one	**any**one	**not … anyone**	**no one**
	everybody	**some**body	**any**body	**not … anybody**	**nobody**
	jeder	jemand	irgendeine(r)	niemand	niemand
Sache	**every**thing	**some**thing	**any**thing	**not … anything**	**nothing**
	alles	etwas	etwas	nichts	nichts
Ort	**every**where	**some**where	**any**where	**not … anywhere**	**nowhere**
	überall	irgendwo	irgendwo	nirgends	nirgends

to **roll** [rəʊl]   rollen
to **roll up** [ˌrəʊl 'ʌp]   zusammenrollen, aufrollen

during ['djʊərɪŋ]   während

MERKE: während	**during** + NOUN	**while** + VERB
	during the night	**while** he was sleeping

Com   **straight** [streɪt]   gerade

*a **straight** line* _____

straight on [ˌstreɪt 'ɒn]   geradeaus

❭❭ *straight ahead*

crossroads ['krɒsrəʊdz]   Kreuzung

Ex13   **town hall** [ˌtaʊn 'hɔːl]   Rathaus
cathedral [kə'θiːdrəl]   Dom, Kathedrale

❭ *a big, important church*

western ['westən]   westlich, West-
arcade [ɑː'keɪd]   Arkade, Einkaufs-passage

❭ *a large building with lots of shops in it*

one hundred and twenty-five   **125**

UNIT 5   Wörterverzeichnis

TYE	**non-white** [ˌnɒn ˈwaɪt]	farbig; Farbige/r	›‹ *white*
	West Indian [ˌwest ˈɪndiən]	westindisch	
	Asian [ˈeɪʃn]	asiatisch; Asiate, Asiatin	
	origin [ˈɒrɪdʒɪn]	Ursprung, Herkunft	
	international [ˌɪntəˈnæʃnəl]	international	›‹ *national*
	ice-rink [ˈaɪs rɪŋk]	Eisbahn	
	to **pull down** [ˌpʊl ˈdaʊn]	abreißen, einreißen	
	concrete [ˈkɒŋkriːt]	Beton	
	homeless [ˈhəʊmləs]	obdachlos	
	crime [kraɪm]	Verbrechen, Kriminalität	Stealing things is a **crime**.
TYE3	**Londoner** [ˈlʌndənə]	Londoner, Bewohner Londons	
TYE4	**modern** [ˈmɒdn]	modern	›› *up-to-date*
	(the) next time [ˌnekst ˈtaɪm]	das nächste Mal	
Read	**terabyte** [ˈterəbaɪt]	Terabyte	› *1 million megabytes*
	memory [ˈmeməri]	Gedächtnis, Erinnerung, Arbeitsspeicher (RAM)	
	inch [ɪntʃ]	Inch, Zoll	› *2.54 cm*
	disk drive [ˈdɪsk draɪv]	Diskettenlaufwerk	
	a dozen [ə ˈdʌzn]	(ein) Dutzend	›› *twelve*
	microwave [ˈmaɪkrəʊweɪv]	Mikrowelle	
	to **include** [ɪnˈkluːd]	einschließen, beinhalten	
	to **mambo** [ˈmæmbəʊ]	Mambo tanzen	
	violin [ˌvaɪəˈlɪn]	Geige	
	to **calculate** [ˈkælkjuleɪt]	rechnen	Can you **calculate** how much it will cost?
	pretty [ˈprɪti]	ziemlich	›› *quite*
	neat [niːt]	ordentlich, sauber, gepflegt	›› *tidy*
	obsolete [ˈɒbsəliːt]	veraltet	›‹ *modern*
	magnificent [mægˈnɪfɪsnt]	prächtig, großartig	›› *very attractive*
	master [ˈmɑːstə]	Meister, Herr	
	prestidigitator [ˌprestɪˈdɪdʒɪteɪtə]	Taschenspieler	
	invisible [ɪnˈvɪzəbl]	unsichtbar	If something is **invisible** you can't see it.
	premier [ˈpremiə]	bedeutendste/r	›› *the most important*
	complete [kəmˈpliːt]	vollständig	
	to **disappear** [ˌdɪsəˈpɪə]	verschwinden	› *to go away so that you can't see it*
	undoubtedly [ʌnˈdaʊtɪdli]	zweifellos	
	lie [laɪ]	Lüge	She told me a **lie**.
	along with [əˈlɒŋ wɪð]	zusammen mit	›› *together with*
	pie [paɪ]	Pastete, Obstkuchen	
	to **confuse** [kənˈfjuːz]	verwechseln, durcheinander bringen	

Wörterverzeichnis   **UNIT 5**

dough [dəʊ]	Teig	
to **sew** [səʊ]	nähen	
to **sow** [səʊ]	säen	
whether ['weðə]	ob	≫ *if* I don't know **whether** I can go there.
to **weather** ['weðə]	wetterfest sein, überstehen	
whatever [wɒt'evə]	was auch immer	*Do **whatever** you like.*

> **MERKE: Übergang in eine andere Wortart (Konversion)**
>
> Wörter können in eine andere Wortart übergehen, ohne dass Vor- oder Nachsilben angehängt werden. So kann eine **Wortform** mehreren **Wortarten** angehören
>
> | | | |
> |---|---|---|
> | He can't **repair** his bike. Where is the **repair** shop? | repair (**Verb**) **reparieren** | repair (**Nomen**) **Reparatur** |
> | It's very **cold** today. I've got a bad **cold**. | cold (**Adjektiv**) **kalt** | cold (**Nomen**) **Erkältung** |
> | Your room isn't **tidy**. Please **tidy** your room. | tidy (**Adjektiv**) **aufgeräumt** | tidy (**Verb**) **aufräumen** |
> | The earth is **round**. It moves **round** the sun. | round (**Adjektiv**) **rund** | round (**Präposition**) **um … herum** |
> | She turned **round**. He does a paper **round**. | round (**Adverb**) **herum** | round (**Nomen**) **Runde** |

Sketches

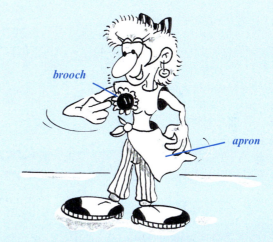

Sket1	**questionnaire** [ˌkwestʃə'neə]	Fragebogen	
	notice ['nəʊtɪs]	Zettel, Notiz	
	to **point** [pɔɪnt]	zeigen	
	expert ['ekspɜ:t]	Experte, Expertin	
	to **count** [kaʊnt]	zählen	
	brooch [brəʊtʃ]	Brosche	
Sket2	**apron** ['eɪprən]	Schürze	
	cart [kɑ:t]	Wagen, Karren	
	wedding ['wedɪŋ]	Hochzeit(stag)	
	meat [mi:t]	Fleisch	
	outlaw ['aʊtlɔ:]	Gesetzlose/r	
	sheriff ['ʃerɪf]	Sheriff	
	cattle ['kætl]	Vieh, Rinder	

Revision

Rev	**fit** [fɪt]	fit, geeignet	≫ *well and strong*
	window-cleaner ['wɪndəʊkli:nə]	Fensterputzer/in	
	seller ['selə]	Verkäufer/in	› *a person who sells sth a flower **seller***
	to **repair** [rɪ'peə]	reparieren	
	hot-air balloon [ˌhɒt 'eə bəlu:n]	Heißluftballon	
	alive [ə'laɪv]	lebendig, am Leben	✕ *dead*
	owner ['əʊnə]	Besitzer/in, Eigentümer/in	*Who's the **owner** of that bike?*
	to **collect** [kə'lekt]	sammeln, einsammeln	
	to **compare** [kəm'peə]	vergleichen	

one hundred and twenty-seven   **127**

Lerntipps: mind maps

Die wesentlichen Lern-und Arbeitstechniken zum Vokabel lernen kennst du ja bereits. Vielleicht arbeitest du mit einer Vokabelkartei oder einem interessant gestalteten Vokabelheft.

Bei allen Möglichkeiten sind zwei Dinge besonders wichtig:
◆ neue Vokabeln solltest du mit bereits bekannten Wörtern vernetzen
◆ du musst in regelmäßigen Abständen gelernte Vokabeln wiederholen.

Besonders gut eignen sich *mind maps*, um bekannte Vokabeln mit neuen Wörtern in Beziehung zu setzen. Hier sind fünf Beispiele:

a Einzelwörter

Bei Einzelwörtern solltest du dir die wichtigsten Kombinationsmöglichkeiten, Besonderheiten in der Schreibung und eventuell einen Beispielsatz aufschreiben.

b Wortfamilien

Du gruppierst um ein Ausgangswort die weiteren Mitglieder der Wortfamilie mit wichtigen Kombinationsmöglichkeiten.

c Wortfelder

Manche Wörter verwendest du deshalb falsch, weil du sie von ähnlichen Begriffen nicht deutlich genug unterscheiden kannst oder weil dich die deutsche Übersetzung dazu verleitet. Hier hilft es, sich Wortfelder zu notieren und Bilder dazu zu zeichnen. Natürlich kannst du sie auch aus Katalogen ausschneiden oder Cliparts verwenden.

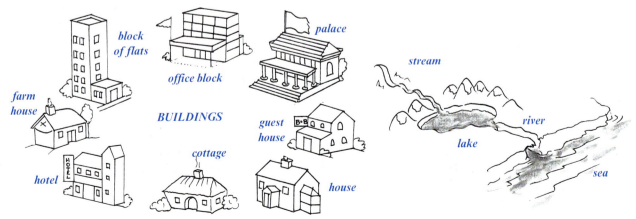

Lerntipps

d Sachfelder

Bei Sachfeldern solltest du darauf achten, die einzelnen Begriffe nicht wild durcheinander aufzuschreiben. Du kommst am einfachsten auf entsprechende Teilbereiche, wenn du W-Fragen stellst:
Wer? Was? Wo? Wann? etc.

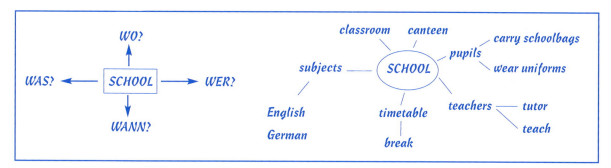

e Mind maps zu Texten

Es ist sehr hilfreich, die wesentlichen Punkte eines Textes zu erfassen und klar zu gliedern. Das ist natürlich nicht nur im Englischunterricht sehr nützlich. Du kommst am schnellsten auf eine sinnvolle Struktur, wenn du folgende Dinge beachtest:
◆ Was ist das Hauptthema? (Das ist der zentrale Begriff.)
◆ Welche wichtigen Ausdrücke lassen sich diesem Thema zuordnen? (Das sind die weiteren Knotenpunkte.)
◆ Was lässt sich bei diesen Knoten noch ergänzen? (Hier kannst du weitere Beispiele einfügen.)

Beispiel zu Unit 1 Words and Pictures:

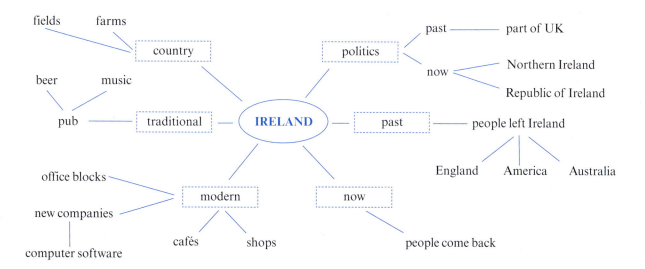

Deine persönliche *mind map* würde vielleicht etwas anders aussehen. Aber das ist ganz normal. Wichtig ist nur, dass die wichtigen Gedanken des Textes erfasst werden. Übrigens, eine solche *mind map* ist auch eine gute Vorbereitung für ein Kurzreferat.

Irregular verbs   Unregelmäßige Verben

Infinitive	Simple past	Past Participle	
to be	was/were	been	sein
to become	became	become	werden
to begin	began	begun	anfangen, beginnen
to bite	bit	bitten	beißen
to blow	blew	blown	blasen
to break	broke	broken	brechen, einbrechen
to bring	brought	brought	bringen
to build	built	built	bauen
to burn	burnt/burned	burnt/burned	(ver)brennen
to buy	bought	bought	kaufen
to catch	caught	caught	fangen
to choose	chose	chosen	wählen
to come	came	come	kommen
to cost	cost	cost	kosten
to cut	cut	cut	schneiden
to dig	dug	dug	graben
to do	did	done	tun, machen
to draw	drew	drawn	ziehen; zeichnen
to drink	drank	drunk	trinken
to drive	drove	driven	fahren
to eat	ate	eaten	essen
to fall	fell	fallen	fallen
to feed	fed	fed	füttern
to feel	felt	felt	fühlen
to fight	fought	fought	kämpfen
to find	found	found	finden
to fly	flew	flown	fliegen
to forbid	forebade	forebidden	verbieten, untersagen
to forget	forgot	forgotten	vergessen
to get	got	got	bekommen
to give	gave	given	geben
to go	went	gone	gehen
to hang	hung	hung	hängen
to have	had	had	haben
to hear	heard	heard	hören
to hide	hid	hidden	(sich) verstecken
to hit	hit	hit	treffen; schlagen
to hold	held	held	halten
to hurt	hurt	hurt	verletzen
to keep	kept	kept	halten, behalten
to know	knew	known	wissen; kennen
to lay	laid	laid	legen
to learn	learnt/learned	learnt/learned	lernen
to leave	left	left	verlassen
to lend	lent	lent	leihen, borgen
to let	let	let	lassen, zulassen
to lie	lay	lain	liegen

Unregelmäßige Verben

Infinitive	Simple past	Past Participle	
to light	lit	lit	anzünden
to lose	lost	lost	verlieren
to make	made	made	machen
to mean	meant	meant	bedeuten, meinen
to meet	met	met	treffen, begegnen
to pay	paid	paid	bezahlen
to put	put	put	setzen, stellen
to read	read	read	lesen
to ride	rode	ridden	reiten
to ring	rang	rung	klingeln; anrufen
to run	ran	run	laufen
to say	said	said	sagen
to see	saw	seen	sehen
to sell	sold	sold	verkaufen
to send	sent	sent	schicken, senden
to shine	shone	shone	scheinen
to shoot	shot	shot	schießen
to show	showed	shown /showed	zeigen
to shut	shut	shut	schließen
to sing	sang	sung	singen
to sink	sank	sunk	sinken; untergehen
to sit	sat	sat	sitzen
to sleep	slept	slept	schlafen
to speak	spoke	spoken	sprechen
to spend	spent	spent	ausgeben; verbringen
to spill	spilt/spilled	spilt/spilled	verschütten
to split	split	split	spalten, teilen
to spread	spread	spread	verbreiten
to stand	stood	stood	stehen
to steal	stole	stolen	stehlen
to stick	stuck	stuck	kleben; stecken bleiben
to swim	swam	swum	schwimmen
to swing	swung	swung	schwingen
to take	took	taken	nehmen
to teach	taught	taught	unterrichten, lehren
to tell	told	told	erzählen
to think	thought	thought	denken, glauben
to throw	threw	thrown	werfen
to understand	understood	understood	verstehen
to wake	woke	woken	aufwecken; aufwachen
to wear	wore	worn	tragen
to win	won	won	gewinnen
to write	wrote	written	schreiben

List of names Liste der Eigennamen

Boys/Men

A
Adam ['ædəm]
Alan ['ælən]
Andrew ['ændru:]
Andy ['ændi]

B
Ben [ben]
Bob [bɒb]
Brian ['braɪən]

C
Chris [krɪs]
Christopher ['krɪstəfə]
Connor ['kɒnə]

D
Daniel ['dænjəl]

F
Finn [fɪn]

G
Gary ['gæri]
Geoffrey ['dʒefri]
Greg [greg]

H
Henry ['henri]

J
Jack [dʒæk]
James [dʒeɪmz]
Jamie ['dʒeɪmi]
Jason ['dʒeɪsn]
Jim [dʒɪm]

K
Ken [ken]
Kevin ['kevɪn]

L
Luke [lu:k]

M
Mark [mɑ:k]
Matthew ['mæθju:]
Michael ['maɪkl]
Mike [maɪk]

N
Nathan ['neɪθn]
Nick [nɪk]

O
Oliver ['ɒlɪvə]

P
Pat [pæt] Kurzform von Patrick
Patrick ['pætrɪk]
Peter ['pi:tə]
Philip ['fɪlɪp]

R
Richard ['rɪtʃəd]
Rob [rɒb]
Royston ['rɔɪstən]

S
Scott [skɒt]
Sean [ʃɔ:n]
Steve [sti:v]

T
Tim [tɪm]
Tom [tɒm]
Trevor ['trevə]

W
Wilfred ['wɪlfrɪd]
Will [wɪl]

Girls/Women

A
Alice ['ælɪs]
Amy ['eɪmi]
Andrea ['ændriə]

B
Britta ['brɪtə]

C
Canice ['kænɪs]
Caroline ['kærəlaɪn]
Charlotte ['ʃɑ:lət]
Claire [kleə]
Crystal ['krɪstl]

D
Diana [daɪ'ænə]
Diane [daɪ'æn]
Donna ['dɒnə]

E
Emily ['eməli]
Emma ['emə]
Ethel ['eθl]

F
Fiona [fi'əʊnə]

G
Geri ['dʒeri]

H
Hannah ['hænə]
Harriet ['hæriət]
Heather ['heðə]
Helen ['helən]

J
Jane [dʒeɪn]
Janet ['dʒænɪt]
Jessica ['dʒesɪkə]
Jodie ['dʒəʊdi]
Julie ['dʒu:li]

K
Kate [keɪt]
Kathy ['kæθi]
Kim [kɪm]
Kirsty ['kɜ:sti]

L
Lauren ['lɔ:rən]
Lehka ['leɪkə]
Liz [lɪz]
Louise [lu:'i:z]
Lucy ['lu:si]

M
Mary ['meəri]
Matilda [mə'tɪldə]
Maureen ['mɔ:ri:n]
Mel [mel]

N
Natalie ['nætəli]

R
Rebecca [rɪ'bekə]

S
Sally ['sæli]
Samantha [sə'mænθə]
Sarah ['seərə]
Sharon ['ʃærən]
Sineád [ʃɪ'neɪd]
Sophie ['səʊfi]
Stacey ['steɪsi]
Susan ['su:zn]

T
Tara ['tɑ:rə]
Tessa ['tesə]
Tracy ['treɪsi]

V
Vicky ['vɪki]
Victoria [vɪk'tɔ:riə]

Z
Zoe ['zəʊi]

Family names

B
Batty ['bæti]
Bentley ['bentli]

C
Cassidy ['kæsədi]
Cox [kɒks]

D
Davis ['deɪvɪs]
Denton ['dentən]
Dexter ['dekstə]
Dooley ['du:li]
Drabble ['dræbl]
Dunston ['dʌnstən]

F
Foster ['fɒstə]
Freeman ['fri:mən]

G
Gardner ['gɑ:dnə]
Gordon ['gɔ:dn]

H
Hibbert ['hɪbət]
Hobbs [hɒbz]
Hurst [hɜ:st]

J
Jenkins ['dʒeŋkɪnz]
Jones [dʒəʊnz]
Jordan ['dʒɔ:dn]

M
MacInnes [mə'kɪnɪs]
McCarthy [mə'kɑ:θi]
Megson ['megsn]
Minako [mi:nakɔ:]
Moss [mɒs]

N
Nolan ['nəʊlən]

O
O'Byrne [əʊ'bɜ:n]

P
Pinman ['pɪnmən]

N
Nesbitt ['nezbɪt]

T
Thompsett ['tɒmpset]
Thorpe [θɔ:p]
Trevis ['trevɪs]
Tucker ['tʌkə]

U
Usher ['ʌʃə]

W
Wan [wæŋ]
Wilkins ['wɪlkɪns]
Williams ['wɪljəmz]
Willis ['wɪlɪs]

132 one hundred and thirty-two

List of names

Famous people

A

All Saints [ˌɔːl ˈseɪnts] britische Popgruppe

Catherine of Aragon [ˌkæθrɪn əv ˈærəgɒn] 1. Frau Henry VIII (1485–1536)

B

David Beckham [ˌdeɪvɪd ˈbekəm] britischer Fußballspieler(*1975)

Victoria Beckham [vɪkˌtɔːrɪə ˈbekəm] „Posh Spice" (*1975)

Ann Boleyn [æn bəˈlɪn] 2. Frau Henry VIII (1507–1536)

Boyzone [ˈbɔɪzəʊn] irische Boygroup

Jenson Button [ˌdʒensn ˈbʌtn] britischer Rennfahrer (*1980)

C

King Charles II [kɪŋ ˌtʃɑːlz ðə ˈsekənd] (1630–1685)

Prince Charles [ˌprɪns ˈtʃɑːlz] 1. Sohn von Elizabeth II, (*1948)

Anne of Cleves [ˌæn əv ˈkliːvz] 4. Frau Henry VIII (1515–1557)

The Corrs [ðə kɔːz] irische Band

Cindy Crawford [ˌsɪndi ˈkrɔːfəd] amerikanisches Fotomodell

D

Diana, Princess of Wales [daɪˈænə, ˌprɪnses əv ˈweɪlz] ehemalige Gattin von Prince Charles (1961–1997)

Leonardo DiCaprio [ˌliːəʊˈnɑːdəʊ di ˈkæprɪəʊ] amerikanischer Schauspieler (*1974)

E

Elizabeth I, (Virgin Queen) [ɪˌlɪzəbəθ ðə ˈfɜːst, ˌvɜːdʒɪn ˈkwiːn] englische Königin, Tochter Henry VIII (1533–1603)

Elizabeth II, Queen [kwiːn ɪˌlɪzəbəθ ðə ˈsekənd] englische Königin (*1926, Königin seit 1953)

F

Guy Fawkes [ˌgaɪ ˈfɔːks] Berühmtester der Verschwörer, die 1605 das Parlament in die Luft jagen wollten

G

Debbie Gibson [ˌdebi ˈgɪbsn] am. Popsängerin (*1970)

H

Emperor Hadrian [ˌempərə ˈheɪdrɪən] (76–138 AD)

Mia Hamm [ˌmiːə ˈhæm] amerikanische Fussballspielerin (*1972)

King Harold [kɪŋ ˈhærəld] (ca. 1020–1066)

Prince Harry [ˌprɪns ˈhæri] Sohn von Prinz Charles und Lady Diana (*1984)

Henry VIII (Henry Tudor) [ˌhenri ði ˈeɪtθ, ˈtjuːdə] englischer König (1491–1547)

Hans Holbein [ˌhans ˈhɒlbaɪn] deutscher Maler, der in England zur Zeit von Heinrich VIII wirkte (1497–1543)

Catherine Howard [ˌkæθrɪn ˈhaʊəd] 5. Frau Henry VIII (1521–1542)

M

Madonna [məˈdɒnə] erfolgreiche amerikanische Popsängerin (*1958)

N

New York Yankees [ˌnjuː jɔːk ˈjæŋkiz] Baseballmannschaft in den USA

P

Catherine Parr [ˌkæθrɪn ˈpɑː] 6. Frau Henry VIII (?–1548)

St Patrick [sənt ˈpætrɪk] Nationalheiliger Irlands (389–461)

Philip, Duke of Edinburgh [ˈfɪlɪp, ˌdjuːk əv ˈedɪnbərə] Gatte von Königin Elizabeth II (*1921)

Philip of Spain [ˌfɪlɪp əv ˈspeɪn] (1527–1598)

Elvis Presley [ˌelvɪs ˈprezli] amerikanischer Sänger und Gitarrist (1935-1977)

S

Jane Seymour [dʒeɪn ˈsiːmɔː] 3. Frau Henry VIII (1509–1537)

William Shakespeare [ˌwɪljəm ˈʃeɪkspɪə] englischer Dichter und Dramatiker (1564–1616)

Britney Spears [ˌbrɪtni ˈspɪəz] amerikanische Popsängerin (*1981)

Spice Girls [ˈspaɪs gɜːlz] britische Popgruppe

Sting [stɪŋ] englischer Popsänger (*1951)

W

Westlife [ˈwestlaɪf] irische Boygroup

William I (William the Conqueror) (Duke William of Normandy) [ˌwɪljəm ðə ˈkɒŋkərə] englischer König nach der Schlacht von Hastings (1066)

Sir Frank Williams [sə ˌfræŋk ˈwɪljəmz] Gründer des Williams Rennteams (*1942)

Kate Winslet [ˌkeɪt ˈwɪnslət] britische Schauspielerin (*1975)

Other names

A

Armada [ɑːˈmɑːdə] spanische Flotte

Arsenal [ˈɑːsnəl] englischer Fußballclub

King Arthur [kɪŋ ˈɑːθə] legendärer britischer König

B

Bayeux tapestry [baɪˌɜː ˈtæpɪstri] Gestickter Wandteppich, der die Schlacht bei Hastings und deren Vorgeschichte darstellt

Blarney Stone [ˈblɑːni stəʊn] Stein an der Außenmauer von Blarney Castle bei Cork

C

Chippy [ˈtʃɪpi] Name eines Wellensittichs

Church of England [ˌʃɜːtʃ əv ˈɪŋglənd] Unabhängigkeit von der römisch-katholischen Kirche seit der Zeit Henry VIII

D

D of E, Duke of Edinburgh's Award (Scheme) [ˌdjuːk əv ˈedɪnbərəz əˈwɔːd skiːm] Aktionsprogramm für Jugendliche im Alter von 14–23

List of names

DSPCA: The Dublin Society for Prevention of Cruelty Against Animals [ðə ˌdʌblɪn səˈsaɪəti fɔː prɪˌvenʃn əv ˌkruːəlti əˌgenst ˌænɪmlz] Tierschutzverein in Dublin

E

Eastenders [ˌiːst ˈendəz] Seifenoper

F

Frosty [ˈfrɒsti] Schneemann

G

Gareth [ˈgærəθ] Ritter von König Arthurs Tafelrunde
Guinevere [ˈgwɪnɪvɪə] Gattin König Arthurs
Gypsy [ˈdʒɪpsi] Name eines Ponys

H

Hector [ˈhektə] Ziehvater Arthurs in der Arthursage
Home and away [ˌhəʊm ənd əˈweɪ] beliebte Seifenoper

I

Igraine [ɪˈgreɪn] Mutter König Arthurs

K

Kay [keɪ] Ritter von König Arthurs Tafelrunde

L

Leprechauns [ˈleprəkɔːnz] irische Feen

M

Manchester United [ˌmæntʃɪstə juˈnaɪtɪd] engl. Fußballverein
Marion [ˈmæriən] Gefährtin Robin Hoods
Mary Rose [ˌmeəri ˈrəʊz] Kriegsschiff von Henry VIII
Merlin [ˈmɜːlɪn] Zauberer und Ratgeber König Arthurs
Merlo [ˈmɜːləʊ] Name eines Taschenspielers
MGM, Metro-Goldwyn-Mayer [ˌem dʒiː ˈem] bekannte Filmgesellschaft in Hollywood

N

Neighbours [ˈneɪbəz] Seifenoper
Nipper [ˈnɪpə] Name eines Hundes

R

Robin Hood [ˌrɒbɪn ˈhʊd] legendärer Held, der zur Zeit von Richard Löwenherz die Reichen beraubte und den Armen half.

S

Santa Claus [ˈsæntə klɔːz] Weihnachtsmann (besonders in den USA)
Sir Bedivere [sə ˈbedɪvɪə] Ritter von König Arthurs Tafelrunde
Sir Lancelot [sə ˈlɑːnsəlɒt] der berühmteste Ritter von König Arthurs Tafelrunde, Liebhaber von Guinevere
Smash Hits [ˈsmæʃ hɪts] Titel einer Jugendzeitschrift

T

The Merry Men [ðə ˌmeri ˈmen] die Gefährten von Robin Hood
Titanic [taɪˈtænɪk] Name eines Passagierschiffes, das 1912 sank
Tristan [ˈtrɪstən] Ritter von König Arthurs Tafelrunde

U

Uther Pendragon [ˌjuːθə penˈdrægən] König Arthurs Vater in der Arthursage

V

Viking [ˈvaɪkɪŋ] Wikinger/in

W

Wannabe [ˈwɒnəbi] Titel eines Songs der „Spice Girls"

Place names

A

Atlantic, the [ði ətˈlæntɪk] Atlantischer Ozean

B

Bahamas [bəˈhɑːməz] westindische Inselgruppe
Ballymun [ˌbæliˈmʌn] Stadtteil von Dublin
Bayeux [baɪˈɜː] Stadt in der Normandie, Nordfrankreich
Birmingham [ˈbɜːmɪŋəm] zweitgrößte Industriestadt in Mittelengland
Black Country [ˈblæk kʌntri] Gegend bei Birmingham, erhielt ihren Namen vom Rauch der Fabriken im 19. Jahrhundert
Black Country Living Museum [ˈblæk kʌntri ˌlɪvɪŋ mjuˈziːəm] Freilichtmuseum, zeigt Leben und Arbeitsweisen im 19. Jhdt.
Brighton [ˈbraɪtn] Stadt in Südengland
Brindley Place [ˈbrɪndli pleɪs] Platz in Birmingham
Bristol [ˈbrɪstl] Industrie- und Hafenstadt im Südwesten Englands
Brookfield [ˈbrʊkfiːld] Name einer Schule
Buckingham Palace [ˌbʌkɪŋəm ˈpæləs] Buckingham-Palast in London
Burnley [ˈbɜːnli] Ortsname

C

California [ˌkæləˈfɔːniə] Bundesstaat der USA
Cardiff [ˈkɑːdɪf] Hauptstadt und wichtigster Hafen von Wales
Central Park [ˈsentrəl pɑːk] großer Park in Manhattan/New York
China [ˈtʃaɪnə] China
Cork [kɔːk] Stadt in der Republik Irland
Cornwall [ˈkɔːnwəl] Verwaltungsbezirk im Südwesten Englands
County Kerry [ˌkaʊnti ˈkeri] Verwaltungsbezirk in der irischen Republik

List of names

D

Dartford ['dɑːtfəd] Stadt in Südengland
Denmark ['denmɑːk] Dänemark
Dublin ['dʌblɪn] Hauptstadt der Republik Irland
Dudley ['dʌdli] Stadt in der Nähe von Birmingham

E

Edinburgh ['edɪnbərə] Hauptstadt Schottlands
Eton ['iːtn] Stadt und gleichnamige Schule in der Nähe von Windsor

F

Fiji ['fiːdʒiː] Inselgruppe im Südwest-Pazifik
Finchley ['fɪntʃli] Stadtteil von London
France [frɑːns] Frankreich

G

Galway ['gɔːlweɪ] Stadt in der Republik Irland
Giant's Causeway [ˌdʒaɪənts 'kɔːzweɪ] Damm des Riesen, Felslandschaft in Nordirland
Glasgow ['glɑːsgəʊ] Industrie-und Universitätsstadt in Westschottland
Grove Farm ['grəʊv fɑːm] Name eines Bauernhofs
Gwynllan ['gwɪnθæn] Stadt in Nordwales

H

Hadrian's Wall [ˌheɪdriənz 'wɔːl] Hadrianswall
Hastings ['heɪstɪŋz] Stadt an der Südostküste Englands; in der Nähe fand die Battle of Hastings (1066) statt
Hong Kong [ˌhɒŋ 'kɒŋ] bis 1997 brit. Kolonie in Südost-China
Hyde Park [ˌhaɪd 'pɑːk] großer Londoner Park

I

Ireland ['aɪələnd] Irland

J

Jorvik Museum ['jɔːvɪk mjuːˈziːəm] Wikingermuseum in York

K

Kent [kent] Verwaltungsbezirk in Südengland
Kenya ['kenjə] Staat in Afrika
King Edward's School [kɪŋ 'edwədz skuːl] Name einer Schule

L

Limerick ['lɪmərɪk] Stadt und Verwaltungsbezirk im Südwesten Irlands
Liverpool ['lɪvəpuːl] drittgrößte Stadt in Großbritannien
Locksley ['lɒksli] Ortsname
London ['lʌndən] Hauptstadt von Großbritannien
London Bridge [ˌlʌndən 'brɪdʒ] Brücke über die Themse in London

M

Madame Tussaud's [ˌmædəm təˈsɔːdz] Londoner Wachsfigurenkabinett
Manchester ['mæntʃɪstə] Großstadt im Nordwesten Englands
Midlands ['mɪdləndz] Mittelengland, die Midlands
Midway Farm ['mɪdweɪ fɑːm] Name eines Bauernhofs

N

New York [ˌnjuː 'jɔːk] größte Stadt in den USA
Newquay ['njuːki] Ort in Cornwall
Northern Ireland [ˌnɔːðən 'aɪələnd] Nordirland
Norway ['nɔːweɪ] Norwegen
Norwich ['nɒrɪdʒ] Stadt in Mittelengland
Nottingham ['nɒtɪŋəm] Stadt in Mittelengland

O

O'Connell Street [əʊˈkɒnl striːt] Name einer Straße
Oxford ['ɒksfəd] Universitätsstadt in Südengland

P

Paris ['pærɪs] Hauptstadt Frankreichs
Phoenix Park ['fiːnɪks pɑːk] großer Park in Dublin
Portsmouth ['pɔːtsməθ] Hafenstadt in Südengland

R

Regent's Park ['riːdʒənts pɑːk] Park im Nordwesten von London

S

San Francisco [ˌsæn frənˈsɪskəʊ] Stadt in Kalifornien
Scandinavia [ˌskændɪˈneɪviə] Skandinavien
Science Museum ['saɪəns mjuziːəm] Naturwissenschaftliches Museum in London
Scotland ['skɒtlənd] Schottland
Sheffield ['ʃefiːld] nordenglische Industriestadt
Sherwood Forest [ˌʃɜːwʊd 'fɒrɪst] Wald, in dem sich Robin Hood und seine Kameraden versteckten
Smithfield ['smɪθfiːld] Pferdemarkt in Dublin
Stonehenge [ˌstəʊnˈhendʒ] Prähistorischer Steinkreis in Südengland

T

Texas ['teksəs] Bundesstaat der USA
Thames [temz] Englands bedeutendster Fluß
Tintagel [tɪnˈtædʒəl] Burgruine an der Nordküste von Cornwall
Tower of London [ˌtaʊər əv 'lʌndən] Befestigungsanlage im Osten der City of London

U

Uffington ['ʌfɪŋtən] Ort in England
UK, United Kingdom [juˌnaɪtɪd 'kɪŋdəm] Vereinigtes Königreich
USA, US, United States [juˌnaɪtɪd 'steɪts] Vereinigte Staaten

W

Wales [weɪlz] Wales
White Tower ['waɪt taʊə] ältester Teil des Tower of London
Wicklow Mountains ['wɪkləʊ maʊntɪnz] Berggruppe in der Nähe von Dublin
Wimbledon ['wɪmbldən] Stadtteil von London

Y

York [jɔːk] Stadt in North Yorkshire, England

INDEX

Aa

a, an ein, eine, ein **5-U0**, D
abbey Abtei, Kloster, Klosterkirche
    7-U4, Ex7
about ungefähr **5-U7**, T2
about über **5-U2**, T2
above oberhalb, über **6-U4**, T2
absolute absolut, vollständig **7-U3**, T2
absolutely absolut, völlig **7-U3**, T2
accident Unfall **5-U6**, T1
across über, hinüber **6-U4**, T1
act spielen, aufführen **5-U6**, Ex9
action Handlung **5-U6**, Ex6
activity Aktivität, Tätigkeit,
    Beschäftigung **5-U5**, Sit2
actor Schauspieler/in **6-U6**, WPB
act out durchspielen, aufführen
    7-U1, Ex16
actually tatsächlich, in Wirklichkeit
    7-U3, T1
add hinzufügen **5-U5**, Ex5
address Adresse **6-U3**, T1
admit zugeben, eingestehen **7-U2**, T2
adult Erwachsene/r; erwachsen
    7-U5, Ex6
adventure Abenteuer **7-U2**, T2
advertisement Reklame **6-U1**, Ex14
affair Affäre; Angelegenheit **7-U4**, T2
afraid, be Angst haben **6-U2**, Sit4
afraid, I'm ich fürchte, leider
    7-U1, Com
after nach, hinter, danach **5-U5**, WPA
afternoon Nachmittag **5-U1**, Sit6
afterwards danach **7-U2**, Sit3
again wieder, noch einmal **5-U5**, T1
against gegen **6-U2**, Ex10
age Alter **5-U1**, PYE 6
aged im Alter von **7-U3**, T2
ago vor **6-U2**, T1
agree zustimmen, einwilligen **7-U3**, T1
ahead (of) voraus, vor **6-U4**, T2
aid Hilfe **7-U5**, WP
air Luft **6-U2**, WPB
air force Luftwaffe **7-U3**, Read
airport Flughafen **5-U7**, Sit5
alive lebendig, am Leben **7-U5**, Rev
all alle **5-U4**, WPB
all over überall in, auf **7-U3**, WP
all right in Ordnung **5-U3**, T2
almost beinahe **6-U6**, T1
alone, be allein sein **7-U3**, TYE
along entlang **6-U2**, T1

along with zusammen mit **7-U5**, Read
alphabet Alphabet **5-U7**, Ex5
already schon **6-U4**, Sit3
also auch **5-U4**, Sit5
although obwohl **7-U4**, Read
always immer **5-U1**, T2
am bin **5-U0**, A
amazed erstaunt **7-U3**, Sit4
ambassador Botschafter **7-U1**, TYE
ambulance Krankenwagen **6-U2**, T2
American Amerikaner/in;
    amerikanisch **5-U0**, A
and und **5-U0**, A
and so on und so weiter **6-U3**, T1
Angles, the die Angeln **7-U2**, WP
angry wütend, verärgert **5-U6**, T2
animal Tier **6-U2**, WPA
annoying ärgerlich **7-U3**, T1
another ein(e) andere(r, s), noch
    ein(e, es) **6-U4**, WPC
answer Antwort **5-U2**, Sit2
answer antworten, beantworten
    7-U1, Ex10
any (irgend)eine(r, s) **6-U4**, Sit4
anybody irgendeine(r) **7-U5**, Ex12
anyone irgendeine(r) **7-U5**, Ex12
anything irgendetwas **7-U1**, Read
anyway jedenfalls **7-U5**, Sit2
anywhere irgendwo **7-U5**, Ex12
apron Schürze **7-U5**, Sket2
appear erscheinen, scheinen **7-U3**, T2
appetite Appetit **6-U4**, T2
apple Apfel **5-U0**, D
April April **5-U4**, Sit5
arcade Spielhalle, Arkade **5-U7**, WPA
arcade Arkade, Einkaufspassage
    7-U5, Ex13
archery Bogenschießen **7-U2**, T1
are bist, sind, seid **5-U0**, B
argue streiten, argumentieren **7-U5**, T2
argument Streit **6-U1**, T1
arm Arm **5-U5**, T1
armour Rüstung **7-U2**, T2
army Armee **7-U4**, WP
around herum, umher **5-U3**, WPA
arrest festnehmen **7-U1**, T2
arrive ankommen **6-U5**, T1
arrow Pfeil **7-U4**, T1
art Kunst, Kunsterziehung **7-U3**, TYE
as als, während **6-U6**, T1
as als **7-U2**, Proj
as … as so … wie **6-U1**, Sit5

Asian asiatisch; Asiat(e)/in **7-U5**, TYE
ask fragen; bitten **5-U2**, T2
at an, auf, in **5-U1**, WPB
athlete (Leicht)athlet/in, Sportler/in
    7-U3, Read
at last endlich **5-U7**, T1
at least zumindest, mindestens
    7-U3, WP
at (nine o'clock) um (neun Uhr)
    5-U1, Ex 10
at school in der Schule **5-U1**, WPB
at the moment im Augenblick
    5-U4, Sit1
attack angreifen **7-U4**, T1
attention Aufmerksamkeit **7-U3**, TYE
attraction Attraktion, Anziehung
    7-U4, Ex10
audience Zuschauer, Publikum
    7-U3, Sit1
August August **5-U4**, Sit5
aunt Tante **6-U1**, Sit1
auntie Tante **5-U1**, Song
autumn Herbst **6-U4**, WPB
awake wach **7-U5**, T2
award Auszeichnung, Preis **7-U5**, WP
away weg, fort **5-U1**, Sit6
awful schrecklich **5-U1**, Sit2
axe Axt **7-U4**, T1

Bb

baby Baby **5-U3**, Sit3
back zurück **5-U3**, T2
back Rücken **6-U2**, T2
back Rückseite **5-U6**, Ex4
backpack Rucksack **7-U5**, T1
backyard Hinterhof **7-U1**, Read
bad schlecht **5-U2**, Ex17
badger Dachs **6-U2**, T1
bad language Kraftausdrücke,
    unanständige Ausdrücke
    7-U3, Sit3
bag Tasche **5-U0**, D
ball Ball **5-U6**, T1
banana Banane **5-U6**, Sit4
band Band, Musikgruppe **5-U2**, T2
bang peng! **6-U4**, T2
bank Bank(haus) **5-U2**, T1
barbecue Grillparty; Grillgericht
    6-U7, T1
bareback ohne Sattel **7-U1**, Read
bar mitzvah Bar-Mizwa **7-U3**, T2
barrel Fass **6-U4**, T1

Index

baseball Baseball **5-U6**, Sit3
basket Korb **5-U6**, Ex4
basketball Basketball **5-U2**, Ex12
bath Bad **7-U2**, WP
bathroom Badezimmer **5-U1**, T2
batter Schlagmann **6-U7**, Sit3
battle Schlacht **7-U2**, T1
battlefield Schlachtfeld **7-U4**, T1
be sein **5-U0**, F
beach Strand **5-U7**, WPA
bean Bohne **6-U5**, Sit2
beard Bart **7-U4**, Com
beautiful schön, hübsch **7-U2**, T1
because weil **5-U7**, Sit4
become werden **6-U6**, WPC
bed Bett **5-U1**, Sit6
bedroom Schlafzimmer **5-U2**, WPB
beer Bier **7-U1**, Read
before vor, vorher, bevor **5-U5**, Sit2
begin anfangen **7-U4**, WP
beginning Anfang, Beginn **7-U3**, Ex1
begin to do sth anfangen, etwas zu tun **7-U4**, WP
behind hinter **5-U2**, WPA
believe (in) glauben (an) **7-U2**, Sit2
bell Glocke, Klingel **6-U1**, WPA
belong to gehören **5-U5**, T2
below unten, unterhalb **6-U7**, Song
berry Beere **7-U4**, T1
best beste(r, s) **5-U3**, PYE 3
better besser **6-U1**, Sit4
between zwischen **6-U6**, T1
big groß **5-U5**, T2
big time, be/hit the ganz groß rauskommen, ganz oben sein **7-U3**, WP
bike Rad **5-U2**, Sit3
bin Mülleimer, Abfalleimer **7-U3**, T1
bird Vogel **6-U2**, WPB
birthday Geburtstag **5-U0**, G
biscuit Keks **5-U4**, WPA
bit, a etwas, ein wenig **6-U4**, WPB
black schwarz **5-U0**, C
blister Blase **7-U5**, T1
block Block **7-U1**, WP
blow up in die Luft jagen, explodieren **6-U4**, WPA
blue blau **5-U0**, C
board (Wand-)Tafel **5-U0**, D
board Kommission, Gremium, Aufsichtsrat **7-U1**, WP
boat Boot, Schiff **5-U7**, WPD

body Leiche; Körper **7-U4**, T1
bonfire Freudenfeuer, Guy-Fawkes-Feuer **6-U4**, WPA
book Buch **5-U0**, D
bookshop Buchhandlung **5-U6**, WPB
bored gelangweilt **6-U2**, T2
boring langweilig **6-U1**, Sit5
born, be geboren werden **7-U1**, TYE
borrow sich ausleihen, borgen **5-U7**, Ex14
both beide **6-U2**, Sit5
bottle Flasche **5-U5**, PYE 4
bottom Boden, Fuß (Berg) **5-U7**, T2
bowling Bowling, Kegeln **6-U7**, T1
box Kiste, Schachtel, Kasten **5-U5**, T2
boy Junge **5-U1**, WPA
boyfriend fester Freund **5-U1**, WPC
bracket Klammer **7-U1**, TYE 4
bread Brot **6-U5**, Sit2
break (zer)brechen **7-U1**, T1
break Chance **7-U3**, T1
breakfast Frühstück **5-U4**, WPB
break in einbrechen **7-U1**, T1
break-in Einbruch **7-U1**, T2
brick Ziegelstein **6-U1**, Song
bridge Brücke **6-U1**, WPA
bring bringen **5-U4**, Ex6
bring out herausbringen **7-U1**, Sit5
British britisch **7-U3**, TYE
Briton Brite, Britin **7-U2**, WP
broken zerbrochen, kaputt **6-U5**, T2
bronze Bronze **7-U5**, WP
brooch Brosche **7-U5**, Sket1
broomstick Besen(stiel) **7-U2**, Read
brother Bruder **5-U0**, I
brown braun **5-U4**, Ex16
budgie Wellensittich **5-U3**, WPB
build bauen **6-U1**, Song
building Gebäude **6-U7**, T2
burger Hamburger **6-U7**, T1
burn verbrennen, brennen **6-U4**, WPA
burn down niederbrennen **7-U3**, TYE
bus Bus **5-U0**, D
bush Busch, Strauch **5-U3**, T1
bus station Busbahnhof **5-U6**, WPA
bus-stop Bushaltestelle **5-U3**, Sit3
busy beschäftigt, belebt **6-U1**, T1
but aber **5-U1**, Sit2
butter Butter **6-U5**, Sit2
buy kaufen **5-U4**, WPA
by an, bei, neben **6-U1**, WPA
bye Tschüss **5-U0**, B

Cc

cable car Straßenbahn (in San Francisco) **6-U7**, T2
café Imbiss, Café **5-U6**, WPA
cage Käfig **5-U3**, WPA
cake Kuchen **5-U4**, WPC
calculate rechnen **7-U5**, Read
call Ruf, Anruf **7-U1**, T2
call rufen, anrufen, (be)nennen **7-U2**, T1
called, be heißen **5-U3**, WPA
camera Fotoapparat, Kamera **5-U2**, WPC
camp Lager **5-U7**, WPD
camp zelten **5-U7**, Ex14
camping Camping, Zelten **6-U7**, T1
camp site Campingplatz **5-U7**, WPD
can Dose **7-U1**, Read
can können **5-U0**, F
canal Kanal **5-U6**, Ex16
candle Kerze **6-U4**, WPB
cap Mütze **6-U7**, T1
car Auto **5-U1**, Sit6
caravan Wohnwagen **5-U7**, WPB
card Karte **6-U3**, Ex4
careful vorsichtig, sorgfältig **5-U5**, T1
car park Parkplatz, Parkhaus **5-U5**, T2
carry tragen **6-U2**, T2
cart Wagen, Karren **7-U5**, Sket2
cartoon Zeichentrickfilm **6-U6**, WPA
case Koffer **5-U7**, T1
cassette Kassette **6-U5**, T2
castle Schloss, Burg **6-U4**, T2
cat Katze **5-U0**, E
catch fangen **5-U3**, T2
catch a bus einen Bus erreichen **6-U2**, Ex9
catcher Fänger **6-U7**, T1
cathedral Dom, Kathedrale **7-U5**, Ex13
Catholic katholisch; Katholik/in **6-U4**, T1
cattle Vieh, Rinder **7-U5**, Sket2
CD CD **5-U2**, T2
CD player CD-Spieler **7-U1**, Sit5
céilí irische Tanzveranstaltung **7-U1**, T1
cellar Keller **6-U4**, T1
Celt Kelte, Keltin **7-U2**, WP
central zentral **6-U1**, WPB
centre Zentrum **6-U1**, WPA
century Jahrhundert **7-U4**, WP
chair Stuhl **5-U0**, D

one hundred and thirty-seven 137

Index

chalk Kreide **7-U2**, WP
chamber of horrors Gruselkabinett **6-U1**, T1
chance Chance **7-U3**, Sit1
change ändern, verändern **7-U1**, WP
channel Programm, Kanal **6-U6**, T2
character Figur, Charakter **6-U6**, WPA
charge anstürmen, angreifen **7-U4**, T1
cheap billig **6-U1**, Sit2
check überprüfen **5-U5**, Ex17
cheeky frech **7-U3**, T2
cheer zujubeln, bejubeln, anfeuern **7-U3**, T1
cheese Käse **5-U4**, WPB
chess Schach **5-U5**, WPB
child Kind **5-U3**, Sit3
chimney Schornstein **7-U5**, Sit1
chips Pommes frites **5-U4**, WPA
chocolate Schokolade **5-U4**, Song
choose wählen **7-U2**, Proj
Christmas Weihnachten **5-U4**, Sit5
church Kirche **7-U2**, WP
cinema Kino **5-U3**, PYE 3
circle Kreis **6-U1**, WPB
city Stadt, Großstadt **6-U1**, WPA
class Klasse; Unterrichtsstunde **5-U1**, WPB
classroom Klassenzimmer **5-U0**, D
clay Lehm **6-U1**, Song
clean sauber **6-U5**, WPB
clear klar **7-U3**, T2
clever klug **7-U2**, T1
click on anklicken **6-U3**, WPB
climb klettern **7-U5**, T1
close schließen **5-U0**, F
clothes Kleidung **6-U5**, WPB
cloud Wolke **5-U7**, T2
cloudy bewölkt **7-U5**, T1
club Club **5-U5**, WPB
coast Küste **6-U2**, T1
coat Mantel **6-U5**, Sit2
code Kode, Chiffre **7-U2**, Read
coffee Kaffee **5-U4**, WPA
cola Cola **5-U4**, WPC
cold kalt **5-U7**, WPD
collect sammeln, einsammeln **7-U5**, Rev
college College **7-U1**, T1
colour Farbe **5-U0**, C
come kommen **5-U0**, F
Come Komm, Kommt **5-U0**, F

comedy Komödie **6-U6**, WPA
Come on Komm! Komm schon! **5-U4**, Sit1
comic Comic **6-U4**, Sit4
communication Kommunikation, Verständigung **5-U1**, Com
community Bevölkerungsgruppe; Gemeinde **7-U1**, T1
community centre Gemeindezentrum **7-U1**, T1
company Firma **5-U2**, T1
compare vergleichen **7-U5**, Rev
complain sich beschweren **7-U3**, T2
complete vollständig **7-U5**, Read
complete vervollständigen **5-U5**, Ex1
computer Computer **5-U1**, Sit7
concert Konzert **6-U4**, Ex13
concrete Beton **7-U5**, TYE
confuse verwechseln, durcheinander bringen **7-U5**, Read
conquer erobern **7-U2**, WP
contract Vertrag **7-U3**, Sit1
control Kontrolle **5-U7**, Sit5
conversation Gespräch **6-U2**, Ex13
cook kochen **7-U5**, T1
cool kühl **6-U2**, T1
copy kopieren, abschreiben **6-U4**, Ex17
cornflakes Cornflakes **5-U1**, Sit2
correct richtig **5-U5**, Ex15
cost kosten **5-U5**, Sit4
costume Kostüm **7-U2**, Sit4
cottage Hütte, kleines Landhaus **6-U2**, WPA
count zählen **7-U5**, Sket1
country Land **6-U2**, WPA
country Land, Staat **7-U1**, WP
county Verwaltungsbezirk, Grafschaft **7-U1**, T1
couple Paar, Ehepaar **7-U4**, WP
couple of, a ein paar **7-U4**, WP
course Kurs, Lehrgang **7-U3**, Ex11
cousin Cousin, Cousine **6-U1**, Sit1
cow Kuh **6-U2**, WPA
cowboy Cowboy **7-U1**, Read
cowgirl Cowgirl **7-U1**, Read
crane Kran **7-U4**, TYE
crash Krach(en) **7-U1**, T2
crazy verrückt; wütend **7-U1**, Read
creaking knarrend, quietschend **7-U4**, Read
cricket Cricket **7-U1**, TYE

crime Verbrechen, Kriminalität **7-U5**, TYE
criminal Verbrecher/in **6-U1**, T2
crisps Kartoffelchips **5-U4**, T2
cross überqueren **6-U1**, Sit3
crossroads Kreuzung **7-U5**, Com
crowd Menge **7-U2**, T2
cry weinen, schreien **7-U2**, Read
cup Tasse; Pokal **6-U4**, Sit1
cupboard Schrank **6-U5**, T2
cut schneiden, zerschneiden **7-U4**, Sit5
cut off abschneiden **7-U4**, Sit5
cycle Rad fahren **7-U5**, WP

Dd

dad Vati, Papa **5-U1**, WPC
damn verflucht, verdammt **6-U5**, T1
dance tanzen **5-U4**, Ex2
dangerous gefährlich **5-U5**, T1
dark dunkel **6-U2**, T1
date Datum **5-U4**, Ex13
daughter Tochter **6-U1**, Sit1
day Tag **5-U1**, Sit4
day-dream Tagtraum **6-U2**, Sit2
dead tot **7-U4**, T1
dead end Sackgasse **6-U6**, T1
dear lieber, liebe, liebes **5-U4**, Sit4
death Tod **6-U4**, T1
December Dezember **5-U4**, Sit5
decide entscheiden, beschließen **6-U6**, WPC
decide to do sich entschließen, etwas zu tun **7-U2**, WP
deer Reh, Hirsch **6-U2**, WPB
defeat (völlig) besiegen, eine Niederlage zufügen **7-U4**, WP
definition Definition **7-U4**, Ex11
deliver (aus)liefern, austragen **6-U5**, WPA
demo tape Demoband, Musterband **7-U3**, T1
describe beschreiben **6-U6**, Com
desert Wüste **6-U7**, WPA
desk Schülertisch, Schreibtisch **5-U0**, D
detective Detektiv/in **7-U2**, Com
dial wählen (Telefonnummer) **6-U6**, T2
dialogue Dialog **5-U5**, Ex8
diary Tagebuch **6-U2**, Sit2
die sterben **7-U2**, T1
different verschieden, anders **5-U6**, Ex16
difficult schwierig **5-U7**, T1

dig graben **6-U4**, T1
dining-room Esszimmer **5-U2**, WPB
dinosaur Dinosaurier **6-U6**, WPB
dirty schmutzig **6-U5**, WPB
disabled behindert **7-U5**, Sit1
disappear verschwinden **7-U5**, Read
disc Disk, Diskette **6-U3**, WPB
disco Disco **5-U1**, Ex16
disease Krankheit **7-U1**, Read
disk drive Diskettenlaufwerk
 7-U5, Read
display Ausstellung, Vorführung
 7-U1, Proj
distance Entfernung **7-U4**, T1
disturb stören **7-U4**, Read
divorce sich scheiden lassen **7-U4**, T2
do tun **5-U1**, Sit6
doctor Arzt, Ärztin **6-U4**, T2
documentary Dokumentarfilm
 6-U6, WPB
does, he, she, it er, sie es tut **5-U2**, Sit2
dog Hund **5-U1**, WPA
dome Kuppel **6-U1**, WPA
door Tür **5-U0**, D
doorway Eingang **7-U4**, Read
double doppelt **5-U1**, PYE 6
dough Teig **7-U5**, Read
doughnut Berliner, Krapfen
 5-U4, WPA
down unten, nach unten **5-U0**, F
download herunterladen **6-U3**, T1
dozen, a (ein) Dutzend **7-U5**, Read
drama Schauspiel **5-U5**, Sit2
draw zeichnen **5-U4**, Sit2
dream Traum **6-U6**, Ex2
dress Kleid **5-U0**, C
drink trinken **5-U4**, WPB
drink Getränk **6-U5**, T2
drive fahren **5-U1**, Sit7
driver Fahrer/in **6-U5**, WPC
drop fallen lassen, fallen **6-U4**, T1
drug Droge; Medikament **7-U1**, Read
Druid Druide **7-U2**, TYE
drums Schlagzeug **7-U3**, T1
duck Ente **6-U4**, Ex18
duke Herzog **7-U2**, T1
during während **7-U5**, T2
DVD DVD **6-U3**, WPB

Ee
each jeder, jede, jedes **5-U5**, Ex18
ear Ohr **6-U6**, Com
early früh **7-U4**, WP
earn verdienen **6-U5**, WPB
east Osten **6-U1**, WPA
Easter Ostern **5-U4**, Sit5
easy einfach, leicht **5-U6**, T1
eat essen **5-U3**, WPA
eight acht **5-U0**, G
eighteen achtzehn **5-U0**, G
eighty achtzig **5-U4**, WPA
elephant Elefant **6-U3**, WPA
eleven elf **5-U0**, G
else sonst **7-U1**, T1
e-mail E-Mail **6-U3**, WPC
emperor Kaiser **7-U2**, WP
empty leer **6-U4**, T1
encyclopedia Lexikon, Enzyklopädie
 6-U4, PYE4
end Ende **5-U1**, Song
end beenden **6-U2**, Ex6
endless endlos **6-U7**, Song
enemy Feind **7-U2**, Proj
English englisch; Engländer/in **5-U0**, A
enjoy gern haben, genießen
 5-U7, WPC
enjoy doing sth gerne etwas tun
 7-U2, T2
enough genug **6-U4**, Ex11
entrance Eingang **6-U4**, T2
equipment Ausrüstung **6-U7**, T1
er äh **5-U2**, Ex4
especially besonders **7-U3**, T1
etc usw. **6-U5**, Ex12
even sogar **7-U4**, TYE
evening Abend **5-U1**, Sit6
ever jemals **6-U5**, Sit4
every jeder, jede, jedes **5-U1**, Sit6
everybody jede(r), alle **7-U3**, Com
everyone jede(r), alle **6-U2**, Sit2
everything alles **6-U3**, WPC
everywhere überall **6-U2**, Song
exact genau **6-U7**, T2
example Beispiel **7-U4**, T2
except außer **7-U1**, WP
excited aufgeregt, begeistert **7-U2**, T2
exciting spannend, aufregend
 6-U1, WPA
excuse Entschuldigung **7-U2**, Ex3
excuse me Entschuldigung
 5-U6, WPB

execute hinrichten, exekutieren
 7-U4, T2
exercise Übung **5-U1**, Ex1
exercise book Schulheft **5-U0**, D
exhausted erschöpft **7-U5**, T1
exist existieren, vorhanden sein
 6-U5, T1
expect erwarten **6-U6**, Sit1
expedition Expedition,
 Forschungsreise **7-U5**, WP
expensive teuer **5-U7**, WPA
explanation Erklärung **6-U7**, Com
expert Experte, Expertin **7-U5**, Sket1
explain erklären **6-U2**, T2
export ausführen, exportieren
 7-U1, WP
extra zusätzlich **6-U5**, WPB
eye Auge **6-U6**, Com

Ff
face Gesicht **6-U6**, Com
factory Fabrik **6-U5**, WPA
fail scheitern, keinen Erfolg haben
 7-U3, Read
fair fair, gerecht **6-U5**, T1
fair schön, liebreizend **6-U1**, Song
fairground Rummelplatz **7-U5**, Sit1
fair(-haired) blond **7-U4**, Com
fall fallen **5-U5**, T1
fall in love (with) sich verlieben (in)
 7-U2, T1
fall off herunterfallen **6-U2**, T2
family Familie **5-U1**
famous berühmt **6-U1**, WPA
fan Anhänger/in, Fan **5-U2**, T2
fancy mögen **6-U3**, T2
fantastic wundervoll **5-U2**, T1
far weit **5-U5**, T1
farm Bauernhof **6-U2**, WPA
farmer Bauer, Bäuerin **5-U3**, Song
fashion Mode **7-U3**, T1
fast schnell **5-U5**, WPA
fat dick, fett **7-U4**, T2
father Vater **5-U2**, Sit4
fault Fehler **6-U6**, T2
favour Gefallen **6-U6**, T2
favourite Lieblings- **5-U1**, Sit2
February Februar **5-U4**, Sit5
fed up, be die Nase voll haben **6-U1**, T2
feed füttern **5-U3**, WPA
feel (sich) fühlen **6-U2**, T1
feeling Gefühl **7-U2**, T2

one hundred and thirty-nine **139**

Index

female weiblich **7-U3**, Read
fence Zaun **5-U3**, T1
festival Fest, Festival **6-U4**, WPB
fetch holen **7-U5**, T2
few, a ein paar **6-U4**, Sit2
field Feld **7-U1**, WP
fifteen fünfzehn **5-U0**, G
fifty fünfzig **5-U1**, Sit5
fight kämpfen **7-U2**, WP
film Film **5-U1**, Sit1
filthy dreckig **7-U5**, T1
final letzte(r,s), endgültig **7-U4**, T2
finally schließlich **7-U4**, T2
find finden **5-U0**, J
find out herausfinden **6-U3**
fine gut, schön **5-U0**, B
finish beenden **5-U4**, WPA
fire Feuer **6-U4**, WPA
fire feuern, schießen **6-U4**, T2
fire-eater Feuerschlucker **6-U1**, WPA
fireworks Feuerwerk **6-U4**, WPA
first erste, erster, erstes **5-U1**, Sit3
first aid erste Hilfe **7-U5**, WP
first floor erster Stock **5-U2**, WPB
fish Fisch **7-U5**, Ex6
fit fit, geeignet **7-U5**, Rev
five fünf **5-U0**, G
fix befestigen **6-U5**, T2
flat Wohnung **5-U2**, WPA
fleet Flotte **7-U4**, TYE
flight Flug **5-U7**, Ex2
floor (Fuß)Boden **5-U5**, Sit1
flower Blume **6-U2**, WPB
flute Flöte **7-U3**, Ex11
fly fliegen **5-U1**, Sit8
follow folgen **6-U6**, T1
food Essen, Lebensmittel **5-U4**, WPC
fool Narr, Dummkopf **6-U4**, WPD
foot Fuß **5-U5**, T1
football Fußball **5-U1**, Ex10
footballer Fußballspieler/in **6-U1**, Ex2
for seit **7-U1**, Sit4
for für **5-U1**, WPB
for example zum Beispiel **7-U4**, T2
for sale zu verkaufen **7-U4**, Read
forbid verbieten, untersagen **7-U1**, Read
forecast Vorhersage **6-U3**, Sit1
foreleg Vorderbein **7-U1**, Read
forest Wald, Forst **6-U2**, Sit3
forget vergessen **5-U4**, T2
form Form **6-U1**, Ex4

Formula One Formel 1 **5-U2**, T1
forty vierzig **5-U1**, Sit5
forward(s) vorwärts **7-U1**, Ex3
foundation Stiftung; Gründung **7-U3**, Read
four vier **5-U0**, G
fourteen vierzehn **5-U0**, G
free kostenlos, frei **5-U7**, Sit1
freezing kalt, frierend **7-U5**, T1
French Französisch, französisch **5-U1**, Sit3
french fries Pommes frites **6-U7**, Ex1
fresh frisch **7-U1**, Read
Friday Freitag **5-U1**, Sit4
friend Freund/in **5-U1**
friendly freundlich **6-U7**, T2
from von, aus **5-U0**, A
front Vorderseite **6-U2**, T1
frozen gefroren, tiefgefroren **7-U5**, T1
full voll **5-U7**, T2
fun Spaß **6-U4**, WPD
funny witzig, komisch, seltsam **5-U7**, T2
furious wütend **7-U4**, T2
future Zukunft **6-U5**, Sit1

Gg

Gaeltacht Gebiet, in dem Gälisch gesprochen wird **7-U1**, T1
game Spiel **5-U1**, Sit7
garage Garage **5-U2**, WPA
garbage Müll, Abfall **6-U7**, Sit4
garden Garten **5-U2**, WPA
gas Benzin **6-U7**, Ex1
gate Tor **6-U5**, T2
genuine echt, unverfälscht **7-U4**, Ex10
German Deutsch; deutsch; Deutsche/r **5-U0**, A
get bekommen, werden **6-U3**, T2
get holen **5-U3**, T1
get clean sauber machen, sauber bringen **6-U5**, WPB
get home heimkommen **5-U2**, T1
get (in) einsteigen (in) **5-U1**, T2
get on with auskommen mit **7-U3**, T2
get out (of) aussteigen, herauskommen **7-U1**, T2
get ready vorbereiten **6-U5**, Sit2
get to gehen zu, kommen zu **6-U6**, T1
get up aufstehen **5-U1**, Sit6
ghetto Getto, abgesondertes Wohnviertel **7-U1**, Read

ghost Geist, Gespenst **6-U6**, WPA
gig Konzert, Auftritt **7-U3**, Sit1
girl Mädchen **5-U1**, WPA
girlfriend Freundin **5-U1**, Song
give geben **5-U3**, Sit1
give somebody a lift jemanden im Auto mitnehmen **7-U4**, Sit3
glad froh **6-U4**, T2
glass Glas **6-U3**, Ex14
glasses Brille **7-U4**, Com
go gehen **5-U0**, A
goal Tor **7-U3**, Read
God Gott **6-U4**, T1
going to, be werden **6-U3**, Sit1
go-kart Gokart **5-U7**, Sit4
gold Gold **7-U5**, WP
golden golden, aus Gold **6-U7**
good gut **5-U1**, Sit2
goodbye auf Wiedersehen **5-U0**, B
gown Robe, Talar **7-U2**, TYE
grandad Opa **5-U5**, Sit3
grandma Oma **6-U3**, Sit1
grandparents Großeltern **6-U2**, WPA
grandson Enkel(sohn) **7-U3**, T2
grass Gras **5-U3**, WPA
great großartig **5-U1**, Sit2
green grün **5-U0**, C
grey grau **7-U4**, Com
grizzly bear Grizzlybär **5-U0**, Song
ground Grund, Boden **6-U2**, WPB
ground floor Erdgeschoss **5-U2**, WPB
group Gruppe **5-U1**, Ex4
guard Polizist/in (in Irland) **7-U1**, T2
guess raten, schätzen **6-U2**, Ex7
guest Gast **6-U6**, WPA
guest house Gästehaus, Pension **7-U1**, Sit1
guide Führer/in **6-U2**, T1
guitar Gitarre **5-U0**, E
gulf Golf **6-U7**, Song
gun Schusswaffe **5-U3**, Song
gunpowder Schießpulver **6-U4**, T1
guy Typ, Bursche **6-U4**, WPA

140 one hundred and forty

Index

Hh

hair Haar **6-U2**, Sit2
half halb **5-U1**, Sit5
half past (ten) halb (elf) **5-U1**, Sit5
half-term Schulferien **5-U4**, Sit5
hall Flur **5-U2**, WPB
ham Schinken **7-U5**, T1
hamburger Hamburger **5-U4**, WPA
hamster Hamster **5-U3**, WPA
hand Hand **5-U6**, T1
hang around herumlungern,
    herumhängen **7-U1**, Read
happen passieren, geschehen **6-U2**, Ex3
happy glücklich, froh **5-U0**, G
Happy birthday! Herzlichen
    Glückwunsch zum Geburtstag!
    5-U0, G
hard hart, schwer, schwierig **5-U6**, T1
hardly kaum **7-U5**, T1
hate hassen, gar nicht mögen
    5-U5, Sit2
haunted Spuk- **7-U4**, Read
have got haben, besitzen **5-U0**, E
have to müssen **6-U6**, T1
he er **5-U1**, WPA
he's fed up er hat die Nase voll
    6-U1, T2
head Kopf, Oberhaupt **6-U2**, Ex7
headache Kopfschmerzen **7-U1**, Ex14
hear hören **5-U7**, T1
heavy schwer **7-U2**, TYE
hedge Hecke **6-U6**, T1
held hielt **7-U2**, T2
hello hallo **5-U0**, A
help helfen **5-U3**, Com
help Hilfe **6-U5**, Sit2
hen Henne, Huhn **6-U2**, WPA
her ihr, ihre, ihr **5-U1**, T1
her sie, ihr **5-U2**, Sit5
here hier; hierher **5-U0**, F
hero Held **7-U3**, Proj
hers ihr(e, s) **6-U3**, Sit2
hey hey! **5-U7**, T1
hi hallo **5-U0**, A
hide (sich) verstecken **7-U1**, Read
high hoch **5-U7**, T2
high school Oberschule **6-U3**, T2
highway Hauptverkehrsstraße
    6-U7, Song
hill Hügel **6-U7**, WPA
him ihn, ihm **5-U2**, Sit5
Hindu Hindu **6-U4**, WPB

his sein, seine, sein **5-U1**, WPB
history Geschichte **6-U3**, WPE
hit schlagen, treffen **6-U7**, Sit3
hit Hit **7-U3**, T1
hockey Hockey **5-U5**, Sit2
hold halten **5-U4**, T1
hole Loch **5-U3**, T1
holiday Ferien, Urlaub **5-U4**, Sit5
home Heim, Zuhause **5-U1**, Sit6
homeless obdachlos **7-U5**, TYE
homework Hausaufgaben **5-U1**, Sit6
honey Honig **6-U5**, WPA
hoot rufen *(Eule)*; hupen *(Auto)* **7-U2**, Read
hope hoffen **5-U2**, T2
hopeful optimistisch, voller Hoffnung
    7-U3, T2
hopeless hoffnungslos **6-U1**, T1
hope to do sth hoffen, etwas zu tun
    7-U2, TYE6
horrible fürchterlich, schrecklich
    6-U1, T2
horror Horror **7-U4**, T1
horse Pferd **6-U2**, WPA
hospital Krankenhaus **5-U6**, WPA
hot heiß **5-U7**, WPD
hot-air balloon Heißluftballon **7-Rev**
hotel Hotel **5-U7**, WPD
hour Stunde **5-U5**, Sit3
house Haus **5-U0**, G
how wie **5-U0**, B
how many … ? Wie viele … ? **5-U0**, H
how much … ? Wie viel … ? **5-U6**, Sit3
huge riesig **6-U7**, WPA
hundred hundert **5-U4**, WPA
hungry hungrig **5-U4**, WPA
hurry eilen, sich beeilen **5-U1**, Sit6
hurry Eile **7-U1**, T2
hurry (up) sich beeilen **5-U1**, T2
hurt schmerzen, weh tun **5-U6**, T1
husband Ehemann **6-U1**, Sit1
hutch Kaninchenstall **5-U3**, WPA

Ii

I ich **5-U0**, A
iceberg Eisberg **7-U3**, WP
ice-cream (Speise)Eis **5-U4**, WPA
ice-rink Eisbahn **7-U5**, TYE
idea Idee **5-U4**, T2
idiot Dummkopf, Idiot **5-U6**, T2
if ob **7-U2**, T1
if wenn, falls **6-U1**, Sit2

ill krank **6-U2**, Ex1
I'm ich bin **5-U0**, A
imagine sich vorstellen **5-U7**, WPD
I'm fine Mir geht's gut. **5-U0**, B
important wichtig, bedeutend **7-U2**, T1
in in **5-U0**, A
in a hurry in Eile **7-U1**, T2
in a mess durcheinander, in
    Unordnung **7-U5**, T2
inch Inch, Zoll **7-U5**, Read
include einschließen, beinhalten
    7-U5, Read
information Information(en)
    5-U7, Ex3
in front of vor **5-U2**, WPA
in-line skates Inlineskates,
    Rollerblades **5-U5**, WPA
inn Gasthaus **7-U2**, T2
inside innen, drinnen **6-U6**, T1
interest Interesse **7-U2**, Com
interested in, be interessiert sein (an)
    6-U3, T2
interesting interessant **6-U1**, WPA
international international **7-U5**, TYE
internet Internet **6-U3**, WPC
interview interviewen **6-U2**, Ex9
into hinein, in **6-U2**, T1
introduction Einführung **5-U1**, Intro
in trouble in Schwierigkeiten **7-U3**, Sit1
invade einmarschieren in, eindringen in
    7-U4, WP
invader Eindringling, Angreifer/in
    7-U4, WP
invisible unsichtbar **7-U5**, Read
invitation Einladung **7-U1**, Com
invite einladen **6-U6**, WPC
Irish irisch **7-U1**, WP
Irish Tourist Board, das irische
    Fremdenverkehrsamt **7-U1**, WP
iron Eisen **7-U4**, T1
is ist **5-U0**, A
island Insel **6-U7**, Song
it es **5-U0**, B
italics Kursivdruck **7-U1**, Ex6
its sein, seine, sein, ihr, ihre, ihr
    5-U3, Sit1
it's es ist **5-U0**, B
it's fun es macht Spaß **6-U4**, WPD
It's my turn. Ich bin dran. Ich bin an
    der Reihe. **5-U1**, T2
I've got Ich habe, ich besitze **5-U0**, E

one hundred and forty-one 141

Index

Jj

jacket Jacke, Jackett **5-U4**, Ex16
jam Marmelade, Konfitüre **6-U5**, WPA
January Januar **5-U4**, Sit5
jeans Jeans **6-U6**, Com
jet lag Jetlag **6-U7**, T1
job Job, Arbeitsplatz **5-U2**, T1
jockey Jockey **7-U1**, Read
join verbinden, sich anschließen **7-U2**, Sit4
joke Witz, Scherz **6-U1**, Sit4
journey Reise **5-U7**, WPC
judo Judo **5-U5**, WPB
juggler Jongleur/in **6-U1**, WPA
July Juli **5-U4**, Sit5
jump springen **5-U5**, WPA
June Juni **5-U4**, Sit5
just genau, gerade **6-U4**, Sit3
just nur, bloß **5-U4**, T1

Kk

keep halten, behalten **6-U5**, WPC
keep back zurückbleiben, zurückhalten **6-U2**, T2
keep out fernhalten, nicht hereinlassen **7-U2**, WP
key Schlüssel **7-U2**, Read
keyboard Keyboard (Musikinstrument) **7-U3**, T2
kick (mit dem Fuß) treten **7-U1**, T2
kid Kind **5-U5**, WPB
kill töten, umbringen **7-U2**, T1
kind (of) Art, Sorte (von) **7-U4**, T1
king König **6-U1**, T2
kingdom Königreich **7-U1**, WP
kiss Kuss **6-U7**, T2
kitchen Küche **5-U1**, T2
knee Knie **7-U5**, T1
knife Messer **7-U2**, T2
knight Ritter **7-U2**, WP
knock klopfen **7-U4**, Read
know wissen, kennen **5-U2**, Sit2

Ll

label Etikett, Schildchen **6-U5**, Ex17
lady Dame **6-U1**, Song
lake See **5-U7**, T2
land Land, Boden **6-U7**, Song
land landen **6-U2**, T2
landlord Wirt; Vermieter **7-U4**, Read
lane Feldweg, Gasse **7-U1**, T2

language Sprache **7-U3**, Sit3
large groß **5-U4**, Sit4
last letzte(r, s) **6-U2**, Sit2
late spät **5-U1**, Sit1
later später **5-U7**, T1
laugh (at) lachen (über) **6-U4**, T2
law Gesetz, Recht **7-U1**, Read
lay the table den Tisch decken **6-U4**, Sit3
league Bündnis, Liga **6-U3**, T1
learn lernen, erfahren **5-U1**, Sit8
learn to do sth lernen, etwas zu tun **7-U3**, Ex11
leave verlassen, weggehen, abfahren **5-U1**, Sit6
leave lassen, liegenlassen **5-U5**, Sit1
left links **5-U6**, WPB
left verließ **6-U3**, Ex10
left, be übrig sein **7-U3**, Sit1
leg Bein **5-U5**, T1
lemonade Zitronenlimonade **6-U5**, T2
lend leihen **6-U4**, Sit4
lesson Unterrichtsstunde **5-U1**, Ex4
let's Lass(t) uns **5-U0**, A
letter Brief **5-U6**, Sit1
letter Buchstabe **6-U1**, Ex19
let out hinauslassen, herauslassen **5-U3**, WPA
library Bibliothek, Bücherei **5-U5**, T2
lie Lüge **7-U5**, Read
lie liegen **6-U2**, WPB
life Leben **5-U6**, T1
lift Mitfahrgelegenheit **7-U4**, Sit3
lift hochheben **6-U2**, T2
light Licht **6-U2**, T1
light anzünden **6-U4**, WPA
like mögen **5-U1**, Sit7
like wie **5-U7**, WPD
like doing sth etwas gerne tun **7-U1**, Sit1
line Linie, Zeile **6-U1**, WPB
lion Löwe **7-U1**, TYE
list Liste **5-U5**, PYE 6
listen (to) zuhören **5-U1**, Sit8
little klein **5-U0**, Song
live leben, wohnen **5-U0**, A
lively lebendig, rege, lebhaft **6-U1**, WPA
living-room Wohnzimmer **5-U2**, WPB
load laden, beladen **6-U4**, PYE 2
locked verschlossen **7-U2**, T2
Londoner Londoner, Bewohner Londons **7-U5**, TYE3
long lang **5-U1**, T2

look aussehen **6-U1**, T2
look schauen **5-U2**, Sit5
look after sich kümmern um **6-U1**, T1
look for suchen **5-U6**, WPB
look forward to sich freuen auf **6-U1**, Ex5
Look out! Pass auf! **5-U5**, T1
look round sich umschauen **6-U3**, Sit1
Lord Lord **6-U4**, T1
lorry LKW **6-U7**, Ex1
lose verlieren **6-U4**, Sit1
lost, get sich verlaufen **6-U6**, T1
lot of, a eine Menge, viel **6-U1**, Sit2
lots of viel **6-U7**, Sit2
love herzliche Grüße **5-U4**, T2
love Liebe **5-U5**, PYE 4
love lieben **6-U2**, T1
lovely schön, hübsch **6-U2**, WPB
luck Glück **6-U7**, T2
lucky glücklich, Glück haben **5-U1**, T1
lunch Mittagessen **5-U3**, WPA
lunch-time Mittagsstunde **5-U3**, WPA

Mm

machine Maschine **6-U5**, WPD
madam meine Dame, gnädige Frau **5-U7**, Sit5
magazine Zeitschrift **5-U5**, WPB
magic Magie, Zauberkunst **7-U2**, T1
magician Zauberer, Magier **7-U2**, T1
magnificent prächtig, großartig **7-U5**, Read
mail schicken, aufgeben **6-U7**, Ex1
main Haupt-, hauptsächlich **6-U6**, T1
major größer, bedeutend **6-U3**, T1
make machen **5-U4**, Sit1
make a mess of verkorksen, verpfuschen, Mist bauen **7-U3**, T2
make sure sicherstellen, sorgen für **7-U4**, WP
man Mann **5-U3**, Sit3
manager Geschäftsführer, Manager, Filialleiter/in **6-U5**, WPA
many viele **5-U7**, Sit4
map Landkarte **5-U7**, T1
March März **5-U4**, Sit5
market Markt **6-U5**, WPB
marmalade Marmelade aus Zitrusfrüchten **6-U5**, WPA
marriage Ehe, Hochzeit **7-U4**, T2
marry heiraten **7-U2**, T1
marvellous fabelhaft **7-U2**, T2

142 one hundred and forty-two

Index

master Meister, Herr **7-U5**, Read
match passend zusammenfügen, zusammenpassen **7-U4**, Ex5
maths Mathematik **5-U1**, Ex4
matter Angelegenheit **6-U4**, T1
May Mai **5-U4**, Sit5
maybe vielleicht **5-U7**, T2
may I ? darf ich? **5-U7**, Sit5
maze Labyrinth **6-U6**, T1
me mich, mir **5-U2**, Sit5
meal Mahlzeit **5-U4**, WPB
mean meinen, sagen wollen **5-U6**, T2
mean bedeuten **7-U1**, T1
mean gemein, geizig **6-U6**, T2
meaning Bedeutung **7-U5**, Ex4
meanwhile inzwischen **6-U7**, T1
meat Fleisch **7-U5**, Sket2
media Medien **7-U3**, TYE
medium mittelgroß **5-U4**, Sit4
meeow Miau **7-U4**, Read
meet treffen **6-U6**, WPA
member Mitglied **6-U3**, T1
memory Erinnerung, Gedächtnis, Arbeitsspeicher (RAM) **7-U5**, Read
menu Speisekarte **5-U4**, WPA
mess Durcheinander **7-U5**, T2
message Mitteilung, Nachricht, Botschaft **6-U3**, WPC
metre Meter **5-U7**, T2
microwave Mikrowelle **7-U5**, Read
middle Mitte **6-U6**, T1
Midlands Midlands **7-U5**, Sit1
might könnte (vielleicht) **7-U3**, T1
mile Meile **5-U1**, Sit6
milk Milch **5-U4**, WPA
millennium Jahrtausend, Millennium **6-U1**, WPA
million Million **6-U3**, WP C
millionaire Millionär **6-U6**, WPC
mine meine(r, s) **6-U3**, Sit2
minibus Kleinbus **7-U5**, T1
mini-golf Minigolf **5-U2**, Sit1
minister Minister/in **7-U4**, T2
minute Minute **5-U1**, Sit1
miss verpassen **6-U6**, T1
missing fehlend, nicht vorhanden **6-U1**, Ex8
mission Mission, Auftrag, Missionsstation **6-U7**, WPA
mistake Fehler **7-U3**, Ex 12
mixture Mischung, Gemisch **7-U1**, Proj

mobile (phone) tragbares Telefon, Handy **6-U2**, T2
model Modell, Fotomodell **6-U1**, Ex20
modern modern **7-U5**, TYE 4
mom Mama **6-U7**, T1
moment Moment **6-U2**, T1
Monday Montag **5-U1**, Sit4
money Geld **5-U4**, Sit3
monster Ungeheuer, Scheusal, Monster **7-U4**, T2
month Monat **5-U4**, Sit5
more mehr **6-U1**, Com
morning Morgen **5-U1**, Sit6
most meiste (r,s) **5-U6**, T1
mother Mutter **5-U2**, Sit2
motor-racing Autorennen **7-U3**, Read
mountain Berg **5-U2**, Song
mouse Maus **5-U3**, WPB
mouth Mund **6-U6**, Com
move (sich) bewegen, umziehen **5-U5**, T2
movie Film **6-U7**, WPA
Mr Herr **5-U0**, F
Mrs Frau **5-U0**, B
much viel **5-U5**, Sit3
mum Mutti, Mama **5-U1**, WPC
museum Museum **6-U1**, Sit2
music Musik **5-U1**, Sit3
musical Musical **7-U1**, T1
musical instrument Musikinstrument **6-U6**, Ex 2
must müssen **5-U6**, Sit1
mustn't nicht dürfen **7-U5**, Sit3
my mein, meine, mein **5-U0**, A

Nn

name Name **5-U0**, A
name nennen **7-U1**, TYE 1
national national, National- **6-U7**, WPA
near nah **5-U1**, Sit6
neat ordentlich, sauber, gepflegt **7-U5**, Read
need brauchen **5-U4**, Sit1
needle Nadel **7-U1**, Read
needn't nicht müssen, nicht brauchen **7-U5**, Sit3
need to do sth etwas tun müssen **7-U1**, Com
negative negativ **7-U2**, Sit1
neighbour Nachbar/in **5-U3**, Sit1
nervous nervös **6-U6**, Ex 9
never niemals **5-U5**, Sit2

never mind macht nichts, vergiss es **6-U1**, T2
new neu **5-U0**, E
news Neuigkeit(en), Nachricht(en) **6-U3**, WPC
newspaper Tageszeitung **6-U3**, WPD
next nächster, nächste, nächstes **5-U3**, T1
next time das nächste Mal **7-U5**, TYE4
nice nett, schön, hübsch **5-U1**, Sit2
night Nacht **5-U7**, Sit1
nine neun **5-U0**, G
nineteen neunzehn **5-U0**, G
ninety neunzig **5-U4**, WPA
no nein **5-U0**, B
no kein(e) **6-U1**, T1
nobody niemand **7-U2**, Read
noise Lärm **6-U2**, T1
non-white farbig; Farbige/r **7-U5**, TYE
no one niemand **7-U1**, T2
Norman normannisch; Normanne, Normannin **7-U4**, WP
north Norden **5-U7**, T1
northern nördlich, Nord- **7-U1**, WP
nose Nase **6-U6**, Com
not nicht **5-U0**, B
note Notiz **7-U3**, Ex14
nothing nichts **6-U2**, T2
notice bemerken **7-U2**, T2
notice Zettel, Notiz **7-U5**, Sket1
November November **5-U4**, Sit5
now jetzt **5-U0**, F
nowhere nirgendwo **7-U3**, T2
nuisance Ärgernis, Quälgeist **7-U3**, Sit2
number Zahl **5-U0**, G

Oo

observatory Sternwarte, Observatorium **7-U2**, TYE
obsolete veraltet **7-U5**, Read
occur geschehen, vorkommen **7-U3**, Ex1
ocean Meer, Ozean **6-U7**, WPB
o'clock Uhr **5-U1**, Sit5
October Oktober **5-U4**, Sit5
odd word out Wort, das anders ist **6-U2**, Ex16
of von **5-U1**, Sit2
of course natürlich **5-U1**, Sit8
off von … herunter, weg **6-U2**, T2
offer anbieten **7-U3**, T2
office Büro **6-U5**, WPD

one hundred and forty-three **143**

Index

office block Bürogebäude, Bürokomplex **7-U1**, WP
officer Beamte/r, Beamtin **5-U7**, Sit5
often häufig, oft **5-U3**, PYE 3
oh oh **5-U0**, G
Oh, dear! Ach du meine Güte! **5-U4**, Sit4
OK O.K. **5-U0**, B
old alt **5-U0**, G
on auf **5-U1**, T2
once einmal **6-U5**, Sit4
one eins **5-U0**, G
one Wort, das anstelle eines Substantivs stehen kann **7-U2**, Sit5
on foot zu Fuß **7-U5**, Sit3
only nur, bloß **5-U5**, Sit3
on (Monday) am (Montag) **5-U1**, Sit4
on time pünktlich **5-U1**, Sit6
onto auf … (hinauf) **6-U3**, Ex7
on your own (ganz) allein **6-U1**, T2
open offen, geöffnet **7-U1**, TYE
open öffnen **5-U0**, F
opinion Meinung **7-U3**, T2
opposite Gegenteil **5-U5**, Ex16
or oder **5-U0**, I
orange Orange, Apfelsine **5-U6**, Sit4
orange juice Orangensaft **5-U4**, WPA
order Reihenfolge **5-U7**, Ex9
ordinary normal, gewöhnlich **7-U3**, WP
organize organisieren **7-U3**, Sit1
origin Ursprung, Herkunft **7-U5**, TYE
or so ungefähr **7-U4**, Read
other andere(r, s) **5-U4**, Ex6
ought to sollte **7-U4**, T1
our unser, unsere, unser **5-U3**, Sit1
ours unsere(r, s) **6-U3**, Sit3
outlaw Gesetzlose/r **7-U5**, Sket2
out (of) hinaus **5-U1**, Sit7
outside draußen **6-U1**, Sit4
outside außerhalb **7-U2**, Ex6
over zu Ende **7-U1**, T2
over über **5-U3**, T1
over über, mehr als **7-U1**, TYE
overnight über Nacht, ganz plötzlich **7-U3**, Sit1
over there dort drüben **6-U1**, T2
ow Au, Aua **5-U5**, T1
owl Eule **7-U2**, Read
own eigen **5-U2**, WPB
owner Besitzer/in, Eigentümer/in **7-U5**, Rev

Pp

pack (ver)packen, einpacken **7-U5**, T2
packet Paket **5-U5**, PYE 4
page Seite **5-U1**, Ex1
pain Schmerz **7-U5**, T1
paint malen, streichen **6-U5**, T2
painter Maler **7-U4**, TYE4
pair Paar **6-U4**, Ex1
palace Palast **6-U1**, WPA
paper Papier **6-U5**, T2
paragliding Drachenfliegen, Paragliding **7-U5**, WP
paragraph Absatz, Abschnitt **6-U6**, Ex8
paramedic Rettungsassistent/in **6-U2**, T2
pardon? Verzeihung **7-U5**, T2
parents Eltern **5-U2**, T1
park Park **5-U2**, Sit3
parliament Parlament **6-U1**, WPA
part Teil **6-U1**, T1
part Rolle **7-U2**, Sit4
partner Partner/in **5-U5**, WPB
party Party, Feier **5-U4**, WPC
passport Reisepass **5-U7**, Sit3
past Vergangenheit **6-U2**, Sit2
past nach **5-U1**, Sit5
path Fußweg, Pfad **5-U5**, T1
pay zahlen **6-U5**, T2
pen Füllfederhalter, Füller **5-U0**, D
pencil Bleistift **5-U0**, D
penny Penny **5-U4**, WPA
people Leute **5-U3**, Sit3
perform spielen, vorführen **7-U3**, Sit3
perhaps vielleicht **7-U2**, Sit2
person Person **5-U1**, T1
pet Haustier **5-U3**, WPA
petrol Benzin **6-U7**, Ex1
petrol station Tankstelle **5-U2**, T1
pet shop Tierhandlung **5-U6**, WPB
phone telefonieren **5-U5**, PYE 4
photo Foto **5-U1**, Sit2
photocopy fotokopieren **7-U4**, Proj
phrase Ausdruck, Phrase, Satzglied **6-U3**, WPC
piano Klavier **5-U1**, Sit8
pick pflücken, auswählen **7-U4**, T1
picnic Picknick **7-U5**, Ex6
picture Bild **5-U1**, WP
pie Pastete, Obstkuchen **7-U5**, Read
piece Stück, Teil **6-U5**, T2
pig Schwein **6-U1**, Ex19

pitcher Werfer **6-U7**, Sit3
pity, it's a schade **6-U5**, Com
pizza Pizza **5-U4**, WPA
place Ort, Platz **5-U6**, WPA
plan Plan **5-U2**, WPB
plane Flugzeug **5-U7**, WPC
plastic Plastik, Kunststoff **7-U4**, Com
plate Teller **5-U4**, WPA
play (Schau)spiel **7-U2**, Com
play spielen **5-U1**, Sit7
player Spieler/in **6-U7**, T1
playground Spielplatz **5-U6**, Sit2
please bitte **5-U0**, F
plot Komplott, Verschwörung **6-U4**, T1
plotter Verschwörer/in **6-U4**, T1
plug Stecker, Stöpsel **7-U1**, Sit5
pocket Tasche **6-U1**, T1
point zeigen **7-U5**, Sket1
police Polizei **7-U1**, T2
policeman Polizist **5-U5**, T1
polite höflich **6-U1**, Com
polo Polo **7-U1**, TYE
pony Pony **6-U2**, WPA
poor arm **5-U3**, T1
pope Papst **7-U4**, WP
pop (music) Popmusik **5-U1**, Sit7
popular beliebt **6-U1**, Sit2
posh chic, vornehm, nobel **7-U3**, WP
position Stellung, Lage **6-U7**, T1
positive positiv **7-U2**, Sit1
possible möglich **7-U5**, WP
post zur Post bringen, aufgeben **5-U6**, Sit1
postcard Postkarte **5-U7**, WPD
poster Poster **5-U0**, D
postman Postbote **5-U2**, T1
post office Postamt **5-U6**, WPA
potato Kartoffel **6-U5**, T1
pound Pfund **5-U4**, WPA
pour gießen, sich ergießen **7-U5**, Sit1
practice Training, Übung **7-U5**, T1
practise üben **5-U1**, PYE
premier bedeutendste/r **7-U5**, Read
present Geschenk **5-U3**, Sit5
present Gegenwart **6-U5**, Ex6
presenter Moderator/in **6-U1**, T2
president Präsident/in **6-U1**, T2
pretty ziemlich **7-U5**, Read
price Preis **6-U5**, T1
priest Priester/in **7-U2**, TYE
prince Prinz; Fürst **7-U3**, T1

Index

princess Prinzessin **6-U1**, T2
print (out) (aus)drucken **6-U3**, WPB
prison Gefängnis **6-U1**, WPA
prisoner Gefangene/r, Häftling
7-U4, Sit5
prize Preis, Gewinn **6-U4**, Ex3
probably wahrscheinlich **6-U6**, T1
problem Problem **5-U1**, T2
programme Sendung **6-U6**, WPA
project Projekt **6-U2**, Sit2
proper hinreichend, gebührend, richtig
7-U1, Read
proud (of) stolz (auf) **7-U1**, Read
pub Kneipe, Pub **7-U3**, Read
public öffentlich **5-U5**, T1
pull ziehen **7-U2**, T1
pull down abreißen, einreißen
7-U5, TYE
pupil Schüler/in **5-U1**, WPB
purse Geldbeutel **6-U5**, Sit2
push schieben, anrempeln **5-U6**, T1
put setzen, stellen, legen **5-U3**, T1
put in einstecken, einlegen **7-U1**, Sit5
put on anmachen, auflegen (CD)
7-U1, Sit5
puzzle Rätsel, Geduldsspiel **6-U5**, Ex2

Qq

quarter Viertel **5-U1**, Sit5
queen Königin **6-U1**, WPA
question Frage **5-U2**, Sit2
questionnaire Fragebogen **7-U5**, Sket1
queue Warteschlange **6-U1**, Sit2
quick schnell **5-U3**, T1
quiet ruhig, still **5-U1**, T2
quite ziemlich **7-U4**, Com
quiz Quiz **5-U5**, Sit3

Rr

rabbit Kaninchen **5-U3**, WPA
race Rennen **5-U5**, T2
racket Tennisschläger **5-U2**, WPC
radio Radio **5-U1**, T2
rain regnen **5-U4**, Sit1
rain Regen **6-U1**, Ex13
ramp Rampe **7-U2**, TYE
raven Rabe **7-U1**, Sit2
read lesen **5-U1**, Sit7
ready fertig, bereit **5-U1**, T1
real echt **5-U3**, Sit4
really wirklich **5-U5**, Sit3
record aufnehmen **6-U6**, T2

recycle wieder aufbereiten, wieder
verwerten **6-U7**, Sit4
red rot **5-U0**, C
redwood Redwood **6-U7**, WP A
relative Verwandte/r **5-U7**, WPC
relax sich erholen **7-U1**, T1
remember sich erinnern **5-U6**, Ex6
remind erinnern **7-U3**, T1
repair reparieren **7-U5**, Rev
repeat wiederholen **5-U5**, Ex17
report Bericht **6-U3**, T1
reporter Reporter/in **7-U2**, Ex3
republic Republik **7-U1**, WP
residence Residenz, Amtssitz
7-U1, TYE
resolution Vorsatz, Beschluss
6-U3, Ex2
resort Ferienort **6-U7**, WPA
rest Ruhe **7-U4**, T1
rest Rest **6-U6**, Ex14
restaurant Restaurant
result Ergebnis **6-U3**, WPC
rewrite umschreiben, neu schreiben
7-U1, Ex6
rhyme (sich) reimen **7-U3**, T1
rich reich **6-U6**, WPC
ride Karussell, Fahrt **5-U7**, Sit4
ridge Bergkamm, Grat **6-U7**, WPA
riding accident Reitunfall **5-U6**, T1
right rechts **5-U6**, WPB
right richtig **5-U1**, T1
right genau **7-U5**, T2
ring anrufen **6-U2**, T2
river Fluss, Strom **6-U1**, WPA
road Straße **5-U1**, Sit6
robot Roboter **6-U5**, Sit1
roll rollen **7-U5**, T2
roll Brötchen **7-U5**, T1
roll up zusammen-, aufrollen **7-U5**, T2
Roman römisch; Römer, Römerin
7-U2, WP
room Zimmer **5-U1**, Ex4
rope Seil, Tau **7-U2**, TYE
rough uneben, rau **5-U5**, T2
round Runde **6-U6**, WPC
round umher, um … herum **5-U2**, Song
round rund **7-U2**, T2
royal königlich **6-U1**, T2
rubbish Abfall, Müll **6-U5**, T2
ruin Ruine **7-U2**, Sit1
rule Regel **6-U1**, Ex10
ruler Lineal **5-U0**, D

run laufen **5-U3**, WPA
run leiten, führen **7-U1**, Sit1

Ss

sad traurig **6-U2**, T2
safari Safari **6-U6**, WPA
safe sicher **7-U2**, T1
sail segeln **7-U4**, Sit1
salad Salat **5-U4**, WPA
sale Verkauf, Ausverkauf **6-U5**, T2
same gleich **5-U1**, Sit6
sandwich Sandwich, belegtes Brot
5-U1, T2
Saturday Samstag, Sonnabend
5-U1, Sit4
sausage Wurst **5-U4**, WP A
save retten **7-U1**, Read
save sparen **6-U5**, T1
Saxon sächsisch; Sachse, Sächsin
7-U2, WP
say sagen **5-U2**, Sit2
scared, to be Angst haben vor **7-U4**, T1
scene Szene **6-U1**, T2
school Schule **5-U1**, WPB
science (Natur-)Wissenschaft **6-U6**, WPA
score erzielen **7-U3**, Read
screen Bildschirm, Leinwand
6-U3, WPB
sea Meer, die See **6-U2**, Sit3
search (for) suchen (nach) **6-U3**,
WPC
seaside Meeresküste **5-U7**, WPA
seat Sitz, Sitzplatz **5-U7**, T2
secret geheim **7-U1**, T2
see sehen **5-U0**, B
seem scheinen **7-U3**, T2
seem to do etwas zu tun scheinen
7-U3, T2
see you bis dann!, tschüss! **5-U0**, B
sell verkaufen **6-U5**, WPB
seller Verkäufer/in **7-U5**, Rev
send schicken **6-U3**, WPC
sentence Satz **5-U5**, Ex1
separate getrennt **7-U1**, WP
September September **5-U4**, Sit5
series Serie **6-U6**, WPA
serious ernst **6-U3**, T2
seven sieben **5-U0**, G
seventeen siebzehn **5-U0**, G
seventy siebzig **5-U4**, WP A
several mehrere, einige **7-U4**, T2
sew nähen **7-U5**, Read

one hundred and forty-five **145**

Index

sh psst **5-U1**, Sit3

share (sich) teilen, gemeinsam haben **7-U5**, T2

she sie **5-U1**, Sit2

shed Schuppen, Stall **5-U3**, T2

sheep Schaf **6-U2**, WPA

shelf Regal, Ablage **5-U5**, Sit1

sheriff Sheriff **7-U5**, Sket2

shield (Schutz-)Schild **7-U2**, Sit5

ship Schiff **7-U3**, WP

shirt Hemd **5-U0**, C

shock Schock **6-U2**, T2

shoe Schuh **5-U3**, Sit2

shoot schießen, erschießen **7-U1**, Read

shop Geschäft **5-U4**, Sit1

shopping centre Einkaufszentrum **5-U6**, WPB

shore Strand, Ufer **7-U4**, TYE

short kurz **6-U1**, Ex3

should sollte **6-U6**, T2

shout schreien, rufen **5-U6**, T2

show Sendung **5-U5**, Sit3

show zeigen **6-U1**, Ex21

shut up den Mund halten **7-U1**, T1

shy schüchtern, scheu **7-U3**, TYE

side Seite **6-U2**, T1

sight Sehenswürdigkeit **6-U1**, WPA

sightseeing Stadtbesichtigung **6-U4**, PYE 6

sign Schild, Zeichen **5-U7**, T1

signal Signal **6-U4**, T2

silicon Silizium **6-U7**, WP A

silly albern **5-U1**, T1

silver Silber **7-U5**, WP

simple einfach, schlicht **6-U5**, Ex13

since seit **7-U1**, Sit4

sing singen **5-U1**, Ex13

singer Sänger/in **6-U1**, T2

sink sinken, untergehen **7-U3**, WP

sir mein Herr **5-U1**, Ex7

sister Schwester **5-U0**, I

sit sitzen; sich hinsetzen **5-U0**, F

Sit down. Setz dich hin. Setzt euch hin. **5-U0**, F

site Stelle, Platz **5-U7**, WPD

situation Situation **5-U1**, Sit1

six sechs **5-U0**, G

sixteen sechzehn **5-U0**, G

sixty sechzig **5-U4**, WPA

size Größe **5-U4**, Sit4

skate Rollschuh laufen **5-U5**, WPA

skate park Skatinggelände **5-U5**, T1

ski Ski fahren **6-U7**, WPA

skirt Rock **6-U6**, Ex3

sky Himmel **5-U7**, T2

skyway Himmelsweg **6-U7**, Song

sleep schlafen **6-U2**, Sit4

sleeping bag Schlafsack **7-U5**, T1

slogan Slogan, Parole, Wahlspruch **6-U1**, Ex14

slope Gefälle, Hang **7-U4**, T1

slow langsam **5-U5**, Ex1

slums, the Elendsviertel **7-U1**, Read

small klein **5-U2**, WPA

smart schick, elegant, flott **7-U1**, WP

smell riechen **5-U3**, WPB

smile lächeln **6-U1**, T2

smoke Rauch **7-U5**, Sit1

snack Imbiss **5-U5**, PYE 5

snake Schlange **7-U2**, Read

so so **5-U7**, Sit4

soap opera Seifenoper **6-U6**, WPA

soccer Fußball **7-U3**, Read

sock Socke **7-U2**, Ex9

soft weich, zart **6-U4**, T2

softball Softball **6-U3**, T2

software Software **7-U1**, WP

soldier Soldat/in **6-U4**, T1

some etwas, ein wenig; einige, ein paar **5-U4**, Sit1

somebody jemand **7-U3**, Sit1

someone jemand **6-U2**, Sit2

something etwas **5-U4**, Sit3

sometimes manchmal **5-U1**, T1

somewhere irgendwo **7-U1**, T1

son Sohn **6-U1**, Sit1

song Lied **5-U0**, J

soon bald **6-U5**, T1

sorry tut mir leid **5-U1**, Sit1

sound Klang, Laut **5-U5**, Ex17

sound klingen **6-U7**, T1

soup Suppe **7-U5**, T1

south Süden **6-U1**, WPA

sow säen **7-U5**, Read

so what? na und? **7-U3**, T1

space Lücke, Raum, Platz **5-U5**, Ex18

spaceship Raumschiff **7-U2**, Ex3

spare time Freizeit **5-U5**, WPA

speak sprechen **5-U1**, Sit8

speaker Sprecher/in, Redner/in **7-U1**, Ex4

special spezial, besondere(r, s) **6-U4**

spell buchstabieren **5-U0**, J

spelling Rechtschreibung **6-U7**, Sit1

spend ausgeben (Geld) **7-U4**, T2

spider Spinne **6-U4**, WPD

spill verschütten, vergießen **7-U1**, Sit3

splash bespritzen, platschen **6-U7**, T2

sponsor finanziell unterstützen **6-U5**, Com

spoon Löffel **7-U5**, T2

sport Sport **5-U2**, Sit1

sporting Sport(s)-, sportlich **7-U3**, Proj

spot Fleck(en) **5-U7**, Ex13

spray (be)sprühen **7-U4**, TYE

spring Frühling, Frühjahr **6-U4**, T1

square Platz **6-U7**, T2

stamp Briefmarke **5-U6**, Sit1

stamp stampfen **7-U3**, T2

stand stehen; sich hinstellen **5-U0**, F

Stand up! Steh auf! Steht auf! **5-U0**, F

star (Film)star **5-U1**, Sit2

star Stern **7-U3**, Com

star (in) eine Hauptrolle spielen (in) **7-U3**, WP

start Start, Anfang, Beginn **7-U1**, Ex3

start anfangen **5-U4**, WPA

start doing sth anfangen, etwas zu tun **7-U1**, WP

state Staat; Zustand **6-U7**

station Bahnhof, Station **5-U7**, T2

stay bleiben, wohnen **5-U7**, Sit1

steal stehlen **6-U5**, T1

steep steil **6-U7**, WPA

step gehen, treten **7-U1**, Read

stepbrother Stiefbruder **7-U3**, T1

stereo Stereogerät **5-U2**, WPC

stew Eintopf **5-U3**, Song

still (immer) noch **7-U1**, WP

still ruhig **6-U2**, T2

stolen gestohlen **7-U1**, T2

stone Stein **6-U1**, Song

stop anhalten, aufhören **6-U2**, Sit2

storm Sturm **7-U4**, WP

story Geschichte **6-U2**, Ex5

straight gerade **7-U5**, Com

straight ahead geradeaus **5-U6**, WPB

straight on geradeaus **7-U5**, Com

strange merkwürdig **6-U2**, T2

stranger Fremder, Fremde **7-U4**, WP

strawberry Erdbeere **7-U1**, Sit3

stream Bach **6-U2**, WPB

street Straße **6-U1**, WPB

stretcher Tragbahre **6-U2**, T2

strong stark **7-U2**, T1

Index

stupid dumm, blöd **5-U3**, T2
subject Schulfach **5-U6**, T1
succeed (in) gelingen, Erfolg haben (mit) **7-U3**, Sit1
suddenly plötzlich **6-U2**, T2
sugar Zucker **5-U4**, Sit1
suggestion Vorschlag **5-U5**, Ex18
summer Sommer **5-U4**, Sit5
sun Sonne **6-U2**, Sit3
Sunday Sonntag **5-U1**, Sit4
sunny sonnig **7-U5**, T1
supermarket Supermarkt **5-U2**, Sit4
supermodel Supermodel **7-U3**, TYE
support unterstützen **5-U2**, T1
sure sicher **5-U1**, Sit3
surf surfen **7-U5**, Ex7
surfing Surfen **6-U7**, WP A
surprised überrascht **7-U3**, Sit4
swallow Schwalbe **6-U2**, WPB
swap tauschen **5-U2**, Ex1
sweater Pullover **5-U0**, C
sweets Süßigkeiten **6-U4**, T2
sweet talk Schmeicheleien, schöne Worte **7-U1**, Proj
sweet-talk jemandem schmeicheln **7-U1**, Proj
swim schwimmen **5-U1**, Sit8
swimming-pool Schwimmbad **5-U6**, WPA
swing Schaukel **5-U3**, T1
swing schwingen **7-U4**, T1
switch on an-, einschalten **6-U3**, T2
sword Schwert **7-U2**, T1

Tt

table Tisch **5-U1**, T2
take nehmen **5-U4**, WPA
take dauern, Zeit in Anspruch nehmen **6-U5**, Ex2
take a photo ein Foto machen **5-U5**, WPB
take out herausnehmen, herausziehen **7-U1**, Sit5
talk reden **5-U2**, T2
tall groß **6-U6**, Com
tape Tonband, Videoband **6-U6**, T2
tapestry Wandbehang, Wandteppich **7-U4**, WP
taste schmecken **7-U5**, Sit1
taxi Taxi **5-U7**, Ex6
tea Abendessen **5-U3**, Sit1
tea Tee, Schwarzer Tee **5-U4**, WPA

teach unterrichten **6-U3**, T1
teacher Lehrer/in **5-U0**, D
team Team, Mannschaft **5-U1**, Ex17
technician Techniker/in **7-U1**, Sit1
technology Technik **6-U3**, T1
teenager Teenager **6-U6**, WPA
telephone Telefon **5-U1**, PYE 6
(tele)phone box Telefonzelle **7-U1**, T2
television Fernsehen **5-U1**, Sit6
tell erzählen, mitteilen **5-U5**, WPB
temper Laune, Stimmung, Wesensart **7-U4**, T2
temple Tempel, Kultstätte **6-U4**, WPB
ten zehn **5-U0**, G
tennis Tennis **5-U2**, WPC
tent Zelt **7-U5**, T1
term Semester, Trimester **5-U4**, Sit5
terrible schrecklich **5-U6**, T2
test testen, ausprobieren **6-U6**, WPA
test Test **6-U5**, Com
text Text **5-U1**, T1
textbook Lehrbuch **5-U3**, Ex11
than als **6-U1**, Sit3
thanks danke **5-U0**, B
thank you danke **5-U0**, B
that der, die, das (dort) **5-U0**, D
the der, die, das **5-U0**, D
theatre Theater **7-U4**, WP
their ihr, ihre, ihr **5-U1**, WPB
theirs ihre(r, s) **6-U3**, Sit3
them sie, ihnen **5-U2**, Sit5
then dann **5-U1**, Sit7
then also, nun **5-U3**, Sit1
there dort **5-U1**, Ex4
there is es gibt, es ist vorhanden **5-U1**, WPA
these diese **5-U3**, Sit2
they sie **5-U1**, WPB
thick dick, dicht **7-U5**, Sit1
thief Dieb/in **7-U5**, T2
thin dünn **7-U4**, Com
thing Sache, Gegenstand **5-U4**, T2
think denken, meinen **5-U1**, T2
thirsty durstig **7-U5**, T1
thirteen dreizehn **5-U0**, G
thirty dreißig **5-U1**, Sit5
this dieser, diese, dieses, dies **5-U0**, D
those jene **5-U3**, Sit2
thousand tausend **5-U7**, T2
three drei **5-U0**, G
through durch **6-U2**, T1
throw werfen **5-U6**, Ex4

Thursday Donnerstag **5-U1**, Sit4
ticket Fahrkarte; Eintrittskarte **6-U1**, T1
tidy ordentlich **7-U1**, Sit2
tidy aufräumen **5-U5**, Sit1
tiger Tiger **6-U3**, Ex3
time Zeit **5-U0**, B
times mal **7-U2**, Ex7
timetable Stundenplan **5-U1**, PYE 1
tin Büchse, Dose **6-U5**, Sit2
tip Tipp, nützlicher Hinweis **7-U3**, Sit1
tired müde **5-U6**, T1
title Titel **7-U1**, Ex3
to zu **5-U0**, B
toast Toast **5-U4**, WPB
today heute **5-U0**, G
together zusammen **5-U5**, Ex6
tomato Tomate **7-U5**, T1
tomorrow morgen **6-U2**, Sit2
tonight heute Abend **6-U4**, Ex2
ton Tonne **7-U2**, TYE
too auch **5-U0**, G
too zu **5-U5**, Ex1
top Spitze, Gipfel **5-U7**, T2
top Oberteil, Top **7-U1**, Sit1
torch Fackel **7-U2**, TYE
torture Folter, Qual **6-U1**, T2
tough robust, hart, zäh **6-U4**, T2
tour Rundfahrt, Führung **6-U1**, WPA
tourist Tourist/in **6-U1**, Sit2
tower Turm **6-U1**, WPA
town Stadt **5-U6**, WPA
town hall Rathaus **7-U5**, Ex13
toy Spielzeug **6-U5**, T2
traditional traditionell **7-U1**, WP
traffic Verkehr 6 **6-UT**, 2
train Zug **5-U7**, WPA
tram Tram, Straßenbahn **7-U5**, Sit1
trampolining Trampolin springen **6-U5**, Sit4
translate übersetzen **7-U3**, TYE4
travel reisen **5-U7**, WPA
tree Baum **5-U3**, PYE 2
trip Reise **6-U4**, PYE 6
trouble Schwierigkeit **7-U3**, Sit6
truck LKW, Truck **6-U7**, Ex1
true wahr **7-U2**, Sit1
truth Wahrheit **7-U2**, Read
try versuchen **5-U5**, T1
try to do sth versuchen, etwas zu tun **7-U1**, Ex3
T-shirt T-Shirt **5-U4**, Sit3

one hundred and forty-seven **147**

Index

tube U-Bahn **6-U1**, WPB
Tuesday Dienstag **5-U1**, Sit4
tunnel Tunnel **6-U4**, T1
turn einbiegen **5-U6**, WPB
turn drehen **6-U6**, T1
turning Abzweigung **6-U6**, T1
tutor Betreuungslehrer/in,
    Klassenlehrer/in 5 **1-UWP**, B
TV Fernsehen **5-U6**, Ex9
twelve zwölf **5-U0**, G
twenty zwanzig **5-U0**, G
twice zweimal **6-U5**, Sit4
twin Zwilling **6-U6**, WPA
two zwei **5-U0**, G
two out of three zwei von dreien
    7-U1, Read
type Typ **7-U1**, T1
type (in) (ein)tippen **6-U3**, WPC

Uu

umbrella Regenschirm **5-U0**, D
uncle Onkel **5-U1**, Song
uncomfortable unbequem **7-U5**, T1
under unter **5-U3**, T1
underground U-Bahn **6-U1**, WPB
understand verstehen **6-U6**, Sit1
undoubtedly zweifellos **7-U5**, Read
uniform Uniform **5-U1**, WP B
unit Unit, Lektion **5-U1**
United Kingdom Vereinigtes
    Konigreich, UK **7-U1**, WP
until bis **6-U5**, Sit2
up hinauf, herauf, nach oben **5-U0**, F
upset aufgebracht **7-U5**, T2
up-to-date aktuell, modern **6-U3**,
    WPD
urban städtisch, Stadt- **7-U1**, Read
urgent dringend **7-U1**, T2
us uns **5-U2**, Sit5
use gebrauchen, verwenden
    5-U5, WPB
useful nützlich **7-U5**, WP
usually gewöhnlich **5-U5**, WPB

Vv

vacation Ferien **6-U7**, Sit1
valley Tal **6-U7**, WPA
van Lieferwagen **7-U1**, T2
verb Verb, Tunwort **5-U5**, Ex1
very sehr **5-U1**, Sit1
vet Tierarzt, Tierärztin **6-U5**, WPD
video(cassette) Videokassette **5-U4**, T2

video recorder Videorekorder
    7-U3, Sit2
view Ausblick **5-U7**, T2
Viking Wikinger/in **7-U4**, Sit1
village Dorf **6-U2**, Sit3
violin Geige **7-U5**, Read
visit Besuch **7-U1**, TYE 5
visit besuchen, besichtigen **5-U3**, Ex16
visitor Besucher/in **6-U6**, WPD
voice Stimme **6-U2**, T2

Ww

wait warten **5-U5**, T2
wake up aufwachen; aufwecken
    7-U3, T2
walk Wanderung **7-U5**, T1
walk gehen, wandern **5-U2**, Sit3
walkman Walkman **5-U4**, T1
wall Mauer, Wand **5-U2**, T2
want wollen **5-U2**, T2
war Krieg **7-U3**, Com
wardrobe (Kleider)Schrank
    5-U2, WPC
warm warm **6-U3**, Sit1
warn warnen **6-U4**, T2
was war **5-U6**, T1
wash (sich) waschen **6-U2**, Sit2
wash away wegspülen **6-U1**, Song
wash up abspülen **6-U4**, Ex11
watch Uhr **5-U1**, T2
watch sehen, beobachten **5-U1**, Sit6
water Wasser **5-U4**, WPA
waterfall Wasserfall **6-U7**, WPA
wax Wachs **7-U1**, TYE 5
waxwork Wachsfigur **6-U1**, Sit2
way Art und Weise **6-U1**, Ex4
way Weg **5-U1**, Sit7
we wir **5-U1**, Sit1
weapon Waffe **7-U2**, T2
wear tragen **5-U4**, Sit3
weather Wetter **5-U7**, WP D
weather wetterfest sein, überstehen
    7-U5, Read
website Website **6-U3**, WP C
wedding Hochzeit(stag) **7-U5**, Sket2
Wednesday Mittwoch **5-U1**, Sit4
week Woche **5-U1**, Sit3
weekend Wochenende **5-U1**, Sit4
weigh wiegen **7-U2**, TYE
weight Gewicht **7-U5**, Sit3
welcome willkommen **6-U7**, T1
well gut **6-U6**, Sit3

well nun **5-U1**, Sit8
Welsh walisisch **5-U7**, T1
west Westen **6-U1**, Sit1
western westlich, West- **7-U5**, Ex13
West Indian westindisch **7-U5**, TYE
wet nass, feucht **7-U4**, TYE
what was **5-U0**, A
what about? wie wär's mit … ?
    5-U2, WPA
What colour is … ? Welche Farbe hat
    … ? **5-U0**, C
whatever was auch immer **7-U5**, Read
what for? wozu? **7-U1**, Read
what's was ist **5-U0**, A
what's the matter? was ist los?
    7-U2, Read
wheel Rad **5-U3**, WPA
wheelchair Rollstuhl **5-U6**, T1
when wann **5-U4**, Ex14
when als **5-U6**, T1
when (immer) wenn **5-U7**, Sit4
where wo **5-U0**, J
whether ob **7-U5**, Read
which welche(r, s) **6-U1**, WPB
which der, die, das **7-U4**, Sit1
while während **7-U1**, T2
white weiß **5-U0**, C
who wer **5-U1**, T2
whole ganz **7-U2**, Ex8
whose deren, dessen **7-U4**, Sit3
whose wessen **5-U6**, Sit3
why warum **5-U4**, T1
widow Witwe **7-U4**, T2
wife Ehefrau **6-U1**, Sit1
wild wild, ungezügelt **6-U2**, T1
will werden **6-U5**, Sit1
win gewinnen **5-U4**, Sit1
window Fenster **5-U0**, D
window-cleaner Fensterputzer/in
    7-U5, Rev
wine Wein **6-U7**, WPA
wing Flügel **7-U2**, Read
winter Winter **6-U4**, T2
witch Hexe **7-U2**, Read
with mit **5-U1**, Sit2
without ohne **6-U5**, T1
woman Frau **5-U3**, Sit3
wonderful wunderbar **5-U7**, WPD
wood Holz **6-U1**, Song
woof Wauwau **5-U7**, T1
word Wort **5-U0**, J
work arbeiten **5-U2**, Sit4

Index

work Arbeit **5-U1**, Sit7
world Welt **6-U1**, T1
worried besorgt **7-U5**, T2
worry sich sorgen **6-U1**, T1
worse schlechter **6-U1**, Sit4
worst am schlechtesten **6-U1**, Sit4
worth wert **6-U6**, T2
would like möchte gern **5-U4**, WPA
would like to do sth möchte gerne etwas
    tun **7-U1**, Com
would love to do sth möchte gerne etwas
    tun **7-U1**, Com
wow Mann!, Wahnsinn! **6-U3**, T2
write schreiben **5-U3**, Com
wrong falsch **5-U2**, Ex5
wrote schrieb **6-U3**, T2

Yy

year Jahr **5-U1**, Sit3
yellow gelb **5-U0**, C
yes ja **5-U0**, B
yesterday gestern **6-U2**, Sit1
yet, not … yet noch nicht **6-U4**, Sit3
yet, … yet? schon **6-U4**, Sit3
yoghurt Joghurt **5-U4**, WP A
you du, ihr, Sie **5-U0**, A
young jung **6-U2**, WPB
your dein, deine, dein, ihr, ihre, ihr
    5-U0, A
You're lucky. Du hast Glück. Du bist
    gut dran. **5-U1**, T1
yours deine(r, s) **6-U3**, Sit2
you were du warst, ihr wart, Sie waren
    6-U2, Sit1

Zz

zoo Zoo, Tierpark **5-U3**, Ex16

one hundred and forty-nine 149

Activities

Activities Unit 1

saint [seɪnt]	heilig; Heilige/r
patron ['peɪtrən]	Schutzpatron
legend ['ledʒənd]	Legende
century ['sentʃəri]	Jahrhundert
pirate ['paɪrət]	Pirat, Seeräuber
Christian ['krɪstʃən]	christlich; Christ/in
church [tʃɜːtʃ]	Kirche
religion [rɪ'lɪdʒən]	Religion
to chase [tʃeɪs]	jagen
snake [sneɪk]	Schlange
blind [blaɪnd]	blind
goat [gəʊt]	Ziege
giant ['dʒaɪənt]	Riese
darling ['dɑːlɪŋ]	Liebling, Schatz
to step [step]	gehen, treten
to lead, led, led [liːd, led, led]	führen, bringen
nobody ['nəʊbədi]	niemand
volcano [vɒl'keɪnəʊ]	Vulkan
lava ['lɑːvə]	Lava
fairy ['feəri]	Fee
shoemaker ['ʃuːmeɪkə]	Schuhmacher, Schuster
pot [pɒt]	Topf
hidden ['hɪdn]	verborgen
rainbow ['reɪnbəʊ]	Regenbogen
wish [wɪʃ]	Wunsch
to trick [trɪk]	hereinlegen
language ['læŋgwɪdʒ]	Sprache
the Celts [ðə kelts]	die Kelten
Celtic ['keltɪk]	keltisch
Gaelic ['geɪlɪk]	gälisch
official [ə'fɪʃl]	offiziell, amtlich, Amts-
cooked [kʊkt]	gekocht
tablespoon ['teɪblspuːn]	Esslöffel
salt [sɔːlt]	Salz
melted ['meltɪd]	geschmolzen, zerlaufen
flour ['flaʊə]	Mehl
to mash [mæʃ]	zerstampfen
to roll out [ˌrəʊl 'aʊt]	ausrollen
diameter [daɪ'æmɪtə]	Durchmesser
to cut, cut, cut [kʌt, kʌt, kʌt]	schneiden
to fry, fried, fried [fraɪ, fraɪd, fraɪd]	braten (in Fett)

Activities Unit 2

round [raʊnd]	rund
legend ['ledʒənd]	Legende
wedding ['wedɪŋ]	Hochzeit
secret ['siːkrɪt]	Geheimnis
nobody ['nəʊbədi]	niemand
somebody ['sʌmbədi]	jemand
right [raɪt]	Recht
That's fair enough. [ðæts ˌfeər ɪ'nʌf]	Das ist nur recht und billig.
go ahead [ˌgəʊ ə'hed]	nur zu!
symbol ['sɪmbl]	Symbol
to shuffle ['ʃʌfl]	(Karten) mischen
mistletoe ['mɪsltəʊ]	Mistelzweig
to hang up, hung up, hung up [ˌhæŋ 'ʌp, ˌhʌŋ 'ʌp, ˌhʌŋ 'ʌp]	aufhängen
to kiss [kɪs]	küssen
may [meɪ]	kann vielleicht
even ['iːvn]	sogar
snowman ['snəʊmæn]	Schneemann
jolly ['dʒɒli]	fröhlich
soul [səʊl]	Seele
corncob ['kɔːnkɒb]	Maiskolben
pipe [paɪp]	Pfeife
button nose ['bʌtn nəʊz]	Knopfnase
coal [kəʊl]	Kohle
fairy-tale ['feəriteɪl]	Märchen
silk [sɪlk]	Seide
to place on ['pleɪs ɒn]	aufsetzen
alive [ə'laɪv]	lebendig, am Leben
to wave [weɪv]	winken
to cry, cried, cried [kraɪ, kraɪd, kraɪd]	weinen
chimney ['tʃɪmni]	Kamin, Schornstein
to stick, stuck, stuck [stɪk, stʌk, stʌk]	feststecken
to begin, began, begun [bɪ'gɪn, bɪ'gæn, bɪ'gʌn]	anfangen, beginnen
beard [bɪəd]	Bart
soot [sʊt]	Ruß
sack [sæk]	Sack
to tickle ['tɪkl]	kitzeln
atishoo [ə'tʃuː]	Hatschi

150 one hundred and fifty

Activities

Activities Unit 3

daylight ['deɪlaɪt]	Tageslicht
on your own [ɒn jɔːr 'əʊn]	allein
to comfort ['kʌmfət]	trösten
to survive [sə'vaɪv]	überleben
haste [heɪst]	Eile, Hast
to be alone [bi ə'ləʊn]	allein sein
nowhere ['nəʊweə]	nirgendwo
soul [səʊl]	Seele
confused [kən'fjuːzd]	verwirrt
to let someone down	jdn im Stich lassen
[ˌlet sʌmwʌn 'daʊn]	
'coz = because [kɒz]	
to make up, made up,	erfinden
[ˌmeɪk 'ʌp, ˌmeɪd 'ʌp]	
made up [ˌmeɪd 'ʌp]	
one day [wʌn 'deɪ]	eines Tages
to count [kaʊnt]	zählen
to go ahead [ˌgəʊ ə'hed]	weitermachen
to perform [pə'fɔːm]	aufführen, spielen
record ['rekɔːd]	(Schall)Platte
to complain [kəm'pleɪn]	sich beschweren
body ['bɒdi]	Körper
to hide, hid, hidden	sich verstecken
[haɪd, hɪd, 'hɪdn]	
less [les]	weniger
sunglasses ['sʌnglɑːsɪz]	Sonnenbrille
to make it ['meɪk ɪt]	es schaffen

Activities Unit 4

sheriff ['ʃerɪf]	Sheriff
outlaw ['aʊtlɔː]	Geächtete/r, Vogelfreie/r
sponsor ['spɒnsə]	Förderer, Geldgeber
potter ['pɒtə]	Töpfer
shilling ['ʃɪlɪŋ]	Schilling (alte Währungseinhcit)
cheeky ['tʃiːki]	frech
trick [trɪk]	Streich
goods [gʊdz]	Waren
jealous ['dʒeləs]	eifersüchtig
contest ['kɒntest]	Wettbewerb
to turn out [ˌtɜːn 'aʊt]	sich herausstellen
to split, split, split	spalten, teilen
[splɪt, splɪt, splɪt]	
share [ʃeə]	Anteil
gimme = give me ['gɪmi]	gib mir

Activities Unit 5

record company ['rekɔːd kʌmpəni]	Plattenfirma
rucksack ['rʌksæk]	Rucksack
PIN [pɪn]	PIN-Code
to forget (about), [fə'get əbaʊt]	vergessen
forgot, forgotten [fə'gɒt, fə'gɒtn]	
to afford [ə'fɔːd]	sich leisten
to accuse [ə'kjuːz]	beschuldigen, anklagen
to calm down [ˌkɑːm 'daʊn]	beruhigen, beschwichtigen
will do [wɪl 'duː]	ausreichen
would rather [wəd 'rɑːðə]	möchte lieber
offer ['ɒfə]	Angebot
gardener ['gɑːdnə]	Gärtner/in
to shine, shone, shone	scheinen
[ʃaɪn, ʃɒn, ʃɒn]	
to celebrate [selɪ'breɪt]	feiern
to spread, spread, spread	verbreiten
[spred, spred, spred]	
gonna = going to ['gɒnə]	werden
celebration [ˌselɪ'breɪʃn]	Feier
nation ['neɪʃn]	Nation, Staat
to forget (about), [fə'get əbaʊt]	vergessen
forgot, forgotten [fə'gɒt, fə'gɒtn]	
to release [rɪ'liːs]	ablassen, loslassen
pressure ['preʃə]	Druck
to turn around [ˌtɜːn ə'raʊnd]	herumdrehen
troubles ['trʌblz]	Schwierigkeiten

one hundred and fifty-one **151**

Umschlag	David Graham
Illustrationen	Christine Georg, Kim Lane, Angus Montrose
Cartoons	Wendy Sinclair (*Raben*), Peter Muggleston
Fotos	David Graham, Picturefile
zusätzliche Fotos	All Action Pictures *S.15, 33, 37, 38, 43, 44(x2) 45, 46, 86* J Allan Cash Ltd *S.19(x2) 20* Klaus Berold *S.24* The Black Country Living Museum *S.63(x2), 65* British Tourist Authority *S.20, 21, 72, 73* Janet Chipps *S.58(x2)* Udo Diekmann *S.11(x6), 62(all)* DSPCA *S.18(x2)* The Duke of Edinburgh's Award *S.3, 61(all), 64(both), 68, 69, 70(both)* English Heritage *S.19* EuroDisney *S.87(both)* Helga Lade Fotoagentur /H.R.Bramaz *S.10* Intel Ireland Ltd. *Inside front cover* Irish Tourist Board *Inside front cover, S.15* Mary Rose Trust *S.58* Press Association *S.30* The Board of Trustees of the Royal Armouries *S.54* Sportimage *S.46* York Archaelogical Trust *S.49*.
Textquellen	*At your side* Words and Music by The Corrs © Songs of Polygram Int. Inc., Beacon Communications Music Co., Universal Publishing GmbH, Hamburg *(S.38)* *Frosty the Snowman* Words and Music by Steve Nelson and Jack Rollins © CHAPPEL & CO INC./INTERSONG INC. USA. Für D/GUS/Osteuropäische Länder MUSIKVERLAG INTERSONG GmbH, Hamburg *(S.25)* *Holiday* Words and Music by Lisa Stevens and Curtis Lee Hudson © House of Fun Music/Pure Energy Music Publ. Inc. für D/CH/GUS osteur. Staaten, Türkei NEUE WELT MUSIKVERLAG GmbH, München *(S.67)* *Merlo the Magnificent* © 2000, Kenn Nesbitt. All Rights Reserved. Reprinted by permission of the author. www.poetry4kids.com *(S.74)* *New Computer* © 2000, Kenn Nesbitt. All Rights Reserved. Reprinted by permission of the author. www.poetry4kids.com *(S.74)* *Words* Grandpa Tucker © Grandpa Tucker; Reprinted by permission of the author. www.grandpatucker.com *(S.75)* Nicht alle Copyrightinhaber konnten ermittelt werden; deren Urheberrechte werden hiermit vorsorglich und ausdrücklich anerkannt.
Acknowledgements	*The publishers wish to thank the staff, pupils, parents and friends of Alleyn's School, Dulwich, London and Carl-von-Linde-Realschule, Staatliche Realschule, Kulmbach for their continued help and assistance. The publishers also wish to thank the Dublin Society for the Prevention of Cruelty to Animals, Rathfarnham, Co Dublin, The Duke of Edinburgh's Award Trust, Windsor, Berkshire and The Black Country Living Museum in Dudley, West Midlands, for both their help and advice and for use of their stock photos.*
Danksagung	Wir danken den Lehrern und Lehrerinnen, den Schülern und Schülerinnen, ihren Eltern und den Freunden der Alleyn's School, Dulwich, London und der Carl-von-Linde-Realschule, Staatliche Realschule, Kulmbach für ihre Hilfe und Unterstützung. Wir danken außerdem der Dublin Society for the Prevention of Cruelty to Animals, Rathfarnham, Co Dublin, dem Duke of Edinburgh's Award Trust, Windsor, Berkshire und dem Black Country Living Museum in Dudley sowohl für ihre fachliche Unterstützung als auch dafür, dass sie uns ihre Fotoaufnahmen zur Verfügung gestellt haben.